Recent Titles in
Contributions in Military Studies

FEEDING
THE
BEAR

American Aid to the
Soviet Union, 1941-1945

Hubert P. van Tuyll

Contributions in Military Studies, Number 90

Greenwood Press
New York • Westport, Connecticut • London

Library of Congress Cataloging-in-Publication Data

Van Tuyll, Hubert P.
    Feeding the bear : American aid to the Soviet Union, 1941-1945 /
Hubert P. van Tuyll.
        p.   cm.—(Contributions in military studies, ISSN 0883-6884
; no. 90)
    Bibliography: p.
    Includes index.
    ISBN 0-313-26688-3 (lib. bdg. : alk. paper)
    1. Economic assistance, American—Soviet Union—History—20th
century.   2. Lend-lease operations (1941-1945)   3. World War,
1939-1945—Soviet Union.   4. World War, 1939-1945—United States.
5. United States—Foreign relations—Soviet Union.   6. Soviet Union—
Foreign relations—United States.   I. Title.   II. Series.
HC335.6.V36   1989
338.9′173043—dc20   89-7483

British Library Cataloguing in Publication Data is available.

Library of Congress Catalog Card Number: 89-7483
ISBN: 0-313-26688-3
ISSN: 0883-6884

First published in 1989

Greenwood Press, Inc.
88 Post Road West, Westport, Connecticut 06881

Printed in the United States of America

The paper used in this book complies with the
Permanent Paper Standard issued by the National
Information Standards Organization (Z39.48-1984).

10 9 8 7 6 5 4 3 2 1

For Debbie

Contents

List of Tables

Preface

Research on any Soviet-related matter brings home the way in which almost any matter can become controversial or politicized. Lend-Lease is no exception and became a diplomatic and intellectual pawn during the Cold War, part of the argument over which nation did the most to vanquish Hitlerite Germany. In the long run this argument has become political and meaningless. Neither Lend-Lease nor the other Allied contributions to the war effort should obscure the immense sacrifices made by the Soviet people during the war. Lend-Lease, however, should receive its proper share of credit for its role during the Great Patriotic War, rather than being either exaggerated or minimized.

"Soviet peoples" brings up a pedantic but not unimportant question: what does one call the people of the Soviet Union? "Russians" is ethnically inaccurate, but "Soviets" is not much better, as a "Soviet" properly refers to a council as well as a human being. Americans traditionally have used "Russians" and "Russian" to refer to the entire Soviet people and nation, and it is in that sense that these two words are used in the pages that follow.

This work could never have been completed without extensive assistance and support. The U.S. Army Military History Institute and the Texas A&M University Military Studies Institute both provided financial support. Research was greatly facilitated by the staff at the Military History Institute and the National Archives (Modern Military Records Division). Professors Henry Dethloff, Herbert Lang, Larry Hill, and Brison Gooch all furnished much-needed assistance while serving in official capacities with the Texas A&M University Department of History. Professors Arnold Krammer and Chester Dunning of Texas A&M University, Professor William P. Snyder of the Air University, and Professor John Erickson of the University of Edinburgh (Scotland) read the manuscript at various times and made many useful suggestions. I also wish to thank the faculty and staff of Union College (Kentucky) who assisted in many ways during the final stages of manuscript preparation. Without the advice (and careful editing) by Mildred Vasan and Lynn Flint of Greenwood Press, this book would have never reached the publication stage. Most of all, I owe a great debt of thanks to Professor Roger A. Beaumont of Texas A&M University, who helped nurture this project from its inception, and for whose advice (and, more importantly, patience) I will always be grateful. None of these individuals or institutions are in any way responsible for any errors of fact or interpretation in this work, which are my own.

FEEDING
THE
BEAR

1

Introduction

At three in the morning on June 22, 1941, a mighty force of 162 German and assorted allied divisions rolled across the Soviet border. The shocked and terrified defenders did not even have time to abandon their forward positions before they were overwhelmed by the combination of Nazi armor, dive bombers, and infantry assault. Few had received advance warning because the Soviet General Staff, hampered by a mediocre communications system, had only a few hours to alert its formations facing Germany. While the Luftwaffe inflicted staggering destruction on the Soviet air force, German armored units plunged through the Russian lines to attack the "strategic rear": communications, headquarters, and supply lines. In a mere six weeks German forces reached Smolensk, two-thirds of the way to Moscow. To many observers it appeared that Adolf Hitler was destined to add the Soviet Union to his collection of military trophies, with incalculable consequences.

Less than four years later the Red Army battered its way into the Reich, having destroyed or disabled the bulk of the German ground forces. For Germany, *Goetterdaemmerung* had occurred: victory, unity, and the image of invincibility had been replaced by abject surrender, division into zones of occupation, and, later, public humiliation at Nuremberg. The Soviet Union, on the other hand, had reached a new height in terms of power and international prestige, although at the fearful cost of more than15 million dead.

How did this dramatic change in fortune come to be? How did the Soviet Union manage to recover in the midst of desperate struggle and prevail against a foe that had established a European empire on a scale not seen since Napoleon? The reasons for Soviet victory and German defeat are complex. The war in the East is too great a historical event to be explained in terms of a single formulation. Time, space, size of forces, and the Brobdingnagian expenditure of resources and lives by both primary combatants make the Eastern Front unique. The same time and space elements were present in World War I, but Germany was unwilling and Russia was incapable of waging the intense type of war in the East that took place in World War II.

Popular books about the war explain the outcome in the East, when it is extensively discussed at all, in terms of weather, numbers, and Hitler's errors. Undoubtedly the problems faced by the Germans, whether inherent or of their own making, should not be ignored. Operation Barbarossa was an ambivalent concoction of military, economic, and political goals. The Nazi tank force was too small and improperly equipped in relation to the vast spaces of the western Soviet Union, its transport was mostly horse-drawn, and its intelligence about the Soviet state's army and industry was woefully inadequate. Loath to admit their failures, German wartime leaders emphasize the Reich's lack of preparedness.

Yet the focus on German disadvantages is inherently one-sided and minimizes the achievements of the Soviet Union. Soviet writers have bitterly complained that Western publications about the war are distorted and inaccurate and ignore the heavy concentration of German ground forces on the Eastern Front. [1] Their version of the conflict reverses the popular Western bias by interpreting the entire war in terms of the efforts of the Soviet Union. Hence they have tended to belittle many aspects of the Allied war effort, especially the Lend-Lease program.

Soviet writers are correct, however, in denouncing interpretations of the Eastern Front that omit any serious reference to the immense Soviet offensives of 1943-45. German disadvantages can help explain Soviet survival, but not victory. The failure of Germany's great offensives in 1941 and 1942, as well as the disaster at Kursk, robbed the Nazis of any meaningful chance for victory but did not predestine the arrival of Marshal I. Konev in Berlin in 1945. The Soviet Union might have survived the initial onslaught and then sought victory through a defensive war of attrition, but such a strategy would have been pursued at the cost of many years of partial occupation and an unfavorable postwar position. Instead, the Soviet leadership elected to drive Hitler's army from its soil at the earliest possible moment.

The ultimate (if costly) success of the Red Army depended on much more than German errors and Russian climate. The organization of massive offensives required enormous economic and human mobilization, the development of an infrastructure capable of planning, executing, and sustaining offensive operations, and the technical and intellectual capacity to coordinate forces. Add to this the condition of the Red Army (many of its field formations shattered in the first months of the war, valuable officers, NCOs and equipment lost, its skill and initiative still hampered by the arrest and execution of most of its high-ranking officers in the purges), and the magnitude of the task becomes apparent.

The United States and Britain wanted to help the Soviet Union, if for no other reason than self-interest. The only practical way of doing so was by furnishing materiel. An Allied invasion of German-occupied Europe had to wait, for a wide variety of military and political reasons (none of which were viewed very sympathetically by the hard-pressed Soviet government). Britain was militarily overextended, had strategic interests to be protected in the Mediterranean and beyond Europe, and had perhaps not forgotten Stalin's alliance with Hitler during the first 21 months of the war. The United States did not formally enter the war until almost half a year after Germany invaded the Soviet Union, and American forces were not fully prepared for large-scale operations until much later in the war. Stalin may have preferred a "Second Front," that is, a major invasion of Western Europe, but the image of the supremely confident German army caused many misgivings about a premature landing in Europe. As an alternative, the Soviet government twice suggested in late 1941 that 25 to 30 divisions might be sent via Archangel or Iran, a project so far in excess of shipping capacity that Churchill dismissed it as a "delusion."[2] After Stalingrad the Soviet government lost interest in having Allied troops on its soil and rejected almost all Western overtures on the subject.

Material aid was then the only immediate way to help the Soviet Union. This was especially true for the United States, which technically remained neutral until Pearl Harbor. The mechanism for aid to "friendly" powers at war already existed in the form of the Lend-Lease system. As early as November 1939 Congress had repealed certain provisions of the Neutrality Act which forbade belligerents from purchasing arms in the United States. Seven months later President Franklin D. Roosevelt publicly committed his administration to material support for Britain and her Allies, a step taken, ironically, to mollify those isolationists who feared the use of American forces in the conflict. Initially the U.S. government went no further than to issue export licenses for British cash purchases. Roosevelt knew that Britain could not indefinitely continue buying all the arms it needed, and he therefore proposed a system whereby the United States would "lend" war materiel to Britain. After extensive debate the Lend-Lease Act was signed into law on March 11, 1941. The law was extended in 1943 and 1945, with only the addition of provisos prohibiting the use of Lend-Lease aid for postwar reconstruction.[3] This last addendum was to have major diplomatic repercussions.

The act's wording "to Promote the Defense of the United States" was not a technicality, since the program was sold to Congress and the public as a program for American defense. The act allowed the transfer of weapons, machinery, agricultural products, and "any other commodity or article for defense." The president was required to consult with the army chief of staff or the chief of naval operations before he actually transferred any equipment. Repayment arrangements were left to the sole discretion of the president. Convoying was prohibited to protect American "neutrality." The president was further required to report to Congress every three months. Beyond these strictures, however, the president's authority was very broad, and he could authorize the transfer of almost any product to any nation if it were deemed in the best interests of the United States.[4]

Extension of Lend-Lease to the Soviet Union was both practically and politically difficult. U.S.-Soviet relations were hampered by the Russo-Finnish war, the absorption of the Baltic states by the Soviet Union, and the Nazi-Soviet Pact. The United States condemned the first event, refused to recognize the second, and feared the third. The State Department suspected, however, that the Berlin-Moscow agreement was only a matter of convenience to Stalin, and hence instructed Under-Secretary Sumner Welles to begin conversations in the summer of 1940 with Soviet Ambassador Konstantin Umansky with a view to improving relations. These conversations led to a lifting, in January 1941, of the American embargo imposed after the invasion of Finland.[5]

Improving relations at the government level did not overcome domestic hostility toward the Soviet Union. Roosevelt contemplated the extension of Lend-Lease to the Soviet Union in the event of war even before Congress passed the enabling legislation, but steadfastly declined to say so in public because he feared that this might jeopardize his entire program. Unsuccessful efforts were in fact made in both houses of Congress to prohibit the extension of Lend-Lease to the Soviet Union in case of war.[6]

When war came, Roosevelt moved as quickly as possible, given the continued public hostility toward the Soviet Union. On June 23, 1941, he laid the legal foundation for extension of aid by stating that any aid to Hitler's enemies aided the defense of the United States. On June 24, two days after the invasion, he declared that "we are going to give all the aid we can to Russia" and lifted several legal impediments to trade with the Soviet Union. Formal discussions with Soviet representatives began on June 26. The Soviet Union was represented by Umansky, Andrei Gromyko, and officials of the Soviet-American Trading Corporation, Amtorg. The State Department created a temporary interagency committee subject to the general supervision of Welles and Assistant Secretary Dean Acheson to study Soviet aid requirements. The committee included representatives of the Division of Defense Aid Reports, the Office of Export Control, the Office of Price Administration and Civilian Supply, the Office of Production Management, the Army-Navy Munitions Board, and the Maritime Commission.[7]

The Special Committee met five times in early July to consider the initial Soviet aid request, submitted at the end of June, for almost $1.8 billion in aid. By mid-July the committee had recommended immediate clearance for $16 million of the request ($9 million in export licenses were actually issued) and suggested that $172 million be released in the following 12 months. Having completed its task, the committee was dissolved, and on July 21 all Soviet aid matters were referred to the Division of Defense Aid Reports, headed by Major General James H. Burns. This organization looked favorably upon Soviet aid requests, especially because presidential aide Harry Hopkins communicated Roosevelt's strong support for Soviet aid. Furthermore, Soviet aid was handled by a special section under the leadership of Colonel Phillip R. Faymonville, an officer with strong pro-Soviet views.[8] As will be seen later, his appointment would prove controversial.

By the end of July it was clear that the Soviet aid program was not working. Administration was poor. The Soviet Union was last in line for almost all essential items because American needs and Lend-Lease requirements had to be met first. An effort to establish a Soviet-American-British allocation committee got nowhere. Presidential orders to expedite Soviet aid could not overcome the practical problems of complicated administration, tight shipping, payment issues, and military skepticism that the Soviet Union could continue to fight.[9]

The American military's fear that the Soviet Union might surrender was mirrored by Soviet suspicions of whether the Anglo-American alliance actually planned to furnish aid. Roosevelt and Churchill did their best to allay this concern, fearing (despite Stalin's denials) a Soviet withdrawal from the war. A formal U.S.-Soviet agreement to provide aid was made via diplomatic notes between the Soviet Union and the United States on August 2, Hopkins twice visited the Soviet Union during the summer, Britain and the U.S.S.R. began a joint occupation of Iran on August 25, and Britain and the United States decided to modernize the Iranian State Railway (necessary for potential aid shipments). This latter project was partially financed by the United States as part of the British Lend-Lease program.[10]

None of these measures solved the problem of how much to give the Soviet Union and in what way. Roosevelt, believing that "Soviet Russia must be given unstinted aid and kept fighting to the end," ordered Secretary of War Henry Stimson to prepare a list of supplies that could be delivered to the Soviet Union by June 30, 1942. Britain and the United States managed to agree on relative aid allocations, although, according to American envoy Averell Harriman, the negotiations were at times "acrimonious." Finally, on October 1, 1941 an agreement known as the First or "Moscow" Protocol was signed by the United States, Britain, and the Soviet Union.[11]

In the meantime, however, one troubling problem had arisen. How was Soviet aid to be financed? Lend-Lease was the easiest way but also initially unattractive because of congressional opposition and Soviet reluctance to meet Lend-Lease information requirements. The U.S. administration was perfectly willing to proceed via purchases, credits, and loans, but the legal mechanisms were faulty. The Reconstruction Finance Corporation (RFC), for example, could not lend money without collateral. A loan of $50 million was arranged through the Defense Supplies Corporation (an RFC subsidiary) by labelling the money an 'advance' for raw materials that the U.S.S.R. would supply in the future. The Treasury "advanced" $10 million against future Soviet gold deliveries. Sixty million dollars, however, only covered a fraction of the Soviet aid requests.[12]

Roosevelt finally moved to include the Soviet Union in Lend-Lease. Legally he could have done so at any time, but he did not want to jeopardize passage of the Lend-Lease renewal bill. This statute made its way through Congress by October 23 and was signed by Roosevelt on October 28, but far more importantly, efforts to specifically exclude the Soviet Union were overwhelmingly defeated. Roosevelt sent a cable to Stalin on October 30 proposing Soviet participation in the program. Soviet Lend-Lease was described as a 'credit' at Soviet request so that the Soviet Union would not be legally required to submit information. The Soviet embassy filed appropriate declarations for admission to the Lend-Lease program on November 7, 1941. On the same day, the president issued a directive to Edward R. Stettinius, head of the newly created Office of Lend-Lease Administration (OLLA), formally designating the Soviet Union as a Lend-Lease recipient. This constituted a "measure of Roosevelt's willingness to base

American international policy on the principle of the common international interest in supporting resistance to armed aggression."[13]

The administration of Soviet Lend-Lease aid changed little after this point. The Office of Lend-Lease Administration absorbed all aid-related functions of the Division of Defense Aid Reports and the equally important Advisory Commission to the Council of National Defense. OLLA and the Board (later Office) of Economic Warfare were superseded by the Foreign Economic Administration (FEA) on September 25, 1943, which was created to handle all government functions relating to "economic warfare, foreign supply and procurement, and other wartime economic operations." One important exception to this administrative streamlining was the Office of Production Management, a subdivision of the War Production Board, which continued to review the supply of critical materials.[14]

Formal treaties between the United States and the Soviet Union merely ratified ongoing practices. The three protocols signed in 1942 (Washington), 1943 (London), and 1944 (Ottawa) covered periods already under way and formalized aid requests already accepted by the U.S. government. The two supplemental agreements concerning aid against Japan covered much smaller quantities of materiel. The Soviet-American "Master Lend-Lease Agreement" signed on June 11, 1942, did establish formal procedures for aid requests but did not affect the quantity of aid.[15]

Studies of the Soviet aid program include official histories, memoirs, scholarly studies, and, as is inevitable with any topic concerned with Soviet-American relations, polemics. Little has been said or written about the military impact of Lend-Lease. The U.S. government published some important contemporaneous reports, including the official reports to Congress on Lend-Lease,[16] the postwar report of FEA activities,[17] and the State Department's "Report on War Aid Furnished by the United States to the U.S.S.R."[18] No comprehensive American official history of the Soviet Lend-Lease program was ever published. Among the official histories, the best on this topic are Richard M. Leighton's and Robert W. Coakley's studies of global logistics and strategy,[19] the strategic planning volume by Maurice Matloff and Edwin M. Snell,[20] and T. H. Vail Motter's *The Persian Corridor and Aid to Russia*.[21] Hessell Duncan Hall authored one and coauthored another excellent book on the impact of North American resources on the war from the British viewpoint.

The first study to focus on the effect of aid on the Soviet war effort was an unpublished dissertation prepared by John Gardner in 1946.[22] Gardner had to work with very limited material, as little had been declassified and he had few eyewitness accounts and memoirs to rely on. The wartime publications of former U.S. Ambassador to the Soviet Union Joseph Davies (1942)[23] and Lend-Lease Administrator (later Secretary of State) E. R. Stettinius (1944)[24] contain some interesting material, but both authors clearly intended to promote, respectively, Soviet-American relations and Lend-Lease. Far more valuable was General John Deane's *The Strange Alliance*.[25] Deane had served as commander of the U.S. Military Mission in Moscow, an organization that (among other things) controlled local aspects of the flow of aid to the Soviet Union. Deane was a keen observer, and his memoir is useful to anyone studying Soviet-American relations in this period. On the effects of Lend-Lease, however, Deane, like most other authors, speculates, either due to lack of knowledge or reticence concerning still-classified material (the Military Mission files were declassified some three decades after the war).

Other memoirs worth noting include George R. Jordan's *From Major Jordan's Diaries* (1952),[26] William H. Standley's *Admiral Ambassador to Russia* (1955),[27] and Robert Sherwood's *Roosevelt and Hopkins* (1948).[28] Sherwood is invaluable for his description of the inner policy debates of the Roosevelt administration. Standley, ambassador to Moscow in 1942-43, gives fascinating accounts of wartime Moscow and the internal struggles over Lend-Lease which plagued the U.S. embassy. Jordan's memoir is essentially a polemic in which he accuses the U.S. Government of furnishing the Soviet Union with everything from Manhattan project information to unnecessary luxuries. Jordan specifically blamed these peccadilloes on Harry Hopkins (a frequent target of right-wing vitriol).

Scholarly studies of Lend-Lease have focused on its diplomatic aspects. Raymond Dawson's *The Decision to Aid Russia, 1941: Foreign Policy and Domestic Politics* (1959)[29] focused on the complex political, diplomatic, and strategic factors that influenced the move to help the Soviet Union. The beginnings of the aid program were also examined by John Daniel Langer in a dissertation (1975) on the Hopkins-Department of State debate on policy[30] and an article (1979) on the September 1941 Harriman-Beaverbrook mission to Moscow.[31] The most comprehensive study of the diplomacy surrounding Lend-Lease is George C. Herring's *Aid to Russia 1941-1946: Strategy, Diplomacy, and the Origins of the Cold War* (1973).[32] Probably the most exhaustively researched book on Lend-Lease, it gives relatively little attention to the issue of actual impact. Herring did not ignore the issue but, given his concentration on diplomatic questions, had to make do with generalizations, in some cases actually overstating Lend-Lease's effect.[33] Herring's work to establish a connection between Lend-Lease and postwar U.S.-Soviet problems was continued by Leon Martel in *Lend-Lease, Loans, and the Coming of the Cold War* (1979).[34]

Studies on Lend-Lease to the Soviet Union an sich are few and far between. Robert Huhn Jones's *The Roads to Russia: United States Lend-Lease to the Soviet Union* (1969)[35] is the most notable. Jones presented a fair amount of statistics and speculated about what might have been done with American suplies. His research on American documents is outstanding. Some of the most important ones, however, were not available to Jones. Declassification of many of the documents of the U. S. Military Mission did not begin until 1973 (when the Mission's official history was finally made public), and some were declassified as recently as 1983. In addition, Jones did relatively little work synthesizing the many types of statistics and economic data to arrive at conclusions regarding the program's impact. His attitude toward the Soviet Union also affects his book. Certainly his uncritical justification of the lightning-quick cutoff of aid to the Soviet

Union at war's end[36] must be considered in light of the nearly universal condemnation this action received from other historians.

This tendency to go to one extreme or the other permeates much non-Soviet literature on Lend-Lease. Roger Munting's "Lend-Lease and the Soviet War Effort" (1984)[37] echoes the prevailing Soviet view that Lend-Lease was not very important. The program is condemned, however, as having overly benefitted the Soviet Union in Antony C. Sutton's *National Suicide: Military Aid to the Soviet Union.* [38] Sutton had previously written two outstanding volumes on the flow of technology into the Soviet Union,[39] both of which provide invaluable background material for the study of Lend-Lease and the entire Soviet economy.

The Soviet view of Lend-Lease is complicated and will be considered in detail later in this volume. As the Soviet academic and popular press has generally minimized the importance of Lend-Lease, it has logically published little about it. One of the few sources devoted exclusively to the subject, N. Dunaeva's "Lend-Lease: Facts and Falsehoods," is primarily a response to certain selected Western authors who have claimed a substantial role for Lend-Lease in the Soviet victory.[40] There are innumerable Soviet monographs and articles on the war which could be considered relevant, but few directly address Lend-Lease. The official Soviet history of World War II, published in 1977, contains valuable economic and military data which can be used to evaluate the importance of Lend-Lease.[41] Its economic figures are certainly more dependable than those in N. A. Voznesensky's *The Economy of the U.S.S.R. during World War II* (1948).[42] Like their Western counterparts, Soviet authors have concentrated on the diplomatic and political aspects of the aid program.

American authors have neglected the military impact issue because their searches through documentary records of the Lend-Lease bureaucracy yielded little information. This was in part due to some material remaining classified, but also because of the way in which the program was handled. The FEA and its numerous predecessors were never in a position to gather information because they did not make Lend-Lease policy. Roosevelt kept a short leash on the Lend-Lease bureaucracy and imposed his views on them in a number of ways, such as the appointment of Harry Hopkins to administer the program, placing trusted cabinet secretaries on important committees, and frequently dispatching special envoys to the Soviet Union. The State Department had only a limited role in the policy-making process, having been led to believe that Lend-Lease was purely a military affair.[43] The military's role, however, was not much greater, despite the requirement that the president consult the military on Lend-Lease matters. Occasionally, War Plans Division (Operations and Plans Division after 1942) officers did plan the release of specific articles of military equipment and tried to assess the importance of weapons and their use by foreign powers. But "most of the proceedings in this matter . . . were carried on outside the War Department."[44]

While one might assume that all these bureaucracies collectively gathered information about the use and impact of Lend-Lease supplies sent to the Soviet Union, this did not happen because it could not. As explained earlier, the Soviet Union alone among Lend-Lease recipients did not have to file specific proof that its requests were justified by military necessity. "We did not receive," noted Stettinius, "from the Soviet Union the detailed information about its army or about economic conditions within the country which we expected from other Lend-Lease countries."[45] American officials had few opportunities to travel in the Soviet Union and assess the situation. Most important, however, was the effect of policy itself.

Roosevelt did not want Lend-Lease used as a bargaining tool to gain information from the Soviet Union. Lend-Lease personnel in Moscow reported to officials in Washington, not at their own embassy, and did not even share information about the Soviet Union with their own military and naval attaches. In the early years of the war, the U.S. ambassador in Moscow had little control over the Supply Mission which coordinated Lend-Lease arrangements. He received almost no information concerning the Soviet military and was not kept informed about American operational plans. Since the ambassador was the only American stationed in Moscow with access to Stalin, a meaningful military liaison was impossible.[46]

The American military and naval attaches at the Embassy could not gather information because, not being in control of the aid flow, they had nothing with which to bargain. The Supply Mission had the "bargaining chips" but could not gather information because of administration policy to the contrary. Nor could the ambassador do much to rectify the situation. After Averell Harriman was appointed ambassador in 1943, the U.S. embassy was reorganized and the newly-created Military Mission absorbed the Lend-Lease function, administering it through a Supply Division. Even this did not greatly change the situation because most Lend-Lease issues were handled by the Soviet mission in Washington, which dealt directly with the Foreign Economic Administration, and the latter did not include information gathering among its missions. The Supply Division reported to the FEA as well as to the chief of the Military Mission, so that the control issue was never completely resolved.[47]

Harriman's predecessor, Admiral William H. Standley, obtained minimal authority over the Supply Mission but never really controlled it.[48] The Supply Mission during Standley's tenure rarely coordinated its activities with the rest of the embassy, let alone with Standley. This failure of the Supply Mission has been attributed not only to its policy or administrative structure, but also to the Mission's chief in 1941-43, Colonel Faymonville.

Although some of the Faymonville files are still closed,[49] his aversion to bargaining with the Soviet Union for information is well documented. He had no desire to engage in any "horsetrading," nor did he ever demand information, concessions, or Soviet public recognition in return for Lend-Lease aid or technical information.[50] Before the war Faymonville apparently even favored giving foreign secret reports to Soviet authorities.[51] His willingness to give information and to support aid requests without any quid pro quo made it impossible for other embassy officials to pry intelligence from Soviet officials.[52] Faymonville not only refused to cooperate with Standley, he did not even permit Standley to read the messages Faymonville received from Lend-Lease authorities in Washington. [53]

Faymonville was much criticized by his contemporaries, especially those stationed in Moscow, and his departure for an ordnance depot in Texarkana in 1943[54] may have been connected with his unpopularity in some military circles. His methods were often attributed to his well-known pro-Soviet outlook. Faymonville's failure to obtain intelligence information makes study of Lend-Lease impact difficult and, more significantly, may explain in part why contemporary American intelligence reports contained so little specific information about the Soviet Union.

In many ways, however, Faymonville merely followed existing policy. The president's definite views on aid to the Soviet Union were made known to the Lend-Lease bureaucracy, which in turn instructed Faymonville. There is no evidence that he ever acted outside of his instructions from Washington. Most of Roosevelt's contact with the Soviet government was done through special envoys acting on direct presidential instructions. While a more cooperative atmosphere prevailed in the American embassy after the 1943 reorganization, the information flow did not improve, indicating that Faymonville had functioned not as the uncooperative subordinate that Standley saw, but as a political officer executing presidential policy. The White House knew exactly what Faymonville was doing and never permitted Standley to control him. A contemporary of Faymonville's at the embassy was told by Hopkins in July 1941 that Lend-Lease would not be a bargaining chip.[55] Standley conceded in his memoirs that Faymonville, although difficult to work with, was in fact executing administration policy.[56]

Roosevelt and Faymonville both felt that it was more important to keep the Soviet Union as an effective ally than to gain intelligence information. Attaching a price tag to Lend-Lease might have caused unnecessary resentment in Moscow. The Soviet Union suffered horribly during the German invasion, and there was an underlying fear in some Western circles that Stalin might reach an accommodation with Hitler and withdraw from the war if continually provoked by his American ally. Fear of offending the Russians led to Hopkins' rejection of the placing of U.S. agents in Siberia, and the later dissolution of the Persian Gulf Command's G-2 (Intelligence) unit.[57]

The 1943 reorganization of the U.S. embassy was aimed at reducing friction, not changing policy. Harriman's appointment placed a presidential confidant in Moscow, obviating the need for the frequent special envoys who had driven Standley to distraction (and virtually eliminated any standing he might have had with the Soviet government). The new Military Mission, commanded by Major General John R. Deane, absorbed the military, naval, and supply functions of the embassy (the Naval Division retained some of its independence as the result of a separate agreement between Ambassador Harriman and Admiral Ernest King, Chief of Naval Operations). The new Mission was authorized "to discuss with Soviet authorities all information concerning U.S. military strategy, plans and operations" but was not instructed to obtain similar information from the Soviet Union. Deane's occasional suggestions that requests be disallowed until the Soviet government furnished data showing actual need were vigorously overruled by the

White House, and recommendations from senior officers and the various Joint and Combined Boards fared little better.[58]

Not that it mattered. The Soviet Union was less than anxious to furnish specific information on its war effort or even the precise use of Lend-Lease materials. The Russians were even less enthusiastic about having large numbers of Americans travelling around the Soviet Union. Few entry visas were given, and those only after long delays. American officers with Soviet family connections were not particularly welcome (and were sometimes expelled).[59] U.S. missions had to justify the number of members to Soviet authorities or visas would not be forthcoming.[60] Even the commander of the Persian Gulf Command, an organization dedicated almost solely to supplying the Soviet Union, was denied one.[61]

Such denial of entry visas frustrated U.S. officials because they were "unable to ascertain the basis of the Russian reluctance to act on requests for passport visas."[62] Denial of visa requests began early (an American commission formed to give advice on aid was denied entry in September 1941), and many visa requests were simply ignored.[63] American radar technicians were refused entry on the ground that Soviet "personnel were competent to install and operate all types of radar", despite evidence to the contrary.[64] American pilots were not permitted to fly Lend-Lease aircraft into the Soviet Union, ostensibly to avoid offending the Japanese, however doubtful this seemed given the military overcommitment of the Japanese Empire.[65] Some military personnel were given visas: a few navy specialists were admitted to help install marine engines, five or six USAAF officers came to instruct Soviet bombardiers, and a few high-ranking officers made special trips to the Soviet Union. Fifteen hundred Americans were stationed in the Ukraine during the 'shuttle-bombing' raids, although their presence was not particularly appreciated by the Soviet government. In any event, the American presence in the Soviet Union was small compared to the 15,000 Soviet military personnel who visited the United States during the war.[66] The British fared little better. A group of specialists was refused entry to the Soviet Union to help install the complicated ASDIC submarine detection gear in Soviet warships. The British were then blamed when the equipment failed to work.[67]

Whether more would have been known if more Americans and British had been able to enter Russia is doubtful. The experience of those already stationed there suggests that it would have made little difference. The battlefront was almost completely invisible to Western eyes, and the rarely granted and often-delayed visits were usually uninformative. By 1944 not a single American had seen actual forward positions, and glimpses of Western aid on these trips were infrequent.[68] Most visits to the 'front' were tightly organized and did not come close to the actual fighting.[69] Standley questioned all those returning, and "in not a single instance did I discover one person who had actually been at a real front where fighting was currently in progress," while only one had seen evidence of American aid, a wrecked jeep near Viazma.[70] The military and naval attaches were habitually denied permission to go to the front.[71] In general, however, American officers did find Soviet officials to be far more open and flexible when in the field (perhaps partly explaining the Soviet government's reluctance to permit such trips), but the itinerary was usually so tightly organized that such contacts were rarely possible.

Nor were travel limitations imposed only on those who wanted to see fighting. Attempts to move about without official permission could end in arrest.[72] American naval officers asking to see Soviet naval yards were initially told that no navy yards were in operation, although Soviet authorities had requested equipment for these yards.[73] American aircraft were strictly limited in number, route, and frequency of flights into the U.S.S.R. and, after a single accidental forced landing, had to carry a Russian navigator and radio operator.[74] American requests to inspect Siberian airfields for Lend-Lease and, later, Far East operations were unceremoniously denied.[75] Nor could American personnel go east to help locate and assist liberated American prisoners of war.[76]

Little information was gained, and then only after repeated requests or diplomatic pressure. Except for some prewar glimpses,[77] American analysts knew little about the Soviet industrial system. Requests for Soviet factory designs were refused.[78] Secrecy at times seemed to be extreme: an American officer visiting an optics factory was denied information as to the source of the factory's glass.[79] Knowledge about port facilities was mostly prewar: in fact, American travelers were not even allowed to visit liberated Polish ports.[80] Maps showing the location of airfields in the western Soviet Union were denied on grounds that (1) there were so many that planes could land easily without such details, (2) the country was flat enough so that every field could be used, and (3) no such map existed.[81] Travel documents and information only seemed to come forth after vigorous and sometimes public demands.[82] The careful Soviet supervision of American movements contrasted sharply with the freedom of movement given Soviet representatives in the United States.[83]

Sometimes there seemed to be little reason for the refusal of information. The P-63 Kingcobra, a ground-attack aircraft supplied to the Soviet Union in 1944-45, had generated a great many Russian complaints, especially concerning structural defects: the aircraft had a disconcerting tendency to lose its tail in flight. American offers of engineering assistance led to a fruitless round of proposals and refusals. While one engineer was ultimately admitted to help assist in the first assembly of the P-63 in Russia, American engineers were not permitted to see the defective aircraft or talk to the surviving pilots. The Military Mission was finally informed that the structural problem had been solved. Deane wrote two letters in quick succession asking for details. He never got an answer.[84]

The P-63 case was not the only one where Soviet noncollaboration appeared to hurt the Russians. Problems with the routing of Alaska-Siberia shipments led to delays.[85] In the same vein, when the Soviet government requested a highly specialized explosive, a request for detail as to type and composition was refused by the Russians because this would reveal details about their shells and cannon.[86]

None of these frictions affected American wartime policy (although the same cannot be said regarding postwar relations). The Soviet Union, after all, was doing most of the fighting, so there was little that the Americans could do except speculate on the causes of the poor level of collaboration, complain in memoirs, and accept Soviet justifications. Complaining was common, whether about Lend-Lease ("an activity that does all the giving and at the same time does none of the begging"),[87] or about individual Soviet officials ("[Soviet Ambassador Konstantin] Umansky had no redeeming qualities)."[88] The lack of active collaboration was one reason that the Soviet Union was not admitted to the joint U.K.-U.S. Combined Boards.[89]

American analysts seemed at a loss to explain the extent of Soviet secrecy, which covered a staggering number of areas ranging from combat operations to agricultural production.[90] Information seemed to come only directly from Stalin, which led some officials to conclude that "Stalin apparently was the only individual in the Soviet Union who had the authority to give some information."[91] The U.S. Military Mission in Moscow assumed that there might be a quid pro quo that it did not know about. In analyzing the grant of certain valuable refinery equipment, the Mission's official history comments that the offer "may have been an extremely valuable bargaining point, in exchange for some Soviet concession or operation not known here."[92] Undoubtedly Soviet officials were aware that their government would look with suspicion upon any unusual collaboration with the Allies.[93]

The Soviet Union never went to great pains to explain its secrecy. The lack of visits to the front was justified in terms of concern for the Americans' safety.[94] More important was the Soviet attitude regarding the American desire to know more about the specific uses of Lend-Lease materiel. The Russians "have always felt that during this war if we gave them materiel, their objective was to have victories and that it was no concern of ours for what specific purpose the materiel was used so long as they achieved success."[95] One authority noted drily that there "seems not to have been the same complete and cordial effort by Soviet Russia to exchange technical aid and information as there was between the United States and the United Kingdom."[96]

Whatever the reasons for the restrictions on American information gathering, be they American policy or Soviet secrecy, their result was quite simple: U.S. knowledge about Lend-Lease equipment use was minimal. The American Lend-Lease administrator candidly admitted that "we frankly have little detailed knowledge of the use to which the Russians put our weapons."[97] American officials, unable to observe the use made of Western equipment, had to rely on generalizations such as that made by General Rudenko, who told Treasury Secretary Henry Morgenthau that "great quantities" of American equipment were being used in the 1945 offensive.[98] In the same vein, Soviet Ambassador Maxim Litvinov gave a speech to the Lend-Lease staff in 1943 in which he admitted that he had "no statistics at <his> disposal which would enable [him] to quote the exact proportion of American supplies used in any particular battle."[99]

American wartime analyses are (understandably) filled with disclaimers about the accuracy of available information. In some O.S.S. reports there are statements about the various estimated margins of error, followed by the writer's expressed hope that the errors would cancel each other. Conclusions were qualified with words such as "about," "approximate," and "range."[100] Ignorance was almost universal (even the Red Cross did not know what was done with its relief shipments), although a lone visiting Republican politician claimed that "the Soviet government gave me every chance to find out what I wanted to learn."[101]

The United States was (and to some extent remains) ignorant of what actually happened in the Soviet Union during the war. The same is true for our knowledge of the use and effect of Lend-Lease aid. Part of the problem lay in the American military, all too often content with superficial conclusions and lacking serious prewar analysis of the Red Army and personnel with Russian language skills.[102] Many analyses of the Soviet wartime economy, without which evaluation of the impact of Lend-Lease is difficult, have been superficial.[103] Soviet publications do not resolve these problems. Soviet data is sometimes incomplete and verification extremely difficult, although more material has been made available.[104] One frustrated writer concluded that "it is neither possible nor fruitful to try and put a precise measure on the material value of allied aid to the Soviet war economy, if only because of the unavailability of many Soviet production data."[105]

If American wartime sources are vague and Soviet writings sketchy, German sources, which form the basis of most of what we know about the Eastern Front, also contain some ambiguities. These ambiguities mask the peculiarity of the supposedly methodical Germans invading the Soviet Union with completely inadequate intelligence, an act only comprehensible in light of an ignorance-based contempt of the Russians.[106] Only in this light can the German invasion, backed by inadequate armor and air power, be understood at all.[107] Before the invasion German army intelligence had no unit devoted exclusively to long-range political and economic issues, and information gathering on Soviet industrial facilities was frequently insufficient. This may not have mattered, because such information as was obtained was ignored if it failed to suit the prevailing view.[108] German intelligence was competent, but its efforts to function within the collective lunacy of Nazi Germany were doomed to failure. Finally, German intelligence itself had been penetrated by Soviet spies.[109]

This does not mean that German documents based on intelligence assessment should be ignored. At times, German deductions were phenomenally accurate, such as a 1944 estimate of Lend-Lease vehicle shipments which turned out to be within .6 percent of the actual total. Some of their sources, such as the Turkish spy code-named CICERO, furnished detailed information on Lend-Lease. The CICERO affair, once considered the "greatest spy coup of the war," was especially important because Turkey had so much accurate information on the Soviet Union,[110] which may have been passed to the British embassy, where CICERO worked. Whatever its occasional successes, however, German intelligence on the Eastern Front was never a total success. The impact of Lend-Lease was not really known by the Germans, partly because the Persian Gulf and Vladivostok were well beyond the reach of effective German intelligence gathering.[111]

How believable are the memoirs of German officers? The German generals of World War II blame their defeat on the terrain and weather, the numbers, the brutality of Soviet discipline, a lack of gasoline: in fact, everything except their own judgment, doctrine and performance, and Soviet skill.[112] Events which cannot be blamed on weather, supply, or numbers are blamed on Hitler. While much of what the Germans said can be confirmed by documents, they were often beaten in the field by skilled Soviet commanders. Although German generals claimed in their memoirs that the coming of the Soviet counteroffensive at Stalingrad was well known,[113] it was not so obvious to the Nazi high command at the time. While several claimed that they foresaw the invasion of the Soviet Union as a disastrous folly, their premonitions did not prevent them from accepting field marshal's batons and decorations from Hitler and leading the German army to defeat time after time after Stalingrad.

Given that few out of the plethora of sources are both credible and accurate, it is not easy to answer the major questions concerning Lend-Lease aid to the Soviet Union. What did Lend-Lease mean to the Soviet war effort? The diplomatic history of the program has been analyzed in minute detail from conception to sudden termination, but the military impact of the program has received very little attention. Did Lend-Lease help the Soviet Union survive? Did it contribute to the great Soviet offensives of 1943-45? Were Lend-Lease supplies helpful at the front, or mainly an aid to rear (Tyl') functions, logistics, and command, control, and communications? Or were the industrial, raw material, and agricultural items more significant? Since aid flow was not uniform during the war, did these fluctuations affect the conflict?

Nor are these the only questions. How did Lend-Lease affect Red Army operations and tactics? What did individual items mean to the Soviet Union? How did American and British shipments affect their own armed forces? What was the program's effect on worldwide shipping allocation? Finally, did Lend-Lease to the Soviet Union have any significant impact, moral or physical? None of these questions lend themselves to, or deserve, a simplistic answer. The first step is to consider the actual numbers of the aid program.

NOTES

1. Anywhere from two-thirds to three-quarters of the German divisions were present on the Eastern Front. U.S. Army, Assistant Chief of Staff (Intelligence), "History of the War in Eastern Europe, 1941-1945" (Synopsis) (1953), U.S. Army Military History Institute, Carlisle Barracks, PA.

2. Llewellyn Woodward, *British Foreign Policy in the Second World War* (London: Her Majesty's Stationery Office, 1962 [1950]), 155, 157.

3. John Frederick Gardner, "The Lend-Lease Program of World War II: Analysis and Appraisal" (Ph.D. dissertation, University of Pittsburgh, 1946), 1, 2-4, 15-20, 24, 38, 53, 57; Raymond H. Dawson, *The Decision to Aid Russia, 1941: Foreign Policy and Domestic Politics* (Westport, CT: Greenwood Press, 1974 [Chapel Hill, NC: University of North Carolina Press, 1959]), 4, 5, 7-9.

4. U.S. President, *Reports on Operations of the Foreign Economic Administration* (Washington, DC: Government Printing Office, 1944), 48-51; Dawson, *Decision to Aid Russia* , 9-10.

5. Dawson, *Decision to Aid Russia* , 14-17.

6. Ibid., 23, 35, 37; Robert A. Divine, *Roosevelt and World War II* (Baltimore: Johns Hopkins University Press, 1969), 83-84.

7. Dawson, *Decision to Aid Russia* , 118-19, 121-22, 126-29; U.S. Department of State, Protocol and Area Information Staff of the U.S.S.R. Branch of the DIvision of Research and Reports, "Report on War Aid Furnished by the United States to the U.S.S.R." (Foreign Economic Section, Office of Foreign Liquidation, November 28, 1945), 1; "History of the U.S. Military Mission to Moscow," Modern Military Records Division, R.G. 165, Box 146, OPD 336TS, N.A., 351-52. Purely military items had to be approved by the Division of Defense Aid Reports, the Joint Aircraft Committee, and other Anglo-American committees. Dawson, *Decision to Aid Russia* , 130.

8. Dawson, *Decision to Aid Russia* , 128, 143, 151; "History of the U.S. Military Mission," 351-52.

9. Dawson, *Decision to Aid Russia* , 158, 159, 172-79.

10. Ibid., 143, 160-61, 172-79, 179-80, 196-97, 199.

11. Kent Roberts Greenfield, *American Strategy in World War II: A Reconsideration* (Baltimore: Johns Hopkins University Press, 1963), 78; Dawson, *Decision to Aid Russia* , 204, 212-16, 249-50. Roosevelt did not specify whose end.

12. Congressional efforts to exclude Soviet participation in Lend-Lease continued. Divine, *Roosevelt* , 83-84; Dawson, *Decision to Aid Russia* , 145.

13. Dawson, *Decision to Aid Russia ,* 281, 282, 283-84; George C. Herring, Jr., *Aid to Russia, 1941-1946: Strategy, Diplomacy, and the Origins of the Cold War* (New York: Columbia University Press, 1973), 21; Maurice Matloff and Edwin M. Snell, *Strategic Planning for Coalition Warfare 1941-42* (Washington, DC: Office of the Chief of Military History, 1953), 56.

14. U.S. Civilian Production Administration, *Historical Reports on War Administration: War Production Board, Documentary Publication No. 1; Minutes of the Advisory Commission to the Council of National Defense, June 12, 1940, to October 22, 1941* (Washington, DC: Government Printing Office, 1946), 164; John Daniel Langer, "The 'Red General': Phillip R. Faymonville and the Soviet Union, 1917-1952," *Prologue* 8 (Winter 1976), 214; U.S. President, *Foreign Economic Administration*, 7; Gardner, "Lend-Lease Program," 54-55.

15. "Report on War Aid," 1-7; U.S. President, *Reports to Congress on Lend-Lease Operations ,* no. 21 (Washington, DC: Government Printing Office, 1945), 45.

16. U.S. President, *Reports to Congress on Lend-Lease Operations*, nos. 11, 13-16, 18-22, 33 (Washington, DC: Government Printing Office, 1943-52).

17. U.S. President, *Report on Operations of the Foreign Economic Administration* (Washington, DC: Government Printing Office, 1944). A large number of FEA documents are missing. Jay H. Moor, *World War II in Alaska: The Northwest Route (Ferrying Lend-Lease Aircraft to the Soviet Union): A Bibliography and Guide to Primary Sources* (Juneau: Alaska Historical Commision, June, 1985), 4.

18. U.S. Department of State, Protocol and Area Information Staff of the U.S.S.R. Branch of the Division of Research and Reports, "Report on War Aid Furnished by the United States to the U.S.S.R." (Foreign Economic Section, Office of Foreign Liquidation, November 28, 1945).

19. Richard M. Leighton and Robert W. Coakley, *Global Logistics and Strategy 1940-1943* (Washington, DC: Office of the Chief of Military History, 1955); Robert W. Coakley and Richard W. Leighton, *Global Logistics and Strategy 1943-1945* (Washington, DC: Office of the Chief of Military History, 1968).

20. Maurice Matloff and Edwin M. Snell, *Strategic Planning and Coalition Warfare.1941-42* (Washington, DC: Office of the Chief of Military History, 1953).

21. T. H. Vail Motter, *The Persian Corridor and Aid to Russia* (Washington, DC: Office of the Chief of Military History, 1952).

22. John Frederick Gardner, "The Lend-Lease Program of World War II: Analysis and Appraisal" (Ph.D. dissertation, University of Pittsburgh, 1946).

23. Joseph E. Davies, *Mission to Moscow* (London: Victor Gollancz, 1942)

24. Eward R. Stettinius, Jr., *Lend-Lease: Weapon for Victory* (New York: Macmillan, 1944).

25. John R. Deane, *The Strange Alliance: The Story of Our Efforts at Wartime Cooperation with Russia* (New York: Viking Press, 1947).

26. George Racey Jordan, *From Major Jordan's Diaries* (New York: Harcourt, Brace, 1952).

27. William H. Standley and Arthur A. Ageton, *Admiral Ambassador to Russia* (Chicago: Henry Regnery, 1955).

28. Robert E. Sherwood, *Roosevelt and Hopkins* (New York: Bantam Books, 1950 [Harper & Brothers, 1948]).

29. Raymond H. Dawson, *The Decision to Aid Russia, 1941: Foreign Policy and Domestic Politics* (Westport, CT: Greenwood Press, 1974 [Chapel Hill, NC: University of North Carolina Press, 1959]).

30. John Daniel Langer, "The Formulation of American Aid Policy Toward the Soviet Union, 1940-1943: The Hopkins Shop and the Department of State" (Ph.D. dissertation, Yale University, 1975).

31. John Daniel Langer, "The Harriman-Beaverbrook Mission and the Debate over Unconditional Aid for the Soviet Union, 1941," *Journal of Contemporary History* 14 (July 1979), 463-82.

32. George C. Herring, Jr., *Aid to Russia, 1941-1946: Strategy, Diplomacy, and the Origins of the Cold War* (New York: Columbia University Presss, 1973).

33. For example, "By Stalin's own admission, about two thirds of all major industrial enterprise had been rebuilt with equipment or technical assistance from the United States." Herring, *Aid to Russia*, 116. Apparently, Stalin included the effect of all prewar imports as well.

34. Leon Martel, *Lend-Lease, Loans, and the Coming of the Cold War: A Study of the Implementation of Foreign Policy* (Boulder, CO: Westview Press, 1979).

35. Robert Huhn Jones, *The Roads to Russia: United States Lend-Lease to the Soviet Union* (Norman: University of Oklahoma Press, 1969).

36. Ibid., 261.

37. Roger Munting, "Lend-Lease and the Soviet War Effort,"*Journal of Contemporary History* 19 (1984), 495-510.

38. Antony C. Sutton, *National Suicide: Military Aid to the Soviet Union* (New Rochelle, NY: Arlington House, 1973).

39. Antony C. Sutton, *Western Technology and Soviet Economic Development 1930 to 1945* (Stanford: Hoover Institution Press, 1971); Idem, *Western Technology and Soviet Economic Development 1945 to 1965* (Stanford: Hoover Institution Press, 1973).

40. N. Dunaeva, "Lend-Liz: Fakty i vymysly," *Voenno-Istoricheskii Zhurnal* (No. 3, 1977), 102-6.

41. *Istoriia Vtoroi Mirovoi Voiny, 1939-1945*, vol. 8 (Moscow: Voenizdat, 1977). See also *History of the Great Patriotic War of the Soviet Union, 1941-1945* (Moscow: Voenizdat, 1960; OCMH translation).

42. Nikolai A. Voznesensky, *The Economy of the U.S.S.R. during World War II* (Washington, DC: Public Affairs Press, 1948). Current Soviet authors still cite Voznesensky; see, for example, V. S. Prokhorov, "Trudovoi podvig rabochikh i inzhenerno-tekhnicheskoi promyshlennosti v gody velikoi otechestvennoi voiny (1943-45 gg.)," *Vestnik Moskovskogo Universiteta, Seriia 8: Istoriia* (No. 6, 1985), 13-18. Voznesensky was executed shortly after publication of his magnum opus.

43. Langer, "Formulation of American Aid Policy toward the Soviet Union," 122.

44. Ray S. Cline, *Washington Command Post: The Operations Division* (Washington, DC: Office of the Chief of Military History, 1951), 43.

45. Edward R. Stettinius, Jr., *Roosevelt and the Russians: The Yalta Conference* (Garden City, NY: Doubleday, 1949), 7

46. "History of the U.S. Military Mission," 2.

47. Ibid., 357-58.

48. Standley and Ageton, *Admiral Ambassador to Russia* , 237, 251, 314-15, 356-57; "History of the U.S. Military Mission," 2.

49. HIWRP Deputy Archivist to Yeaton (September 24, 1978), Ivan Downs Yeaton Papers, U.S. Army Military History Institute, Carlisle Barracks, PA, Archives.

50. James S. Herndon and Joseph O. Bayle, "Colonel Phillip R. Faymonville and the Red Army, 1934-43," *Slavic Review* 34 (September 1975), 502. When the U.S. Mission in Moscow was reorganized in the summer of 1943, Faymonville and Joseph Michela (military attache) were both recalled. Herring, *Aid to Russia,* 103.

51. Memoirs, Yeaton Papers, 13.

52. Standley and Ageton, *Admiral Ambassador to Russia,* 239-40; Langer, "The 'Red General,'" 218-19.

53. Standley and Ageton, *Admiral Ambassador to Russia,* 243-44, 360.

54. Herring, *Aid to Russia,* 103.

55. Memoirs, Yeaton Papers, 36-37.

56. Standley and Ageton, *Admiral Ambassador to Russia,* 246-47.

57. Robert E. Sherwood, *Roosevelt and Hopkins*, vol 2: *From Pearl Harbor to Victory* (New York: Bantam Books, 1950 [Harper & Brothers, 1948]), 133-34; Motter, *Persian Corridor,* 229-30.

58. Gen. John R. Deane, telegram to AGWAR (January 6, 1944), Modern Military Records Division, R.G. 334, Box 13, Subject File October 1943-October 1945, Folder September 1943-July 31, 1944, N.A.; *Records of the Joint Chiefs of Staff: Part 1, 1942-1945: The Soviet Union* (Frederick: University Publications of America, n.d.), "Cancellation of Convoys to North Russia: Memo, President's Soviet Protocol Committee" (April 3, 1945), 2-8.

59. Memoirs, Wellington Alexander Samouce Papers, U.S. Army Military History Institute, Carlisle Barracks, PA, Archives, 5-6, 9-11.

60. Standley and Ageton, *Admiral Ambassador to Russia,* 106-107.

61. Memoirs, Oleg Pantuhoff Papers, U.S. Army Military History Institute, Carlisle Barracks, PA, Archives, 470.

62. *Joint Chiefs of Staff,* "Allied Communication to the USSR via the Black Sea: Memorandum by the Commander in Chief, United States Fleet and Chief of Naval Operations" (November 11, 1944), 26.

63. Kenny Allred, "The Persian Corridor: Aid to the Soviets," *Military Review* 64 (April 1985), 18; *Joint Chiefs of Staff,* "Memorandum for the United States Chiefs of Staff: Present Relations between the USMM, Moscow, and the Soviet Military Authorities; Memorandum by the Commanding General, USMM" (January 22, 1945), 7-9.

64. "History of the U.S. Military Mission," 457.

65. Richard C. Lukas, "Soviet Stalling Tactics in the Forties," *Aerospace Historian* 14 (Spring 1967), 52.

66. "History of the U. S. Military Mission," 32.

67. Ibid.

68. Report to Walsh of meeting with General Nikitin (July 24, 1944), Robert L. Walsh Papers, U.S. Army Military History Institute, Carlisle Barracks, PA, Archives; Memoirs, Pantuhoff Papers, 466, 630.

69. Memoirs, Yeaton Papers, 42-43.

70. Standley and Ageton, *Admiral Ambassador to Russia,* 332.

71. *O.S.S./State Department Intelligence and Research Reports, Part 6: The Soviet Union, 1941-1949* (Frederick, MD: University Publications of America, 1977), "Morale Organization in the Armed Forces of the U.S.S.R." (April 3, 1942), 1; Langer, "Harriman-Beaverbrook Mission," 466; William Henry Chamberlin, "American-Russian Cooperation," *Russian Review* 3 (Autumn 1943), 5.

72. Memoirs, Yeaton Papers, 32.

73. Kemp Tolley, *Caviar and Commissars: The Experiences of a U.S. Naval Officer in Stalin's Russia* (Annapolis: Naval Institute Press, 1983), 145-46.

74. Walsh to Nikitin (10 August 1944), chronological file, Walsh Papers; Memoirs, Samouce Papers, 15.

75. Standley and Ageton, *Admiral Ambassador to Russia,* 253-54.

76. *Joint Chiefs of Staff*, "Arrangement with the Soviets" (April 3, 1945), 2-3.

77. John Scott, *Behind the Urals: An American Worker in Russia's City of Steel* (London: Martin Secker and Warburg, 1943).

78. Standley and Ageton, *Admiral Ambassador to Russia,* 155-56.

79. Col. Alfred A. Kessler, "Report on Russian Trip" (December 2, 1943), Modern Military Records Division, R.G. 18, Box 1045, File "Report on Russian Trip," Folder 333.1, N.A., 14.

80. U. S. Army, "Bases on the Siberian Coast," Memorandum for the Chief of Staff (May 5, 1941), U.S. Army Military History Institute, Carlisle, PA; *Joint Chiefs of Staff*, "Arrangement with the Soviets" (April 3, 1945), 2-3.

81. F. L. Anderson to C. A. Spaatz, "Report on Visit to Russia by Mission of USSTAF Officers" (May 21, 1944), Walsh Papers.

82. Standley and Ageton, *Admiral Ambassador to Russia,* 216-220.

83. "History of the U.S. Military Mission," 32. Britain was far stricter in this respect.

84. Ibid., 361, 363-64.

85. Wesley Frank Craven and James Lea Cate, eds., *The Army Air Forces in World War II*, vol 7, *Services around the World* (Chicago: University of Chicago Press, 1958), 155.

86. Langer, "Harriman-Beaverbrook Mission," 471.

87. "Personal Report of Russian Assignment" (n.d.), Walsh Papers.

88. Dean Acheson, *Present at the Creation: My Years in the State Department* (New York: W. W. Norton, 1969), 34.

89. Hessel Duncan Hall and C. C. Wrigley, *Studies of Overseas Supply* (London: Her Majesty's Stationery Office, 1956), 241.

90. *Joint Chiefs of Staff*, "Memorandum for Information No. 45: Remarks by Lt. Col. Richard Park, Jr., USA, Former American Military Attache in Russia" (January 31, 1943), 1; *O.S.S.*, "Military Potential of the Soviet Union, Part IIb: The Food Problem under War Conditions" (November 30, 1942), 7.

91. "History of the U.S. Military Mission," 34.

92. Ibid., 372.

93. Robert Conquest, *The Great Terror: Stalin's Purge of the Thirties* (New York: Macmillan, 1969), 231-33.

94. "History of the U.S. Military Mission," 33.

95. "Lessons of ESCOM" (n.d.), Walsh Papers, 7.

96. Gardner, "Lend-Lease Program," 3. Since Gardner wrote this in 1946, a great deal of evidence has come to light which suggests that the British-American relationship was far rockier than it seemed during the war. While most types of information were shared freely, in some areas, such as atomic technology, the United States was not at all willing to share information

97. Stettinius, *Lend-Lease: Weapon for Victory*, 211.

98. Deane, *Strange Alliance*, 97; Henry M. Morgenthau, *Morgenthau Diaries (Germany)* (Washington, DC: Government Printing Office, 1967), 902.

99. Maxim Litvinov, "Ambassador Litvinov on Lend-Lease," *Soviet Russia Today* (May 1943), 24.

100. *O.S.S.*, "Lines of Communication between the United States and Russo-German War Zone, Part II: War Losses of Russian Industry" (October 13, 1941), 2.

101. Standley and Ageton, *Admiral Ambassador to Russia,* 331-32; Wendell L. Willkie, *One World* New York: Simon and Schuster, 1943), 51.

102. Brigadier General Donald P. Booth to Personnel (n.d.), Sidney Gruneck Papers, U.S. Army Military History Institute, Carlisle, PA, Archives; Memoirs, Yeaton Papers, 12; Memoirs, Samouce Papers, 5.

103. Erich Klinkmueller, "Some Economic Reflections on the Great Patriotic War (1941-1952)," *Soviet Union* 4 (1977), 223-25.

104. Ibid., 226, 227. For collections of material, see I. I. Kudriavtsev, "Sborniki dokumentov po istorii velikoi otechestvennoi voiny, 1941-1945 godov," *Sovetskie Arkhivy* (No. 5, 1976), 95-100.

105. Munting, "Lend-Lease and the Soviet War Effort," 505.

106. Reinhard Gehlen, *The Service: The Memoirs of General Reinhard Gehlen* (New York: World Publishing, 1972), 9.

107. Heinz Guderian, *Panzer Leader* (New York: E. P. Dutton, 1952), 143; *World War II German Military Studies: A Collection of 213 Special Reports on the Second World War Prepared by Former Officers of the Wehrmacht for the United States Army*, 24 vols. (New York: Garland Publishing, 1974), 6:(A-3), 16; Frido von Senger und Etterlin, *Neither Fear Nor Hope: The Wartime Career of General Frido von Senger und Etterlin, Defender of Cassino* (New York: E. P. Dutton, 1964), 6.

108. E. H. Cookridge, *Gehlen: Spy of the Century* (New York: Pyramid Books, 1973), 107-9.

109. Paul Kesaris, *The Rote Kapelle: The CIA's History of Soviet Intelligence and Espionage Networks in Western Europe, 1936-1945* (Washington, DC: University Publications of America, 1979), 186.

110. David Kahn, *Hitler's Spies: German Military Intelligence in World War II* (New York: Macmillan, 1978), 185-86, 268, 378, 433.

111. Walter Schwabedissen, *The Russian Air Force in the Eyes of German Commanders* (New York: Arno Press, 1960), 158, 260.

112. Alan F. Witt, "Hitler's Late Summer Pause in 1941," *Military Affairs* 45 (December 1981), 190. Even Soviet sources concede that 1941-42 was an unusually cold winter. U.S.S.R. Red Army General Staff, *Collection of Materials for the Study of War Experience No. 2, September-October 1942* (Moscow: Voenizdat, 1942; U.S. Army Intelligence translation), 111.

113. *The German Army High Command, 1939-1945* (Arlington, VA: University Publications of America, 1975), "Intelligence on Foreign Armies. Military Foreign Service of OKH from 1938 to 1945," 12.

2

Lend-Lease by the Numbers

To understand the effect of Lend-Lease aid on the war in the East, it is obviously necessary to begin with the actual quantity of aid. Unfortunately, this is not as simple as it sounds. Lend-Lease figures are complicated. Aid data are variously expressed in terms of dollars, tonnage, total exports, or amounts actually received, and some sources are unclear as to which standard is being used. Losses in transit are not always taken into account. Dollar totals may either reflect the value of shipments or include the calculated value of services rendered but again, this is not always specified. Estimates of the value of "reverse Lend-Lease," aid given to the United States by its allies, are almost completely hypothetical. There are no precise figures for the value of transfers made in the field (fortunately, this has little relevance to the U.S.-Soviet aid relationship).

Three things make analysis of the data especially difficult. First, there are no meaningful calculations of wastage and losses of materiel after receipt by the Soviet Union. Observer accounts suggest that much may have been lost, but there is no precise way to estimate the loss. Second, much Lend-Lease aid was used in postwar reconstruction and had little impact on the war against Germany. Some industrial plants shipped to the U.S.S.R., for example, were still not operational at war's end. Finally, a comparison of aid to the various recipients (primarily the Soviet Union and the British Empire) can be (and has been) used to yield contradictory conclusions, depending upon the author's bias.

President Roosevelt moved to extend aid to the Soviet Union as quickly as possible, to sustain her as a desperately needed ally against Hitler's growing empire. At first, the supplies were to be paid for by Moscow, but Soviet funds were quickly exhausted despite loans and advances, leading Roosevelt to declare the Soviet Union eligible for Lend-Lease on November 7, 1941.[1] After a slow start, Lend-Lease flooded to the Soviet Union until, by the end of the war, the value of Soviet aid totalled $11 billion, or just under one-fourth of all Lend-Lease aid (see table 1).[2] The U.S. government also transferred equipment from the defunct shuttle-bombing operation to the Soviet government (probably worth less than $10 million).[3] Despite the precipitous and controversial cutoff of Lend-

Lease, the U.S.S.R. received another $76 million after the surrender of Japan.[4] The American people donated $115 million via the American Society for Russian Relief (originally Russian War Relief) and $23 million by means of the Red Cross.[5] In current dollars, the total American expenditure on Soviet aid was about $75 billion.[6]

Nor was the United States the only ally to help the U.S.S.R. Despite being hopelessly overstretched and overcommitted, the United Kingdom moved to help the Soviet Union as soon as Germany invaded. Churchill was no doubt painfully aware of what would happen to Britain's strategic position, both at home and in the Middle East, should the Soviet Union perish.[7] Britain helped the Soviet Union in a variety of ways. The Royal Navy escorted convoys along the dangerous northern route to Murmansk and Archangel. Most Allied merchantmen sunk in the dark and frozen seas to the north of Scandinavia were British. Direct British aid to the Soviet Union totalled more than a billion and a half dollars, hardly a trivial sum. The number of tanks and aircraft sent (see table 2) was substantial given the condition of British forces, exceeding until 1943 the number delivered by the United States. In 1941 Britain even filled part of America's quota for Soviet deliveries.[8] U.S. supplies originally allocated to Britain were sent instead to the Soviet Union, including some aircraft produced under cash contract for the British.[9]

Soviet writers ignore British aid to the U.S.S.R., complaining instead about the disparity between the British and Soviet shares of Lend-Lease, which they calculate as being 69 percent and 22 percent, respectively.[10] It was inevitable that Britain would receive more Lend-Lease aid than the Soviet Union. Not only was Lend-Lease originally designed to help Britain, but, more importantly, the difficulties of getting materiel to the Soviet Union would have kept the Soviet aid total lower under almost any circumstances. As in all theatres of war, shipping constraints shaped aid distribution as much as policy or ideology.

Yet the accusation levelled by some Soviet authors that the United States deliberately and unfairly disadvantaged the Soviet Union for the benefit of the British Empire is serious enough to require a closer look. How did the positions of the two major aid recipients compare? Britain was seriously overextended, having to defend its home islands, conduct an air war, prepare to invade Europe, protect global sealanes, conduct war in North Africa, the Mediterranean, and the Far East, maintain imperial garrisons and bases, and equip Indian, Australian, Canadian, and African forces. Certainly Lend-Lease aid to Britain was never superfluous. Soviet needs, on the other hand, even more critical. Soviet resources, however, were far greater and, outside of western Russia, much less vulnerable to attack. Soviet munitions production exceeded that of Britain throughout the war (table 3), although invasion losses slowed the growth rate somewhat.(table 4). In fairness to the Soviet viewpoint, it should be noted that its munitions production was never the equal of the United States and Britain combined and lagged behind its opponents; in 1944, for example, Soviet munitions production totalled $16 billion, compared to $23 billion for the Axis and $55 billion for the United States, Britain, and Canada.[11]

Arguments about relative need aside, was there any deliberate American effort to limit aid to the Soviet Union so that the aid flow to Britain could be maintained? At the beginning of the war in the East, some American officials feared that all aid would fall into the hands of the advancing Nazi forces, but this concern did not affect aid policy. In fact, American officials wanted to shift part of the British allotment to the Soviet Union.[12] The British viewpoint was understandably ambivalent because, although Britain understood the need for aid to the Soviet Union and participated in the Soviet aid program, the British government resented the diversion of badly needed aid (especially aircraft).[13]

In terms of "total aid," which includes the value of services rendered, the British Empire as a whole received $30.3 billion, while the Soviet Union got $10.8 billion (25 percent). In terms of actual aid, the Soviet Union did a little better, getting 29 percent, while the United Kingdom, as opposed to the British Empire as a whole, received 43 percent (table 5). The disparity between Soviet and British Lend-Lease is far less in munitions but far greater in petroleum products than for the program as a whole (table 6). With large U.S. forces on its soil and overseas bases, Britain was in a far better position to furnish "reverse Lend-Lease" aid than the U.S.S.R. The Empire as whole contributed $5.9 billion in such aid, of which the United Kingdom contributed $4.2 billion. The Soviet contribution was understandably negligible.[14] Reverse Lend-Lease is difficult to calculate and in some cases may have been given an overly enthusiastic value.[15] Nevertheless, crude as these figures may be, they do provide a basis for comparing British and Soviet Lend-Lease 'total aid.' If the role of reverse Lend-Lease and British aid to the Soviet Union is considered, the British Empire received about 58 percent of all Lend-Lease, the United Kingdom about 40 percent, and the Soviet Union, 32 percent (table 7). Lend-Lease to Britain began eight months earlier than the Soviet aid program, reflecting the earlier British entry into the anti-Hitlerite struggle.

By October 1, 1945, actual Lend-Lease exports totalled $32.5 billion, of which $9.5 billion (29 percent) went to the Soviet Union.[16] Of this amount, $9.16 billion was delivered during the war against Germany.[17] The final total of deliveries, including quantities still in the pipeline when the war ended, was approximately $10 billion.[18] Lend-Lease represented approximately one-third to one-half of all Soviet imports.[19] As can be seen in tables 8 and 9, nonmilitary goods predominated, partly because of Soviet requirements, partly due to shipping problems and Western shortages.

For the sake of clarity, figures for goods actually received by the Soviet Union have been used whenever possible, to avoid the frequent mistake of citing export figures without considering losses, sinkings, and diversion of vessels headed for the Soviet Union.[20] Careless use of export figures not only misstates what the Soviet Union actually got, but also obscures when it arrived, a potentially crucial point.

The calculation and analysis of Lend-Lease data are further complicated by the fact that data are variously expressed in terms of quantity, value, or tonnage. Values and tonnage figures given by various authors do not always agree.[21]

Some writers fail to clarify whether their tonnage figures refer to short or long tons, a difference of about 12 percent (all tonnage figures cited herein have been converted to short tons, unless otherwise specified). Information about the amount of a particular item by itself does not indicate whether it got there in time to be of any importance in the war. Tables 10, 11, 12, 13, 14 and 15 include some material delivered after the surrender of Germany but exclude supplies still in transit by September 1945. Some authors give only estimates, which vary as much as 10-15 percent from the correct information.[22]

Lists of military equipment delivered to the Soviet Union (table 10) show certain items predominating (planes, trucks, field telephones) while other ordnance items are virtually lacking. This is hardly surprising, as the Soviet Union expressed strong preferences for some items, and a dislike for others. Shipping also affected the pattern, since its scarcity made the Soviet Union more selective in ordering. This was especially true for supplies sent by the tenuous Northern route, on which bulky, heavy equipment made little sense (although often there was no alternative). Perhaps the most important aspect of Table 10 is the huge quantity of communications and transportation equipment: one-half of all Lend-Lease motor vehicles went to the Soviet Union.[23]

Food and clothing, popular items on the Soviet shopping list (table 11), were easily available in the United States. Furthermore, they could be shipped directly to Vladivostok as a result of a Soviet-Japanese understanding which permitted "nonmilitary" goods to go via this route.[24] The only condition was that the carriers be under the Soviet flag, a condition easily complied with by transferring American freighters to Sovfrakht (table 12). The tonnage figures for food are deceptive, understating its actual value because so much of it was shipped in dried or concentrated form.

Warships and naval gear made up only a small share of Soviet Lend-Lease, although the return of these vessels became a major stumbling block during postwar aid settlement negotiations. Ironically, the American vessels, plus those sent by the British (including a battleship) constituted a good share of the Soviet surface fleet. This reflects the state of the Soviet navy in the war more than it does the extent of Allied naval aid.

As already noted, some industrial equipment shipped to the Soviet Union had little impact on the war. The Persian Gulf Command transferred two entire truck plants (as well as a quantity of large truck cranes and railroad equipment) to the U.S.S.R. near the end of the war: little of this materiel could have been in use before the German surrender. A Ford Motor Company tire plant designed to produce 1 million tires per year was shipped by October 1944 but apparently was not operational during the war. On the other hand, the United States provided equipment for several petroleum refineries, power plants (including 60 portable units), rolling mills, auxiliary steel mills (designed to expand existing capacity), and some miscellaneous plants. Although not all these facilities were ready by tte end of the war against Germany, the value of industrial aid (Table 13) should not be reduced by more than 6 or 7 percent to account for the incomplete factories.[25] The Soviet Union received over half of all Lend-Lease industrial shipments.[26]

Why are there so many different items on the Lend-Lease shopping lists? Tables 14 and 15 contain only a partial listing because many smaller categories have been combined. The official postwar State Department report listed about 500 categories of supplies, perhaps reflecting the breadth as well as the depth of Soviet need.[27] The length of the list, however, may have another explanation. Soviet officials may have ordered equipment and supplies not available in the Soviet Union in order to copy them, which would not have been a departure from earlier Russian practices. Soviet engineers had carefully copied imported industrial machinery before World War II, so why should this practice have stopped? Certainly any complaints of patent infringement were and must be balanced against the horrendous Soviet losses of the war.

As suggested earlier, arguments, policy disputes, and historical disagreements over the size of the Soviet aid program must take into account the existence of a variety of practical problems. Shipping was always scarce during the World War II. The problem of allocating enough shipping space for Lend-Lease was a perennial headache, one that got worse as the United States embarked upon an active military role. In the case of the Soviet Union, geography posed an even greater problem. During the war five routes were used for deliveries, but none was free of disadvantages and problems. In sheer tonnage the trans-Pacific (Vladivostok) route was most significant, followed by the Persian Gulf, the Northern, the Black Sea, and the Arctic (table 16).

The northern route was most important early in the war, before the transport net in the Persian Gulf had been developed to accommodate supply shipments. It was vital because military supplies could not be sent to Vladivostok, and it had the advantage of being a relatively short voyage from British ports, which may explain Stalin's preference for this route.[28] It was, however, by far the most dangerous way to send shipments. The convoys sailed within striking range of German forces, and losses were at times disastrous. A British intelligence specialist described the route as "from a naval point of view, completely unsound. Climatically the conditions were appalling . . . the chances of crews of sunken ships surviving were minimal." During their voyage, cargo ships were "within easy reach of German air and U-boat bases . . . if surface ships were to join in, then losses would be unacceptable."[29] The dangers were compounded by the weakness of British-furnished and coordinated escort forces and the limited Soviet commitment to protecting the route.[30]

These hazards were exacerbated by the 'get through at any cost' attitude of the British and American governments.[31] The results of this policy were costly. Of 780 vessels making the Northern run from August 1941 to May 1945, 60 were sunk before reaching the U.S.S.R. and 36 more were lost on the return trip. For example, convoy PQ 17 (June-July 1942) lost 23 of its 34 ships.[32] Thus did Allied sailors on this route earn a disproportionate number of the Soviet medals awarded to Westerners.[33] Yet there were sound reasons for using this route. The fine natural harbor at Murmansk easily lent itself to expansion.[34] Despite the losses of ships and materiel (about 295,000 tons), the 40 convoys which reached the Soviet Union brought over 4.1 million tons of supplies (including 1.1 million tons from Britain).[35]

The logical alternative to the Northern route was the path across the Pacific, which involved no military risk. Japan had reached a neutrality agreement with the Soviet Union in April 1941 which ultimately permitted shipments from the United States to reach Vladivostok without interference. The active entry of the United States into the war actually complicated Lend-Lease shipments to the Far East, but this was remedied by leasing American merchant vessels to Sovfrakht.[36] Unfortunately, this agreement prevented the shipment of military supplies by this route. In addition, the movement of supplies from Vladivostok to the front imposed an immense strain on the Soviet transport net.[37] Even so, the Vladivostok route accounted for almost half of all tonnage.[38]

The Persian Gulf route was quite safe and, unlike the Pacific route, could be used for combat equipment. In fact, the immense effort that went into its development was justified as a way of avoiding the dangers of the Northern route and the strictures of the Pacific route. Gulf shipments, however, had to make a very long voyage and then had to be transported across the inhospitable desert of Iran. Roads and railways were poor, and the existing port facilities at Basra were inadequate.[39] Preparation of the route required the deployment of 30,000 Americans by the middle of 1943.[40] Besides the difficulties of constructing an overland conduit, there were two problems on the Soviet side, one logistical, one political. Soviet officials were skeptical about the ability of the British and Americans to develop the trans-Iranian railway and were slow to build up their own facilities in the area. Criticism of the Soviet logistical system still touches a raw nerve.[41] Perhaps more importantly, the Soviet government feared that expansion of Allied facilities in northern Iran might be accompanied by increased British influence.[42] Once this problem was diplomatically resolved by joint Anglo-Soviet occupation of Iran (with no consultation with the Iranian government), the "Persian corridor" quickly surpassed the Northern route. Total deliveries amounted to almost 5.79 million tons, including almost one-half of all truck deliveries and more than half a million tons of fuels via pipeline. The corridor, staffed by more than 70,000 British and American soldiers by the end of the war, was probably the single most important reason that the final two protocols were exceeded.[43]

Together, more than 18 million tons went to the Soviet Union via these three major routes, while the two smaller routes accounted for over a million more. The Black Sea route was opened so late in the war that its effect was necessarily limited. The Arctic route, which included the Alaska-Siberia (ALSIB) aircraft shuttle, was more important, although only during one month were promised deliveries exceeded. American support for this route was partly based on the hope that eventually Siberian air bases could be used for bombing raids on Japan.[44] In an examination of the Lend-Lease numbers and consideration of the reasons behind them, the routes cannot be ignored. The various problems encountered in setting them, whether physical, military, or diplomatic, go much further toward explaining the Lend-Lease totals than the internal machinations of the Allied governments. It is unfortunate that Soviet authors have not given more attention to these problems in their explanations of and views about Lend-Lease.

NOTES

1. "History of the U.S. Military Mission to Moscow," Modern Military Records Division, R.G. 165, Box 146, OPD 336TS, N.A., 352.

2. Ibid., 351-52; Samuel Eliot Morison, *History of United States Naval Operations in World War II*, vol. 10, *The Atlantic Battle Won:,May 1943-May 1945* (Boston: Little, Brown, 1956), 314. The figure is sometimes given as $10.8 billion. U.S. President, *Reports to Congress on Lend-Lease Operations*, no. 21 (Washington, DC: Government Printing Office, 1945), 14, 18.

3. Col. C. R. Bond to Robert Walsh (September 8, 1944), and Col. F. J. Sutterlin to Maj. Gen. F. L. Anderson, Notations on Park House Meeting 25 May 1944 (May 26, 1944), Robert L. Walsh Papers, U.S. Army Military History Institute, Carlisle Barracks, PA, Archives.

4. U.S. President, *Reports to Congress on Lend-Lease Operations*, no. 22 (Washington, DC: Government Printing Office, 1946), 22. This constituted material already in the pipeline.

5. U.S. Department of State, Protocol and Area Information Staff of the U.S.S.R. Branch of the Division of Research and Reports, "Report on War Aid Furnished by the United States to the U.S.S.R." (Foreign Economic Section, Office of Foreign Liquidation, November 28, 1945), 30.

6. Calculations based on data in U.S. President, *Economic Report of the President* (Washington, DC: Government Printing Office, 1986), 252-54. No single source accurately summarizes all Soviet Lend-Lease supplies. Relatively small quantities were supplied under various special or ad hoc agreements. For example, $12 million in communications gear went to Russia via northern Siberia and was not included in the Supply Protocols. Antony C. Sutton, *National Suicide: Military Aid to the Soviet Union* (New Rochelle, NY: Arlington House, 1973), 84.

7. Roger Munting, "Lend-Lease and the Soviet War Effort," *Journal of Contemporary History* 19 (1984), 497, 507; Michael Howard, "Strategy and Politics in World War II: The British Case," in Arthur L. Funk, ed., *Politics and Strategy in the Second World War* (San Francisco: International Committee for the History of the Second World War, 1975), 37.

8. Winston Churchill, *The Hinge of Fate* (New York: Bantam Books, 1974 [Boston: Houghton Mifflin, 1953]), 241; Hessel Duncan Hall, *North American Supply* (London: Her Majesty's Stationery Office, 1955), 332.

9. Wesley Frank Craven and James Lea Cate, eds., *The Army Air Forces in World War II*, vol. 6, *Men and Planes* (Chicago: University of Chicago Press, 1955), 408; Hessel Duncan Hall and C. C. Wrigley, *Studies of Overseas Supply* (London: Her Majesty's Stationery Office, 1956), 137.

10. Nikolai Sivachyov, "Franklin Delano Roosevelt: On the Occasion of his 100th Birth Anniversary," *Soviet Life* (February 1982), 16.

11. Hall, *North American Supply*, 421. If the vast differences in labor costs were taken into account, Soviet production would appear to be far closer to the Axis and probably the British and American figures as well.

12. Maurice Matloff and Edwin M. Snell, *Strategic Planning for Coalition Warfare, 1941-42* (Washington, DC: Office of the Chief of Military History, 1953), 207; R. W. Coakley, "Roosevelt et le pret-bail," *Revue d'Histoire de la Deuxieme Guerre Mondiale* 21 (April 1977), 96.

13. Hall and Wrigley, *Studies of Overseas Supply,* 23, 137; Hall, *North American Supply,* 332, 392, passim. The British view was related to her lower production of war materiel. See Hall, *North American Supply,* 419, 426, 429. Over half of all Canadian military production went to the Soviet Union. Hall, *North American Supply,* 488.

14. Hall, *North American Supply,* 421.

15. Margaret Saxton Haltom, "Discrepancies in the Lend-Lease Program," *Southern Quarterly* 4 (July 1966), 448.

16. The figure is sometimes given as $9.8 billion. *Great Soviet Encyclopedia,* vol. 14 (New York: Macmillan, 1980), 370.

17. U.S. President, *Reports to Congress on Lend- Lease Operations* , no. 21, 11, 14, 18-24; no. 22, 17-18, 20, 22, 28-29.

18. M. M. Kozlov, ed., *Velikaia Otechestvennaia Voina, 1941-1945: Entsiklopediia* (Moscow: Soviet Encyclopedia, 1983), 400 ($9.8 billion); "Report on War Aid," 8 ($10.2 billion); Hall, *North American Supply,* 430 ($10.67 billion).

19. In 1942-43, for example, Soviet imports totalled $10.1 billion. Nikolai A. Voznesensky, *The Economy of the U.S.S.R. during World War II* (Washington: Public Affairs Press, 1948), 43-44.

20. This is at times done even in official studies. See, for example, U.S. Army, Assistant Chief of Staff (Intelligence), "History of the War in Eastern Europe, 1941-1945" (Synopsis) (1953), U.S. Army Military History Institute, Carlisle Barracks, PA.

21. Dollar amounts give some indication of the value a product had to the United States but are not terribly informative about its usefulness to the Soviet Union. As all values are in 1945 dollars, they are best used for comparative purposes only. British pounds present a problem in that writers have not always applied a consistent rate of exchange when translating U.K. aid into dollars. Tonnage is a further complication, since there are "short" or "net" tons of 2,000 pounds known to most Americans and "long" tons of 2,240 pounds springing from British mercantile and insurance usage. "Metric" tons (2,204.62 pounds) are occasionally used for agricultural products. Authors (and some government reports) sometimes fail to specify which is being used. All figures used herein are expressed in short tons unless otherwise specified.

22. See, for example, G. Buehlmann, *The Supply Services of Foreign Armies (Economic Principles, Organization and Supplies, Transportation, and Problems*

of the Supply Services) (Frauenfeld, CH: Huber & Co.,1949; U.S. Army Intelligence translation), 41.

23. U.S. President, *Reports to Congress on Lend-Lease Operations* , no. 22, 22.

24. George C. Herring, Jr., *Aid to Russia, 1941-1946: Strategy, Diplomacy, and the Origins of the Cold War* (New York: Columbia University Press, 1973), 72.

25. Author's estimate, based upon data in "Report on War Aid," 16, 17, 28.

26. U.S. President, *Report to Congress on Lend-Lease Operations,* no. 22, 22.

27. "Report on War Aid."

28. Kenny Allred, "The Persian Corridor: Aid to the Soviets," *Military Review* 64 (April 1985), 17.

29. Patrick Beesly, *Very Special Intelligence: The Story of the Admiralty's Operational Intelligence Centre, 1939-1945* (London: Sphere Books, 1978), 173-74.

30. Robert E. Sherwood, *Roosevelt and Hopkins,* vol. 2, *From Pearl Harbor to Victory* (New York: Bantam Books, 1950 [Harper & Brothers, 1948]), 161; Beesly, *Very Special Intelligence,* 137 (convoys were administered by the British Home Fleet).

31. Sherwood, *Roosevelt and Hopkins,* 124-25.

32. Beesly, *Very Special Intelligence,* 172, 175. The loss figures are also given as 63 and 27, respectively. Morison, *History,* 313-14. See also Godfrey Herbert Winn, *PQ 17: The Story of a Ship* (London: Hutchinson, 1947). It has been suggested that PQ 17 was used as bait to lure the German surface forces into battle. "Soviet Honoring American Civilian Sailors Who Risked Lives to Help U.S.S.R. in World War II," *Birmingham News,* June 30, 1987.

33. Morison, *History,* 4 (Northern route sailors received 70 medals and 127 orders); Joel Sayre, *Persian Gulf Command: Some Marvels on the Road to Kazvin* (New York: Random House, 1945), 75. American merchant sailors have received very little official recognition for their work. Recently a number were honored by the Soviet government. "Soviets," *Birmingham News,* June 30, 1987.

34. U.S. War Department, *Murmansk Railway and Kola Peninsula* (Washington, DC: Government Printing Office, 1918), 27, 28-29, 33.

35. Morison, *History,* 313-14.

36. Allred, "Persian Corridor," 14, 16.

37. Sherwood, *Roosevelt and Hopkins,* 125.

38. U.S. Army Assistant Chief of Staff (Intelligence), "History of the War in Eastern Europe," 159; Munting, "Lend-Lease and the Soviet War Effort," 498.

39. Morison, *History,* 313-14.

40. Allred, "Persian Corridor," 18.

41. See, for example, L. I. Zorin, "Osoboe zadanie," *Voprosy Istorii SSSR* (No. 3, 1985), 79.

42.Col. C. R. Bond to Walsh, "ESCOM Logistical Notes with Respect to Russia" (August 17, 1944), Walsh Papers; Beesly, *Very Special Intelligence,* 173-74.

43. "Persian Gulf Command" (pamphlet, 1945), Sidney Gruneck Papers, U.S. Army Military History Institute, Carlisle Barracks, PA, Archives; U.S. Army, Assistant Chief of Staff (Intelligence), "History of the War in Eastern Europe," 159 (gives Persian Gulf total as 5,560,000 tons); Col. D. P. Booth to W. A. Harriman, "Capacity of the Persian Gulf Corridor" (May 31, 1944) (gives extensive details on system capacity); Memoirs, Oleg Pantuhoff Papers, U.S. Army Military History Institute, Carlisle Barracks, PA, Archives, 473; Allred, "Persian Corridor," 18.

44. Jay H. Moor, *World War II in Alaska: The Northwest Route (Ferrying Lend-Lease Aircraft to the Soviet Union): A Bibliography and Guide to Primary Sources* (Juneau: Alaska Historical Commission, June 1985), 1, 2.

3

The Soviet View

On June 1, 1942, President Franklin D. Roosevelt informed Soviet Foreign Minister Vyacheslav Molotov that Lend-Lease shipments during the next twelve months might be reduced from 4.1 million to 2.5 million tons to make shipping available for a "Second Front," the Anglo-American invasion of northwest Europe for which the Soviet Union had clamoured since July 1941. Roosevelt had not informed Molotov of this proposal in advance, but given the Soviet enthusiasm about the "Second Front," he probably expected Molotov to respond enthusiastically.

Molotov was anything but enthusiastic. He hoped that "such non-military supplies as metals and railroad materiel, which have a direct bearing on the solidarity of the present front, would not be cut too much, as they also were in large degree essential." Molotov feared that Lend-Lease cuts would "impose restrictions on the Russian rear, e.g. on electric plants, railroads, and machinery production," which he described as "comparatively vital."

Roosevelt, perhaps surprised by this response after constant Soviet insistence on a "Second Front," pointed out that shifting tonnage away from Soviet Lend-Lease would help bring the "Second Front" closer. Molotov retorted that the "Second Front" would be stronger if the "first front" stood fast. He then asked Roosevelt what would happen if Soviet aid shipments were cut and the "Second Front" did not appear.[1] Molotov allegedly even argued for more supplies at the expense of the "Second Front" at this meeting with Roosevelt.[2]

This brief exchange between Molotov and Roosevelt would not seem significant but for the fact that it does not fit at all within the typical Soviet viewpoint toward Lend-Lease. Postwar authors have given varied views about American aid but most tend to downgrade it, arguing that a "Second Front" would have been far more valuable and focusing on Lend-Lease's shortcomings, whether quantitative or qualitative. Some imply that Lend-Lease was no more than a gesture, in fact, a self-interested gesture; yet clearly Molotov, who could hardly have presented this position if it did not reflect the Soviet government's views, thought that Lend-Lease was important and resisted the effort to shift shipping from aid to troops. Which position represents the 'real' Soviet view on Lend-Lease?

Soviet vacillation on the value of Lend-Lease should come as no surprise. There is no single 'Soviet view' of Lend-Lease or any other aspect of the war, although there are important commonalities. Soviet writings on the war range across a spectrum of technical studies, self-glorification, and discussion of the diplomacy and domestic politics of the time. Sometimes all three elements can be found in a single book or article. As all nations publish self-serving materials to justify conduct or glorify themselves, Soviet self-congratulatory literature is not unique but does at times seem exaggerated in tone. Even so, its content is hardly uniform. The highly centralized nature of the Soviet state means that all publications receive approval from some higher authority. Since Soviet literature cannot be easily divided into "official" and "unofficial," inconsistencies between different sources are all the more interesting.

Soviet publications about the Great Patriotic War are designed to reinforce ideology as well as teach history. Communist historians castigate their Western counterparts for omitting the former in 'bourgeois' explanations of the conflict. Soviet historians, however, are bedevilled by the tension between ideological and national explanations of the war. Why did the Soviet Union win the war? A national explanation might consider the inherent strengths of the Soviet Union (geography, climate, numbers) as well as such less deterministic factors as the skill of the leadership, both civilian and military, the courage and self-sacrifice of the people, and strengths that spring forth from the culture. The ideological explanation attributes all successful achievements (including courageous behavior) to the system, whether directly or indirectly. That is to say, the Soviet Union won the war because its productive resources were superior due to Marxist-Leninist planning and management, its workers and soldiers were motivated by their belief in socialism, and its military strategy was guided by ideological theory.

The problem for the Soviet historian is simultaneously to prove that (A) Soviet victory was inevitable (due to the superiority of Marxism-Leninism), and (B) Soviet victory would not have occurred but for the heroism of the people and the brilliance of the leadership, the latter a highly variable consideration depending upon date of publication. This is closely connected to the problem of establishing the legitimacy of both state and ideology; that is, the interpretation of the war may depend on which it is more important to 'legitimize' at the time of publication. During the war, for example, Stalin was desperate enough to invoke Russian heroes of the past such as Kutuzov, Suvorov, and various tsars, and even called for help from the Orthodox church. The reintroduction of rank and insignia made the Red Army look more and more like its tsarist predecessor, whose deeds were recalled to raise the national spirit. 'Great Patriotic War' sounds much like 'Patriotic War,' the Russian sobriquet for the victorious War of 1812, in which the Russians defeated the legendary Napoleon. The implication now, of course, was that the Soviet Union would do the same to Hitler.

Postwar authors from socialist states have had to interpret these events in terms of ideology. Whether or not they succeed is of great interest to political philosophers, but in the matter of analyzing Lend-Lease, it is important to be aware that many Soviet and East European writers write as they do because they strive to resolve problems of intepretation and still receive the *imprimatur* and *nihil obstat* necessary for publication.

Historical theory is, however, hardly the only, or even the major, determinant of what is written in the Soviet Union. Repeated emphasis on the immense wartime losses of the Soviet Union is not only propaganda. Since the ratio of Soviet to American deaths was about 66 to 1, it is understandable that Soviet writers have tended to downgrade other combatants' sacrifices. Midway, for example, is described as a "victory of a Japanese squadron," while the Axis surrender of 250,000 troops in Tunisia is described as the "suspension of military operations by the Anglo-American forces in Tunis." The Western allies are pictured as willing to enter into a separate peace with Germany.[3] If all this seems one-sided, it should not be forgotten that many Western texts, films, television documentaries, and popular histories have ignored or minimized the Eastern Front. In addition, Soviet publications are designed to inform (occasionally misinform) and influence foreign readers. That Soviet literature has a political purpose is something that the Soviet Union does not deny.

Soviet histories have been an unstable source of data due to the need to justify or condemn (as the case may be) the actions of particular leaders. During Stalin's lifetime he could do nothing wrong; after he had been denounced by Khrushchev in 1956, he was predictably said to have done very little right, and a wealth of new information came to light. Stalin has been somewhat rehabilitated since Khrushchev's retirement.[4] In any case, Soviet interpretations have varied over time for political reasons. While mentions of *perestroika* have crept into the literature, it is too early to speculate about the extent to which current changes in the Soviet Union will affect historical scholarship on the war.[5]

The writing of Soviet history is also influenced by highly practical considerations. The Soviet military, more so than many other modern armies, has shown a strong predilection for the use of military history in military education and formulation of doctrine. One reason for this is to justify the evolution of the Soviet military in terms of the Marxist theory of history, and more specifically in terms of 'Marxist-Leninist military art and science.' More important is the Soviet military's strong belief in the "lessons of history," as part of "military-historical science." The process of compiling a historical bibliography of the war began as early as 1945.[6] Conclusions stemming from military-historical experience are communicated to the mass of middle- and junior-level officers through courses of study and publications. The latter can tell us a great deal but often contain little specific information, perhaps to avoid running afoul of the extremely rigorous Soviet secrecy laws.

All these considerations and problems are visible throughout Soviet publications concerning the war, but especially so when they apply to the outbreak of the conflict. If Soviet historians are troubled by having to prove that the result of the war was both inevitable and in doubt, they face a far trickier dilemma when explaining how the Soviet Union was both prepared and surprised in 1941. If surprised, who among the leadership in 1941 was to blame? If prepared, why were Soviet military forces propelled backward to the very gates of Leningrad, Moscow, and Stalingrad, with over four million casualties in the first four months? This problem is crucial to understanding Soviet views on Lend-Lease, because Soviet requests for war and war-related materiel offer a way to chart areas where the state was not properly prepared for war or where production had been most harmed by the invasion, as well as to aspects of tactics, strategy, and "operational art."

In the first months of the war, the Red Army was thrown back to the edge of the capital city, giving up most of the western Soviet Union. During Stalin's regime this poor military performance was either explained as a planned, phased withdrawal or attributed to tremendous German superiority in armor. The former met with skepticism during the war, but the latter was accepted by Western governments until the war was over and it became known that German tank strengths on the Eastern Front in 1941 had been overstated by a factor of seven. Recent Soviet works give the correct numbers for German armor but underestimate the size of the Soviet tank park, most notably by omitting Soviet (but not German) light tanks.[7]

Wartime publications denied that there had been surprise: "The attack made by Hitlerite Germany did not catch our country unawares." The initial withdrawals were attributed to Germany's "considerable superiority in the number of tanks and aircraft."[8] There is some truth in the former statement, because the Soviet leadership did expect an eventual war with Germany. The rate of Soviet military spending increased by about one-quarter in the year before the war. The American military attache noticed some evidence of mobilization before the attack.[9] In 1938 U.S. Ambassador Joseph Davies observed that "all Russia, including ourselves, were thinking and talking in terms of the war preparations in which the Soviets were so intensively engaged." According to Davies, plans for the establishment of partisan detachments in German-occupied areas were under way as early as 1937.[10] Soviet raw material imports also rose after 1939.[11] Perhaps this represented stockpiling of supplies for war.

Nevertheless, the invasion was not expected when it came, despite warnings from Soviet spy Richard Sorge in Tokyo, the "Red Orchestra" spy ring in Germany, and even Churchill. The Soviet armed forces were not ready. This lack of preparedness did not fit well with the image of Stalin's omniscience and was not truly addressed until Khrushchev became general secretary. The official Soviet history of the war (1960) blamed the lack of tactical readiness on three individuals: Stalin, Marshal Zhukov and Marshal Timoshenko. The effects of the 1938 purge of the Red Army were not ignored, but rather addressed indirectly. "The cult of the individual of I. V. Stalin had a negative effect on the development of Soviet military science, especially after 1937." The postpurge break-up of armored formations is attributed not to the incompetence of post-1938 generals, but to "Spanish Civil War experience." The purge itself is blamed on the machinations of "western imperialists" who "in search of ways to weaken the Red Army, used Beria and his accomplices to destroy many of the most experienced and trained commanding officers and political workers."[12]

While the 'Great Stalin' demigod never returned, criticism of Stalin became less popular after Khrushchev retired. Rather than denouncing unpreparedness, Soviet sources have sought a more moderate way of criticizing surprise. In 1966, for example, a Soviet journal admitted that Stalin's "mistake was in a misconception of the date of the conflict."[13] Professor Nikolai Yakovlev has suggested that Roosevelt and Stalin had made the same mistake in this respect.[14] By 1976 the portrayal of surprise as tactical rather than strategic had become the main Soviet explanation of the events of 1941: "Though the Soviet people knew that the war was inevitable and prepared for it, it nevertheless broke out unexpectedly, like any great misfortune."[15] Studies of prewar military efforts emphasize the level of preparation.[16]

Expected or not, and regardless of preparations, the invasion was certainly a "great misfortune." What role did Lend-Lease have in speeding Soviet recovery? According to most Soviet sources, very little. In fact, there is the implicit suggestion in many Soviet accounts that Western aid is not really worthy of much attention, especially in the context of the losses and achievements of the Soviet armed forces. Soviet authors picture Lend-Lease as too limited in 1941-42 to have influenced events, and as too small in 1943-45 relative to Soviet production to have been significant. In some publications the increasing material wealth of the Red Army is attributed solely to Soviet war industry, with no mention of Lend-Lease at all.[17] Marshal Zhukov conceded in his memoirs that Lend-Lease supplies were "of certain help," but argued that (A) Western writers had exaggerated its role, (B) Lend-Lease was shipped in much smaller quantities than promised, and (C) the aid was insignificant when compared to overall requirements.[18] This minimization of the significance of Western aid is visible in Soviet military education.[19]

Downgrading of Lend-Lease is frequently coupled with implied and explicit criticisms of Western authors. The official Soviet history of the war (1960) describes the Soviet government as "grateful" for the aid rendered but argues that it could not be compared with the military effort and sacrifices of the Soviet Union, which were "quite obvious to the Americans themselves."[20] A more recent work (1984) condemns "reactionary historians and politologists" for arguing that the U.S.S.R. "would not have been able to stand the pressure of the Nazi juggernaut and would have surely lost the war" without Western aid, a contention "spread in every way by the Western mass media."[21] Another source criticizes "bourgeois politicians" for falsifying historical reality by exaggerating the significance of Lend-Lease deliveries to the Soviet Union.[22] Western writers are denounced for their failure to compare Lend-Lease to Soviet production figures, for exaggerating the role of American aid, and for even considering it as a factor in the Soviet victory.[23]

Specifically, Soviet authors criticize Lend-Lease in three ways. First, deliveries were insignificant, especially when compared to Soviet needs and production. Second, Allied equipment was frequently of poor quality. Third, Allied governments delayed and cancelled shipments, thereby diminishing deliveries beyond even their meager promises.

Soviet writers contend that Lend-Lease amounted to only 4 percent of Soviet industrial production (less than 3 percent in the last year of the war), although they do allow for the greater Western proportion of tanks (7 percent) and aircraft (13 percent).[24] The usual view is that "deliveries of this size could not have possibly had any marked effect on the course of the war," and Allied deliveries were "an insignificant supplementary source" of supply for the armed forces.[25] Most supplies were received after Stalingrad when they were "no longer needed," while during the most acute phase of the war, the first six months, they amounted to 0.1 percent of total Soviet production.[26]

The quality of Allied equipment also has come in for a good deal of criticism. "The tactical and technical characteristics of this equipment also left much to be desired." Allied tanks and aircraft have been described as "obsolescent" and "inferior."[27] A number of experienced Soviet pilots were killed in accidents involving American aircraft.[28] Soviet soldiers allegedly preferred domestic over imported clothing and equipment.[29] Criticism was also directed at the condition in which some of the equipment arrived.[30]

The most vigorous criticism concerns the perceived failure of the United States and Britain to honor delivery commitments in their entirety. Deliveries are described as "erratic," and the convoy cancellations in 1942 and 1943 meant that "Britain and the United States defaulted on half of their aid commitments."[31] Soviet writers imply that such changes in delivery plans, and the resulting shortfalls, were the result of Western Allied policy, although they cite no documentary evidence for these accusations.[32]

Nor did Soviet authorities have much good to say about Lend-Lease during the war. The commander of the American shuttle-bombing bases complained that the Soviets "rarely mentioned" Lend-Lease.[33] The names on U.S. equipment were even removed or changed.[34] Ambassador William Standley's irritation with Soviet silence about Lend-Lease led to a public denunciation on his part, noted, incidentally, in Joseph Goebbels' diary, as the latter luminary was always on the lookout for evidence of discord among the United Nations.[35] This speech finally led to several acknowledgments by the Soviet government of Lend-Lease, both in public and in conversations with American officials and journalists. Frequently these statements were coupled with explanations of the military burden being borne by Soviet arms, requests for timely deliveries, and calls for a "Second Front."[36]

In recent years Soviet authors have at least conceded a role to Lend-Lease in the war, although without giving specifics as to where and how Western equipment was used. Recent Soviet military journal articles do occasionally note the receipt of Allied aid.[37] Soviet historians do now state verbally that Lend-Lease contributed to the war effort, although they still emphasize its small size in relation to Soviet production.[38] Indeed, it is now suggested that Soviet sources "have never denied the importance of Allied assistance." The same author argues that "Soviet history books have never ignored or underestimated the importance of American and British wartime assistance," but adds that "they seek to give a correct, fair and balanced assessment of this aid."[39]

In fact, the Soviet assessment of Lend-Lease has changed over time. During the war the attitude of the Soviet government was much more positive than in later years, at least in private. Stalin described the initial $1 billion American loan as "exceptionally substantial assistance to the Soviet Union in its great and difficult struggle" and later wrote to Roosevelt to convey his "sincere gratitude" for a later $1 billion aid grant.[40] At the Teheran conference Stalin went much further, stating that the war would have been lost without American aid, describing it as an "absolute necessity."[41] Other Soviet officials expressed similar views. American officers travelling in the Soviet Union found that "great appreciation for lend-lease supplies was expressed by authorities who regard these supplies as a major contribution to the war effort."[42] The relatively small number of field commanders and local officials with whom the Americans had contact were enthusiastic about the supplies and equipment received from the United States.[43]

Even during the war, however, the Soviet view of Lend-Lease contained ambiguities. On the one hand, occasional radio broadcasts and official statements stressed the importance of Lend-Lease. Between May 3 and June 15, 1943, Soviet radio broadcast a series of reports on Western aid, including detailed information on shipments.[44] On June 17, 1944, the anniversary of the aid protocol, "a comprehensive survey of Allied material aid to the Soviet Union gave generous recognition and gratitude for Allied bombings and Allied aid in supplies."[45] American aid was repeatedly featured on foreign-language broadcasts.[46] Contemporary Western writers argued that the average Russian knew about and appreciated the help which the United States gave Russia.[47] At the same time, a statement by Foreign Minister Viacheslav Molotov to the effect that Lend-Lease played an important part in Soviet victories was immediately followed by a Sovinformburo statement proclaiming that Soviet industry was producing "all that it, the army, needs."[48] This viewpoint became more noticeable as the war progressed. Finally, Soviet aid officials were frequently less than cooperative, and requests for better protection for the Northern route went unheeded.[49] This is particularly puzzling, as the Soviet government became vitriolic if shipments via this route were delayed.

There were good reasons for this seeming vacillation on Lend-Lease. Politically, Lend-Lease presented the wartime Soviet government with several dilemmas. Too much emphasis on American aid constituted admission either of poor preparation or of such tremendous losses of materiel at the front that Soviet industry could not replace them. The omniscience of the state, not to mention the wisdom of Stalin's 'wise peace policy,' might have been questioned, however quietly. Aside from obvious political problems, a loss of confidence in the system could undermine the morale of the country at an inconvenient moment.

The tendency to devalue the importance of Lend-Lease was also based on the nature of the war, as the Soviet Union expended vast quantities of lives, supplies, and funds to expel *fashistskaia Germaniia* from its soil. The destruction and losses were on a scale wholly beyond American experience and, the Soviet Union still contends, understanding as well. The Soviet Union's absorbing of the brunt of the German war effort for almost four years, albeit involuntarily, allowed the

Western Allies to wage a relatively limited war against Hitler. To the "average Russian," let alone the leadership, a few shiploads of supplies cannot be compared to the Soviet contribution to the war.

As the war progressed, the Soviet attitude toward Lend-Lease underwent some subtle changes. Practical barriers to the aid flow were eased, but public and private statements on the subject became less positive. In a sense this was ironic, because only in the last three years of the war did the Allies manage to solve most of the shipping problems that had bedevilled the aid program. The Nazi menace to the Northern route had been neutralized, the Persian corridor reached full operational capacity, and enough vessels were finally available to compensate for the Soviet cargo tonnage bottled up in the Baltic and Black seas.[50] Nevertheless, as the aid situation improved, the Soviet attitude deteriorated.

This trend continued after the war ended, as the entire American and British contribution to the war effort (not just Lend-Lease) came in for systematic downgrading. Lend-Lease, it was argued, had favored the British Empire, because the United States wanted to weaken the Soviet Union as much as possible. The aid program was, and is, pictured as an effort to expand the economic, military, and political power of the United States.[51]

Why this attitude? The role of Cold War politics cannot be ignored. In addition, the quasi-canonization of Stalin would not admit of any foreign factors in the Soviet victory. Finally, the Soviet attitude toward Lend-Lease must be seen in light of the postwar dispute over repayment for supplies, which alone would furnish a motive for minimizing aid value. In 1951 the Soviet Union refused to offer more than $300 million in full settlement of Lend-Lease, arguing that it was being required to pay proportionately far more than the United Kingdom.[52] Given the devastation suffered by the U.S.S.R. during the war, its refusal to pay was understandable.

While more information about the war in general and Lend-Lease in particular came to light after Stalin's death, condemnatory assertions concerning the program continued. The Soviet Union had been deliberately 'starved' of supplies. The program was an extension of American imperialism. Western writers were accused of falsifying historical facts. For example, General John R. Deane, commander of the Military Mission in Moscow and author of *The Strange Alliance*, was alleged to have ignored "well-known facts and documents" (although these were not specified).[53] Aid to Britain was described as an effort to weaken both Germany and the Soviet Union. [54]

This is not to say that all statements about Lend-Lease in the post-Stalin era were derogatory. Many of the assertions in the official history of the war were analytical, not polemical. The United States sent aid to the Soviet Union in order to "slow down and hinder Hitlerite Germany" and use Soviet resistance to gain time "for the strengthening of the mobilization of their own forces and resources." Implementation of Lend-Lease was delayed due to "traditional hostility" for the Soviet Union, but "part of the representatives of the ruling classes, realistically assessing the situation, tried to render immediate aid to the U.S.S.R." On the controversial question of delays in shipments, the official history attempts to have it both ways. Delivery of war materials to the Soviet Union was "fraught with considerable difficulties" (a point acknowledged by Stalin during the war), but lack of deliveries was caused by the goal of "protracting the war and the exhaustion and weakening of both Germany and the Soviet Union."[55]

Soviet criticism of Lend-Lease continues, but often with less vitriol than in the past. Most criticism suggests that the Soviet Union should have received more, both in absolute terms and relative to the British program.[56] In addition, the postwar repayment issue is pictured as an American effort to gain influence in European and Asian countries.[57] Praise is given, however, to many Americans and Britishers involved in the aid program. During the war the Soviet government gave decorations and awards to a number of Westerners, and it recently honored seamen who had served on the Murmansk run.[58] Acknowledgments of the supply program have become more frequent, as have public statements of gratitude, although these are still accompanied by a certain reticence about the use made of Lend-Lease supplies.[59] The tone of statements about the United Nations coalition has also changed. Although emphasis on the contribution of the Soviet Union has not unnaturally remained at the forefront, there is more frequent reference to wartime cooperation and "working together" as part of the "antihitlerite coalition." Western opposition to cooperation is blamed on "conservative forces," not entire nations.[60]

This shift in Soviet style is part of a general trend to write about the war with somewhat less rhetoric and glorification of state, system, and leaders than in the past, and more emphasis on technical, tactical, and strategic aspects.[61] More attention is given to non-Soviet publications, whose authors are no longer inevitably described as 'bourgeois.' "In some of their works on the Second World War western historians give a true picture of the role and significance of lend-lease." Soviet writers approvingly quote Alan Clark: "The Russians could have won the war on their own, or at least fought the Germans to a standstill, without any help from the West," and Lend-Lease "was marginal, not critical."[62] The use of this quotation, incidentally, is more interesting than might appear. Soviet authors do not quote their Western counterparts carelessly. The inclusion of "at least fought the Germans to a standstill" is a rare tacit suggestion that Lend-Lease might have affected the speed with which the Nazis were ejected from the U.S.S.R. Such a quotation would not have appeared in a Soviet publication thirty years earlier.

Although modern Soviet publications still consider Lend-Lease a minor factor in the outcome of the war, these same sources are less likely to reject other aspects of the Allies' war effort. This is especially true of works directed at American audiences. In a 1982 article in *Soviet Life,* Professor Nikolai Sivachyov wrote that "the Soviet Union, during the war, and in postwar times (both in speeches by Soviet statesmen and in historical works), always noted the significance of the American deliveries to our country." The reader is still reminded that Lend-Lease only amounted to 4 percent of Soviet military production and "played a secondary role," but the latter point is extended to its role in the American war effort as well. "The direct operations of the U.S. Armed Forces in the Pacific, in Africa and, finally, in Europe were the main contribution of the American people in routing the aggressors."[63]

The many nuances in the Soviet view of Lend-Lease can be explained, but not in any simplistic way. Certainly Lend-Lease was not as irrelevant as Soviet writers in the 1950s claimed: their view does not square with the steadily increasing Soviet requests for every conceivable item.[64] Nor does it explain the Soviet failure to release detailed information about the use of Western supplies. The downgrading of Western contributions to victory does make sense in terms of domestic Soviet politics and propaganda, and occasionally sycophancy. Since the Soviet state was legitimated by victory, pride in military achievement is understandable, especially given that the Soviet victory had been predicted by few outside observers (most of whom were unaware of post-1940 reforms and the eastward shift of Soviet industry). Whatever the shortcomings of the Soviet military system, its ability to regenerate itself in the midst of conflict is especially remarkable.

To the distress of many Soviet writers, the successes of the Red Army received little foreign attention.[65] American high school and college texts virtually ignored the Soviet role in World War II, as did Hollywood after 1945. Problems of access to Soviet documents, conditions facing researchers in the U.S.S.R., and language barriers discouraged many.

Western scholars and writers have had to contend with the proverbial Russo-Soviet passion for secrecy. Westerners have difficulty either penetrating or understanding this. Soviet officials, for example, sometimes refused foreign technical assistance that would require the release of information, even that concerning clearly obsolete equipment. American officials suspected that the primitive facilities they were shown were only a blind.[66] Fortunately, the situation has begun to change in two ways. First, a great many technical studies of the war have been published in the Soviet Union, such as the exhaustive study of the Soviet wartime transportation system which appeared in 1981.[67] Second, controversies concerning important events during the war have received more public attention. In 1974, for example, a study of the battle of Kursk revealed that "some scholars" denied that the famous tank battle at Prokhorovka, the single largest armored encounter ever, had taken place, an assertion vigorously denied by the Soviet commander there.[68]

Even recent histories and apparently thorough technical works, however, frequently omit important details. These studies are still far more informative than wartime and immediate postwar material. There were certainly practical reasons for both the state and the individual Soviet author to be reticent. Soviet military authorities attributed some of their successes to the secrecy with which they concealed their strength. Stalin suggested that "public ignorance of the capacity of railroads is the best guarantee against treason."[69] During the war the Russians may have feared that secrets communicated to Washington might 'leak' and find their way into the American press and eventually to the Germans (much of whose North American intelligence program consisted of newspaper subscriptions routed through neutral countries).[70] This fear was stimulated by concern about pro-

Fascist elements in British and American military, government, and private circles.

How much did secrecy aid Soviet victory? Germany was generally ignorant of Soviet military and economic resources (and virtually unaware of the prewar eastward relocation of industry). Whether this benefitted Russia hinges on the complicated dynamics of deterrence and balance of power (not to mention Hitler's psyche). Deterrence depends more on a potential aggressor's perception of strength (assuming rational behavior) than on the intended victim's actual strength. Would Germany have attacked even if Soviet strength had been more visible? Contrary to popular impression, Hitler was not alone in his confidence about the outcome of Barbarossa, even when the magnitude of Soviet resources and capabilities was clearer. As late as the summer of 1942, the arch-pessimist Chief of Staff General Franz Halder still thought that Germany would win, and even in 1943 victory was not deemed impossible. The pros and cons of strict secrecy are numerous and the issue is complex. Excessive secrecy can not only undercut deterrence but can confuse the system itself if its members are denied adequate knowledge of operations. In this regard, one may consider the role of the special teams of Soviet General Staff officers used to conduct major offensives.

Whatever the actual merits of the issue, Soviet analysts can certainly make an honest claim that secrecy is an advantage in wartime. Secrecy and the war did not, however, end simultaneously. Again, there were practical reasons for both government and individuals to withhold information. Information about the precise flow of Lend-Lease supplies, for example, would have revealed a great deal about the Soviet logistical system and more. In addition, individual officials and authors faced certain disadvantages if they were too open or cooperative. Excessive wartime collaboration with foreigners brought suspicion on Soviet officials.[71] Writers, then as now, worked under a rigorous Soviet secrecy law. As elsewhere, the intentional transfer of state secrets is considered treason, and even merely losing or divulging secret information is a criminal offense. What makes the Soviet situation somewhat different (other than strict law enforcement and the lack of private commercial publishers) is a definition of 'state secret' which includes both military and economic information. The former consists of all information concerning the strength, armament, location, equipment, and planning of the armed forces, as well as information about border protection. The latter includes data about military and metal industries, mineral resources, inventions of military importance, and inventions of economic importance.[72]

An examination of the basis for Soviet secrecy should never exclude the Soviet psyche. During the war American officials, like foreign observers over the centuries, found the Russians to be paranoid and somewhat xenophobic. "Every request or proposal that we make to the Soviet Union is viewed with suspicion." Even American liberality and informality did not soften them. "Our attitude is beyond their understanding, hence they do not trust us."[73] The implementation of the Alaska-Siberia airplane delivery route was delayed due to Soviet suspicions of

American motives, especially when U.S. officials expressed an interest in information such as the type and location of airfields in Siberia.[74]

Paranoia may not be a surprising state of mind for a country invaded as often as Russia. American interest in Siberian facilities may have been viewed by some Soviet officials in terms of the American military presence there in 1919. Relations with the United States had developed rather slowly, hampered by delayed recognition, ideological friction, and perhaps the very limited U.S. support of Finland in the Russo-Finnish war, although this aid was minimal compared to French and British efforts.[75] The American commander of the shuttle-bombing force in the Ukraine conceded that U.S. actions often contributed to Soviet paranoia.[76] The sudden cutoff of Lend-Lease at the end of the war seemed reasonable enough to Americans but embittered the Soviet government, a bitterness still echoed by some current writers.[77]

The individual Soviet citizen also had reason to be paranoid. The domestic policies of the Russian state, whether tsarist or Communist, have not encouraged free expression. Stalin-era Soviet officials had reason to be at least uncertain about their future, and not just from the normal dangers of demotion or arrest. Returning POWs were considered traitors and sent to the prison camps.[78] During the occupation of Berlin some American officers suspected that several Soviet generals had been poisoned.[79] True or not, it gives some indication of the atmosphere surrounding the Soviet system.

Finally, Soviet efforts to minimize and distort the role of Lend-Lease, as well as the tendency to withhold specific information on the subject, may have been motivated by considerations of national prestige and image. Rigid restrictions placed on travel by the Allied missions in Russia were, it was believed, somehow related to a desire for more prestige through presenting an image of invincibility.[80] It was not clear how much the denial of information concealed Soviet weakness versus strength. Throughout the war (and after) Soviet officials were extraordinarily sensitive about any evidence that Western equipment, supplies, or techniques were superior to their own, but at the same time they did their level best to acquire all of these.

The Soviet attitude toward Lend-Lease, complex and contradictory as it is, must be viewed in the context of history, tsarist and Soviet, politics, law, and psychology.[81] On the surface, the Soviet view of Lend-Lease seems pejorative and slighting. It is Soviet sources, however, which prove that the program was in some way important. So many Soviet writers have censored, minimized, or rationalized the role of Lend-Lease. Would they have done so if the program were truly meaningless?

NOTES

1. Robert E. Sherwood, *Roosevelt and Hopkins,* vol. 2, *From Pearl Harbor to Victory* (New York: Bantam Books, 1950 [Harper & Brothers, 1948]), 159.

2. William H. Standley and Arthur A. Ageton, *Admiral Ambassador to Russia* (Chicago: Henry Regnery, 1955), 82.

3. *History of the Great Patriotic War of the Soviet Union, 1941-1945* (Moscow: Voenizdat, 1960; OCMH translation), vol. 3: 78-79, 488; "The Armored and Mechanized Troops of the Soviet Armed Forces" (n.d.), (U.S. Army Intelligence translation), U.S. Army Military History Institute, Carlisle Barracks, PA, 64, 95.

4. The reasons for this are very complicated and uncertain, but one factor was that many senior Kremlin functionaries would have been threatened by unlimited criticism of and investigation into the Stalin era.

5. See A. N. Mertsalov, "O kritike burzhuaznoi istoriografii vtoroi mirovoi voiny," *Voprosy Istorii* (No. 12, 1987), 50.

6. A. O. Zilberman, "Velikaia otechestvennaia voina v bibliograficheskikh izdaniiakh: obzor," *Istoriia SSSR* (No. 3, 1980), 162.

7. Oleg Rzheshevsky, *World War II: Myths and the Realities* (Moscow: Progress Publishers, 1984), 103, 211.

8. "Armored and Mechanized Troops," 5.

9. G. Buehlmann, *The Supply Services of Foreign Armies (Economic Principles, Organization and Supplies, Transportation, and Problems of the Supply Services)* (Frauenfeld, CH: Hubert & Co., 1949; U.S. Army Intelligence translation), 50, 53; memoirs, Ivan Downs Yeaton Papers, U.S. Army Military History Institute, Carlisle Barracks, PA, Archives, 28-29.

10. Joseph E. Davies, *Mission to Moscow* (London: Victor Gollancz, 1942), 305, 363. I find Davies' observations somewhat doubtful.

11. Hessel Duncan Hall, *North American Supply* (London: Her Majesty's Stationery Office, 1955), 93.

12. *History of the Great Patriotic War*, 1:149, 562, 563;2: 10.

13. "Stalin in Command," *Atlas* (May 1966), 271 (translated from *Oktiabr'*).

14. Nikolai Yakovlev, "USSR-USA: 50 Years of Diplomatic Relations," *Soviet Life* (November 1983), 37.

15. I. K. Koblyakov, *USSR: For Peace against Aggression, 1933-1941* (Moscow: Progress Publishers, 1976), 233.

16. B. A. Platonov, "Uzel sviazi general'nogo shtaba v gody velikoi otechestvennoi voiny," *Voprosy Istorii* (No. 2, 1978), 95.

17. V. I. Chuikov, *The End of the Third Reich* (Moscow: Progress Publishers, 1978), 72.

18. Georgii K. Zhukov, *The Memoirs of Marshal Zhukov* (New York: Delacorte Press, 1972), 92, 391.

19. Zbigniew Brzezinski, ed., *Political Controls in the Soviet Army* (Ann Arbor: Edwards Brothers, 1954), 36.

20. *History of the Great Patriotic War,* 3:501.

21. Rzheshevsky, *World War II,* 181-83. The quotations he cites refer either to the Anglo-American role in general or to specific Soviet victories.

22. M. M. Kozlov, ed., *Velikaia Otechestvennaia Voina, 1941-1945: Entsiklopediia* (Moscow: Soviet Encyclopedia, 1983), 400.

23. S. V. Baranov, "Rost tekhnicheskoi osnashchenosti sovetskikh vooruzhennykh sil v gody velikoi otechestvennoi voiny," *Voprosy Istorii* (No. 5, 1975), 31; V. A. Sekistov, "Kritika burzhuaznykh fal'sifikatsii itogov i urokov mirovoi voiny," *Voprosy Istorii KPSS* (No 4, 1975), 81-92.

24. Kozlov, *Velikaia Otechestvennaia Voina,* 400; Baranov, "Rost tekhnicheskoi osnashchenosti," 31; V. A. Matsulenko, "Velikaia pobeda sovetskogo naroda i ego vooruzhennykh sil," *Voprosy Istorii KPSS* (No. 9, 1963), 116-17. The 4 percent figure is still used. Jeffrey Kimball, "1st Soviet-American Symposium on US-USSR Relations during World War II, Moscow, USSR, Oct. 20-29, 1986," *SHAFR Newsletter* 18 (June 1987), 43.

25. Rzheshevsky, *World War II,* 185; N. Dunaeva, "Lend-Liz: Fakty i vymysly," *Voenno-Istoricheskii Zhurnal* (No. 3, 1977), 104.

26. Baranov, "Rost tekhnicheskoi osnashchenosti," 31.

27. Rzheshevsky, *World War II,* 185.

28. L. I. Zorin, *Osoboe Zadanie* (Moscow: Izdatel'stvo Politicheskoi Literatury, 1987), 122-23.

29. Gen. Istvan Beleznay, "The Logistical Service of the Soviet Army," *Honved* (December 1949; U.S. Army Intelligence translation and abstract), 2.

30. Dunaeva, "Lend-Liz," 103.

31. Rzheshevsky, *World War II,* 184-85.

32. Maurice Matloff and Edwin M. Snell, *Strategic Planning for Coalition Warfare, 1941-42* (Washington, DC: Office of the Chief of Military History, 1953), 205n; Robert A. Divine, *Roosevelt and World War II* (Baltimore: Johns Hopkins University Press, 1969), 81-82.

33. "Lessons of ESCOM" (n.d.), Robert Walsh Papers, U.S. Army Military History Institute, Carlisle Barracks, PA, Archives, 12.

34. Memoirs, Wellington Alexander Samouce Papers, U.S. Army Military History Institute, Carlisle Barracks, PA, Archives, 47. In general, World War II Soviet newsreels did not show Lend-Lease equipment until the 1960s.

35. Standley and Ageton, *Admiral Ambassador to Russia,* 341-49; Louis P. Lochner, ed., *The Goebbels Diaries* (New York: Universal-Award House, 1971), 328.

36. See, for example, Joseph Stalin's reply to Moscow AP correspondent Henry C. Cassidy, October 3, 1942. Joseph Stalin, *The Great Patriotic War of the Soviet Union* (New York: International Publishers, 1945), 163.

37. V. Konovalov, "Iz opyta popol'neniia sostava severnogo flota v gody velikoi otechestvennoi voiny," *Voenno-Istoricheskii Zhurnal* (No. 8, 1978), 109; V. Bakaev, "Morskoi transport v velikoi otechestvennoi voine," *Morskoi Sbornik* (No. 6, 1976), 28.

38. Kimball, "1st Soviet-American Symposium", 43.

39. Rzheshevsky, *World War II,* 184, 190-91.

40. U.S.S.R. Ministry of Foreign Affairs, *Correspondence between the Chairman of the Council of Ministers of the U.S.S.R. and the Presidents of the U.S.A. and the Prime Ministers of Great Britain During the Great Patriotic War of 1941-1945* (London: Lawrence & Wishart, 1958), 2:14-15, 20-21.

41. Edgar L. Erickson, Foreword to Robert Huhn Jones, *The Roads to Russia: United States Lend-Lease to the Soviet Union* (Norman: University of Oklahoma Press, 1969), vii.

42. Gen. John Deane and Gen. Sidney Spalding to AGWAR (June 21, 1944), Modern Military Records Division, R.G. 334, Box 13, Subject File October 1943-October 1945, Folder September 1943 through July 31, 1944, N.A.

43. U.S. Department of State, *Foreign Relations of the United States*, vol. 12 (Washington, DC: Goverment Printing Office, 1966), 1080-81; Jones, *Roads to Russia,* 235-36.

44. *O.S.S./State Department Intelligence and Research Reports, Part 6: The Soviet Union, 1941-1949* (Frederick, MD: University Publications of America, 1977), "Soviet Domestic Shortwave Broadcasts -- Their Scope and Content" (27 September 1943), 12-13.

45. *Records of the Joint Chiefs of Staff: Part 1, 1942-1945: The Soviet Union* (Frederick, MD: University Publications of America, n.d.), "Memorandum for Information No. 275: Ambassador Harriman's Interpretive Comment on the Soviet Press" (July 26, 1944), 1.

46. *Foreign Relations of the United States,* vol. 3 (Washington, DC: Government Printing Office, 1961), 553.

47. William Henry Chamberlin, "American-Russian Cooperation," *Russian Review* 3 (Autumn 1943), 4-5.

48. *Foreign Relations of the United States,* 3:545, 548.

49. Jones, *Roads to Russia,* 111, 153-54.

50. "Military Notes from around the World," *Military Review* 21 (October 1941), 48.

51. A. Alexeyev, "Lend-Lease as 'Weapon of U.S. Imperialism'," *Current Digest of the Soviet Press* 3 (September 1951), 8-9. See also Oleg A. Rzheshevsky, "Noveishaia burzhuaznaia istoriografiia o korennom perelome v khode vtoroi mirovoi voine," *Istoriia SSSR* (No. 3, 1985), 166.

52. U.S. President, *Reports to Congress on Lend-Lease Operations*, no. 33 (Washington, DC: Government Printing Office, 1952), 7.

53. B. I. Marushkin and N. N. Yakovlev, "Vopros o bzaimootnosheniiakh SSSR i SSHA v period vtoroi mirovoi voiny v amerikanskoi burzhuaznoi istoriografii," *Novaia i Noveishaia Istoriia* (No. 3, 1957), 162.

54. *History of the Great Patriotic War,* 1:435.

55. Ibid., vol. 2:180, 365; Sherwood, *Roosevelt and Hopkins,* 544-47.

56. A. L. Narochnitskii, "Vneshniaia politika S.S.S.R. i problemy evropeiskoi bezopasnosti mezhdu dvumia mirovimi voinami," *Novaia i Noveishaia Istoriia* (No. 5, 1974), 19; Dunaeva, "Lend-Liz," 103; V. S. Prokhorov, "Trudovoi podvig rabochikh i inzhenerno-tekhnicheskoi intelligentsii podshipnikovoi promyshlennosti v pervyi period velikoi otechestvennoi voiny (1941-1942 gg.)," *Vestnik Moskovskogo Universiteta, Seriia 8: Istoriia* (No. 5, 1985), 22-28; Rzheshevsky, "Noveishaia burzhuaznaia istoriografiia," 155-68.

57. Kozlov, *Velikaia Otechestvennaia Voina,* 400.

58. Zhukov, *Memoirs,* 643; B. Nikitin, "Za tysiachi mil' ot fronta," *Morskoi Sbornik* (No. 10, 1976), 58; "Soviets Honoring American Civilian Sailors Who Risked Lives to Help U.S.S.R. in World War II," *Birmingham News,* June 30, 1987; Zorin, *Osoboe Zadanie,* 105.

59. Kozlov, *Velikaia Otechestvennaia Voina,* 400; Pavel D. Pavlov, Second Secretary of the Soviet Embassy to the United States, speech at the Student Conference on National Affairs, Texas A&M University, February 10, 1982. Pavlov said that the Soviet Union was "grateful" for the moral and especially the material support provided during the war.

60. Zorin, *Osoboe Zadanie,* 174-75.

61. See Otto P. Chaney, Jr., "The Agony of Soviet Military Historians," *Military Review* 48 (June 1968), 24-28.

62. Rzheshevsky, *World War II,* 186.

63. Nikolai Sivachyov, "Franklin Delano Roosevelt: On the Occasion of His 100th Birth Anniversary," *Soviet Life* (February 1982), 16. Note the veiled reference to the belated Anglo-American entry into northwest Europe.

64. Jones, *Roads to Russia,* 86.

65. Dunaeva, "Lend-Liz," 103.

66. Memoirs, Oleg Pantuhoff Papers, U.S. Army Military History Institute, Carlisle Barracks, PA, Archives, 632-33.

67. I. V. Kovalev, *Transport v Velikoi Otechestvennoi Voine, (1941-1945)* (Moscow: Izdatel'stvo Nauka, 1981); V. A. Matsulenko, *Operativnaia Maskirovka Voisk* (Moscow: Voenizdat, 1975).

68. Ivan Parotkin, ed., *The Battle of Kursk* (Moscow: Progress Publishers, 1974), 171.

69. Buehlmann, *Supply Services of Foreign Armies,* 43.

70. "History of the U.S. Military Mission to Moscow," Modern Military Records Division, R.G. 165, Box 146, OPD 336TS, N.A., 2.

71. Robert Conquest, *The Great Terror: Stalin's Purge of the Thirties* (New York: Macmillan, 1969), 231-32.

72. F. J. M. Feldbrugge, ed., *Encyclopedia of Soviet Law* (Dobbs Ferry, NY: Oceana Publications, 1973), 2:600-601.

73. *Joint Chiefs of Staff,* "Revision of Policy with Relation to Russia: Memo, Commanding General, USMMUSSR" (April 16, 1945), 2.

74. Sherwood, *Roosevelt and Hopkins,* 133.

75. Mark Skinner Watson, *Chief of Staff: Prewar Plans and Operations* (Washington, DC: Historical Division, Department of the Army, 1950), 311.

76. "Final Report," Walsh Papers, 6-7.

77. See Oleg A. Rzheshevsky and Evgeni Kulkov, "Politik und Strategie der UdSSR und der Westmaechte gegenueber dem faschistischen Deutschland in den letzten Monaten des Krieges in Europa," *Militaergeschichte* 24 (No. 1, 1985), 3-17.

78. Stephen F. Cohen, "Stalin's Terror as Social History," *Russian Review* 45 (October 1986), 379.

79. A. E. Schanze Papers, U.S. Army Military History Institute, Carlisle Barracks, PA, Archives. A group of American officers in Berlin received a case of vodka that turned out to be poisoned. The vodka had apparently been intended for some Russian officers (including A. A. Grechko), who simply sent it on. According to Schanze, a number of Russian generals died mysteriously at about this time.

80. "Lessons of ESCOM" (n.d.), Walsh Papers, 7; John W. O'Daniel Papers, U.S. Army Military History Institute, Carlisle Barracks, PA, Archives.

81. As for the psychological factor, American officers suggested that "I understand the Russians," like "liquor doesn't affect me," belonged in the "famous last words" category. O'Daniel Papers.

4

Lend-Lease and the Road
to Stalingrad

The titles of John Erickson's magisterial two-volume work on the Eastern Front, *The Road to Stalingrad* and *The Road to Berlin*, focus our attention on the true nature of the conflict.[1] By using the names of the two greatest Soviet victories, the one the destruction of an entire Nazi field army and the other the final act in the destruction of the Third Reich, Erickson reminds us that the Soviet Union won, that the Red Army overcame the appalling losses and incalculable suffering brought by the Nazi invasion to win a ground war which in size, scope, and destruction has no equal. His titles also remind us that the Great Patriotic War was not uniform, but that it consisted of the advance and retreat of huge forces which in a smaller area might have been condemned to a World War I-like stalemate. The war does not divide simply into a period of German victories and a period of Soviet counteroffensives. Even after Stalingrad the Nazis were able to mount the immense but unsuccessful Kursk offensive, and even after that bloodbath the German army was able to survive for almost two years. Nevertheless, Stalingrad was a turning point in many different ways, not only in the physical and material sphere, but in the psychological as well. It requires no imagination to realize that the surrender of the German Sixth Army had an undoubted effect on the faith that the rank and file had on their respective leaderships.

It is therefore a useful step to divide the analysis of Lend-Lease aid over time into pre- and post-Stalingrad phases. The effect of Lend-Lease, if any, could not have been uniform throughout the war. The flow of aid to the Soviet Union was understandably uneven in volume and frequency, although the general trend was definitely upward. This growth was mostly due to improvements in transport, the construction of new railway and port facilities in Iran, more vigorous protection for the northern route, the late opening of the Black Sea, and a general increase in shipping space, although this remained fairly tight. Increasing aid, however, did not automatically mean increasing effect. Despite the losses caused by the invasion, the Soviet economy did not collapse and by approximately the middle of the war had recovered, outstripping German production of most weapons (although this production increase may have been helped by Western aid). In other words, as Lend-Lease imports grew, so did the Soviet Union's capacity to meet its own military needs. The reverse is also true: Lend-Lease imports in 1941-42 were comparatively limited, but Soviet production was barely adequate, if that.

Soviet writers disagree among themselves about the relative importance of Lend-Lease during various phases of the war. When Marshal Zhukov criticized Western writers for exaggerating the role of aid, he carefully referred to 1941 and 1942, not the entire war.[2] Other Soviet sources claimed instead that Lend-Lease could only have been important during the first part of the war, at a time when Soviet industry "could not replace the losses of 1941" and "production in the Urals and Siberia was only developing." Lend-Lease deliveries of "aircraft, tanks, ammunition, motor vehicles, and various strategic raw materials helped the USSR in the war."[3]

When and how did Lend-Lease have its greatest impact on the Eastern Front? Certainly the war was too vast and complex a phenomenon to be viewed as a whole; even when a single facet of the conflict is examined, evidence must be broken down into manageable units. In the case of the effect of Lend-Lease supplies, this is easier said than done. A considerable time lag existed between the time that an item was delivered and the time that it actually came into use, which, in turn, varied depending on need for a particular item, complexity, and whether it was a finished product or raw material.

There is also a qualitative dimension, insomuch as composition of shipments changed throughout the war, and quality, complexity, and usefulness of materiel varied. Raw materials, for example, had an indirect effect on the great battles, difficult to precisely determine. It is especially hard to find out when weapons made with these raw materials arrived at the front. At the same time, some supplies, such as food and clothing, could have been used by combat forces, or rear service troops, or civilians.

Early in the war, Soviet requests emphasized weapons. The Americans and British obliged by sending, among other things, several thousand tanks. Their narrow treads, relatively thin armor, light guns, and mechanical complexity made them unsuited to the Eastern Front. While using these vehicles as an example of the shortcomings of Lend-Lease, Soviet sources pay much more public attention to foreign weapons, visible to friend and foe alike, than to less glamorous items, such as clothes, food, and communications equipment, which probably were more important to the Red Army than any imported weapons, aircraft possibly excepted.

Neither individual military successes nor general improvements can be automatically attributed to Lend-Lease. Neither the Red Army's admittedly dramatic improvement by 1943 nor its victories in particular battles were mainly the result of foreign aid.[4] Lend-Lease was certainly a factor, but to what extent? Lend-Lease being one variable of many, it is exceedingly difficult to control for the others, since it is impossible to determine, let alone to gather accurate data about, all other variables.

This does not prevent drawing conclusions about effects of the changing flow of Lend-Lease supplies. It is certainly significant that the Soviet share of Lend-Lease (as well as the absolute aid total) rose continuously throughout the war. This reflects a continuous Soviet demand for war materiel and may possibly indicate persistent domestic shortages. The demand could not be met instantly. In 1941 only 6.3 percent of all Lend-Lease aid was sent to the Soviet Union, primarily because of shipping and organizational problems and the U.S.S.R.'s late entry into the war. By June 1942 the cumulative total rose to 19.8 percent. In the twelve months ending in July 1943, 26.4 percent of all aid went to the Soviet Union, in the ensuing twelve months, 30 percent, and for the war as a whole, almost one-third.[5] The aid flow was fairly constant from mid-1943 to mid-1945, especially when compared to earlier fluctuations.[6]

This trend is reflected in the flow of individual items as well as in aggregate totals. Aircraft, motor vehicles, foodstuffs, and clothing moved to the Soviet Union at a steady pace. Rail cars and locomotives only arrived in quantity at the beginning of 1944, increasing in number rapidly thereafter.[7]

Table 17 shows the increasing flow of supplies, while tables 18, 19, and 20 demonstrate aid-flow variations in monthly and quarterly terms. The average annual aid flow increased every year except 1945, and that only because of the end of the war. Quarterly statistics fluctuate a bit more, showing a noticeable drop in the second quarter of 1943, followed by an enormous jump in the latter part of the year; shipments in the last quarter of 1943 were greater in value than those of any other, and the Soviet Union's share of all Lend-Lease was exceeded only once, in the second quarter of 1945.

Montly totals show even more variety. In the summer of 1942 vigorous German attacks on the Northern route led to a drop in shipments, which, as shown by table 19, did not regain the April level until November. The same thing happened again in 1943, but the growth of the Persian Gulf route almost matched the decrease in Northern route shipments. The effect of variations in monthly shipments was not uniform, since cancellations and delays were obviously of less significance if a high percentage of the ships did not get through anyway. Losses were much higher in 1942 and 1943 than in the last two years of the war. Tables 19 and 20 both reflect losses in transit. Wastage and loss inside the Soviet Union, virtually impossible to estimate but known to be substantial, slightly reduced the effect of imports and shipment cancellations. For example, if losses inside the Soviet Union during transport and storage amounted to 10 percent, the shipment or cancellation of 100 tons of supplies translated into 90 tons available for or lost to the Red Army.

Beyond all that, the effect of Lend-Lease help could not have been immediate, since it had to make its way through the Soviet logistical system, and recipients often needed time to learn how to use new equipment, especially if it was technically complex. While difficult to estimate, the time lag between shipment and actual use was probably one to three months, and substantially longer for some raw materials and complex machinery.

Since periodic reductions in the quantity of aid were vigorously criticized by the Soviet government, which received Allied explanations of shipping problems with little sympathy, it is especially perplexing that the Soviet Union occasionally slowed the flow of supplies. As mentioned earlier, the United States and the Soviet Union established an Alaska-Siberia (ALSIB) route for aircraft delivery in 1942. Stalin refused to allow American pilots to fly these machines into the Soviet Union. Moreover, Soviet aircraft inspectors initially rejected 31 of the first 400 aircraft made available, a rate of 8 percent.[8] Nevertheless, almost 8,000 aircraft were delivered via this route (mostly fighters and attack planes), as shown in table 21.

TO THE GATES OF MOSCOW: JUNE-DECEMBER 1941

Both American and Soviet sources agree that American aid, Lend-Lease and otherwise, played a small role on the Eastern Front in 1941. Quantities sent to the Soviet Union were small (see table 22), including only 150 aircraft, 180 armored vehicles, and 8,300 motor vehicles.[9] Of these, only 29, 35, and 1,506, respectively, arrived by the end of the year, along with 25,000 tons of fuel and 11,000 tons of other supplies. The British managed to deliver 676 aircraft and 446 tanks, 867 vehicles, and 76,000 tons of other supplies in 1941.[10] Supplies were limited due to scarce shipping, shortages of supplies, and fears in some American official circles that the Soviet Union would collapse.

Most of the 1941 aid was secured through American loans and, in few cases, cash purchases. Lend-Lease alone for 1941 totalled less than a million dollars.[11] By September, 186,000 tons of supplies had been exported, almost four-fifths of it petroleum.[12] Most Lend-Lease petroleum products were highly specialized blending agents with a potential impact not indicated by shipment size alone, as not all these products could be manufactured inside the Soviet Union. Aircraft deliveries increased slowly: 1,200 American and British planes by February of 1942 and 1,311 U.S. machines by June, by which time the Soviet air force had begun to recover from the postinvasion disaster.[13] The Soviet Union obtained export licenses for $145 million in supplies, but only $28.5 million worth of cash purchases made it out of the country.[14]

The Soviet Union was not happy with the slow pace of deliveries in 1941 and did not conceal this view from the American government. The Americans, however, were equally distressed. President Roosevelt was so displeased with the slow progress of deliveries that he personally informed all U.S. war agencies that commitments to the Soviet Union were to be met "regardless of the effect of these shipments on any part of our war program." Presidential aide Harry Hopkins, equally concerned with the Soviet Union's ability to survive the early Nazi onslaught, and thus with the safety of the West, echoed that call at a Supply Priorities and Allocation Board meeting on October 15, 1941.[15]

Presidential rhetoric neither satisfied the Soviets nor compensated for the many practical problems of providing aid to the Soviet Union. Western help in 1941 remained limited. A Soviet source emphasizes that American aid was too small prior to Stalingrad to matter and did not even meet commitments, although an emigre study written for the U.S. Army suggested that American assistance "played a great part in supplying the Red Army during the critical period."[16] Neither author provides much specific support for his or her respective conclusions.

Such generalizations about Western aid tend to overlook the dire plight of the Soviet Union in 1941. By the end of the year the Nazis occupied 38 percent of the Soviet Union's grain and cattle regions, 84 percent of its sugar-growing lands, and 60 percent of its hog-raising area. The precipitate retreat of the Red Army led to immense loss of livestock; grain output declined by two-thirds; crops for cloth manufacture, and cattle and milk, by almost half; potatoes, sheep, and goats, by one-third; eggs and hogs, by three-quarters; and sugar, by almost nine-tenths.[17]

Industrial production fared slightly better, given the substantial prewar expansion of the Ural industrial base. The losses, however, from destruction of industrial plants, disruption of production due to plant movements, loss of raw materials, and transportation problems, were near-catastrophic. After two months of war, Soviet iron production had declined by 60 percent, electricity by 25 percent, aluminum production by three-quarters, and pig iron and steel by almost one-half.[18] Stalin admitted to Hopkins in August 1941 that the supply situation "could be serious by the following Spring."[19] Privately his expectations were probably even worse.

Could even the meager help from abroad have been important under these circumstances? At first glance, the number of Western tanks, for example, seems insignificant, especially given their qualitative shortcomings. The 481 machines sent by the end of 1941, plus the additional 550 which arrived from the United Kingdom in January 1942, did not seem to be many, given the huge area of operations and the weakness of their armament (although this was also true of German tanks).[20] Most British tanks in 1941 were armed with 40-mm guns, while Soviet machines were built with 76-mm weapons. The mere handful of American tanks delivered in 1941 were lightly armed and oddly configured. Allied tanks were often rearmed after their arrival in the Soviet Union.[21] Alteration of armament can be explained either as a reflection of the Western tanks' shortcomings or as a move to standardize ammunition. The foreign tanks were also more vulnerable than Soviet machines, especially because they were gas-powered and more likely to explode when hit. Even given all these problems, however, it must be kept in mind that the Soviet Union only produced 2,819 of the excellent T-34, KV-I, and KV-II tanks in the second half of 1941 (compared to 24,000 in 1942).[22] Enough Allied tanks arrived in the Soviet Union in 1941 to fully equip seven 65-machine tank brigades. The Red Army began the conflict with 78 tank and mechanized brigades, the latter supposedly having 41 machines each, but many were understrength and equipped with obsolete tanks.[23] Given the increasing quantity and quality of Soviet armor as the front closed on

Moscow, the number of Western machines may well have been important until the growing supply of KV and T-34 tanks could be committed.[24]

A far more important aspect of foreign aid, even in the first year and a half of the war, has to do with the Red Army's mobility. Mobile warfare had interested the Red Army long before 1941. The invasion, however, caught the Soviet forces with serious deficiencies in the transport system. It did not take long for motor vehicles to move to the top of the Soviet shopping list. Since trucks and armored vehicles both used much shipping space, an obvious trade-off existed. Stalin's requests for combat equipment soon gave way to orders for motor vehicles, the importance of which was recognized by later Soviet writers.[25] During a meeting with American officials on September 29, 1941, Stalin evinced little enthusiasm until motor vehicles were mentioned and the next day stressed his need for transport, telling the Americans that "winning this war depends on the gasoline engine," and that "the country which can produce the greatest number of gasoline engines will be the victor."[26] The Soviet Union did have some 800,000 vehicles of all types before the war, but so many were lost in 1941 that even production and imports could not prevent that total from declining slightly by 1942.[27]

Western aid was certainly not a major factor in the survival of the Soviet Union in 1941. Translating aid figures into division-days is difficult because the size of the 'average' division was so unsteady, and little was known about the requirements of the 'average' Soviet soldier before 1945. The tanks and vehicles could at most have equipped four to six divisions. Machinery and raw materials probably had little effect before late 1942. American, British, and Canadian aid administrators did gain a clearer picture of Soviet needs and put this to use in planning the years ahead.

The physical effect, then, was small. But what of the psychological impact? This is admittedly an imponderable factor. The Soviet people must have felt isolated at the beginning of the war. The invasion was not expected. The government had expressed no sympathy for the powers resisting Hitler in 1939-41. The ideology of the state certainly furthered the vision of isolation of the Soviet Union, picturing itself as the only socialist state in a bourgeois world which might attack at any time. Certainly the knowledge that a foreign power was providing some assistance must have boosted morale out of all proportion to the economic and military value of the supplies. At the same time, the Soviet people showed no predisposition to surrender at any time, making the effect on morale of foreign aid difficult to calculate.

MOSCOW TO STALINGRAD: JANUARY-DECEMBER 1942

Shipments of Allied aid to the Soviet Union increased considerably in 1942. The U.S.S.R. received 2.74 million tons of supplies, including 2,500 aircraft, 3,000 tanks, and 79,000 motor vehicles. Quarterly shipments rose from $168 million in the first quarter of 1942 to $493 million in the last.[28] The value of Lend-Lease aid in 1942 is shown in table 23.

The Eastern Front in 1942 is best remembered for the Soviet counteroffensive at Stalingrad, which, if it did not paralyze the Wehrmacht, certainly inflicted vast physical and perhaps psychological damage on the Nazi hierarchy. Substantial Allied aid had arrived in time for that battle, almost 1.5 million tons of supplies reaching the Soviet Union in the first half of 1942.[29]

Most Western assistance by this time consisted of food, petroleum, and raw materials (see table 24), all items which could be sent via the safe Vladivostok route, but combat vehicles and aircraft were still included. The United States and Britain together sent over a thousand tanks in the first two months of 1942, almost 1,400 by May, and, in the twelve months ending in October 1942, over 4,000.[30] Soviet tank production during this period has been estimated at anywhere from 1,400 to 2,000 per month, the lower figure apparently applying to early 1942. Allied deliveries of about 225 tanks per month therefore equalled about 11-16 percent of Soviet production. If American estimates were correct, Western machines made up about 13 percent of all Soviet tanks. Again, the drawbacks of some of the foreign vehicles must be noted. Sixty percent of the imported tanks were light, the balance medium.[31] Most of the British machines were either 17-ton Valentines or 26-ton Matilda IIs, and although the latter were not 'light,' their gunnery was inadequate. The American Lee and Grant tanks were classified as 'medium,' given their 30-ton weights, 75-mm guns, and 57-88 mm of armor. It is often overlooked that in all these categories they matched the vaunted Soviet T-34. Technically, however, they were inferior because of their high profile, narrow tracks, and unusual configuration (a very small turret with a 37-mm gun, with the larger weapon in the lower right corner of the tank).[32] Even if they were not seen as useful by the Soviets for tank-to-tank combat or assault roles, however, the smaller tanks could have been used in training, reconnaissance, rear-area security, and infantry support missions.

The pattern of aircraft shipments was much the same, exceeding 500 in the first two months of 1942, 1,500 by May, and 3,000 in the year ending in October.[33] Over 2,300 American planes were delivered in 1942.[34] Estimates of Soviet aircraft strength varied greatly (high losses partially offset an increase in monthly production from 1,200 to 2,260) causing estimates of the Anglo-American proportion of the Soviet air fleet to vary from 11 to 25 percent.[35] The imported aircraft were not the most advanced in the Western arsenal, but proved reasonably useful on the Eastern Front. The British Hurricane fighter was not equal to better German fighters by 1942. In a similar vein, the American P-39 Airacobra was considered an inferior fighter by the U. S. Army Air Forces (USAAF) as well as by the Royal Air Force (RAF), which quickly donated its P-39s to the Soviet Union. Both planes, however, were heavily armed and proved highly successful as ground-attack aircraft.

As useful as the aircraft and tanks may have been, they were not the most important items supplied by the Allies. Admittedly the military situation on the Eastern Front was sufficiently in doubt that every plane and tank was useful.

Lend-Lease supplies were undoubtedly important in terms of aircraft, perhaps helpful as far as tanks were concerned, but virtually irrelevant in relation to artillery.[36] More important, however, was the help given the U.S.S.R. which enabled the assembling and husbanding of a powerful group of reserve armies, without which Stalingrad might have been lost. This force, directly controlled by the General Staff, was considered so valuable that it was kept in reserve, even in early 1942 when Soviet offensives ran into trouble. Unless this force could be quickly moved and carefully coordinated, its strategic value was limited to the defensive. Lend-Lease supplied increasing quantities of petroleum, mostly specialized fuels and blending agents, and oil-refining equipment. The latter was important because Hitler's surprisingly successful strike at the Caucasus fields threatened 84 percent of the Soviet oil supply and much of its refining capacity.[37] Understandably, Stalin closely monitored (and criticized) the defense of the Caucasus, although he was not so desperate as to accept the offered deployment of American air units in the region. Lend-Lease also furnished communications equipment, wire, and field telephones, as well as about 30,000 motor vehicles; unfortunately, it is not known how many of them were used at Stalingrad. Of other Lend-Lease supplies, the most important in 1942 was probably food, which (in dehydrated and canned form) absorbed 14 percent of Lend-Lease tonnage. Most went to the Red Army, where (in 1942) it could have fed over 1 million soldiers for a year.[38]

How important was Lend-Lease to the Soviet Union in 1942? In his communiques to Roosevelt, Stalin revealed some ambivalence, insisting that aid was necessary, but clearly more confident about the outcome of the war. While he informed Roosevelt in early 1942 that "delivery of materials in May . . . is of the utmost urgency," he did not seem concerned about the Soviet Union's survival.[39] This view was shared by American analysts, who based their view in part on the growing strength of the Red Army (see table 25). They did not, however, expect the Soviet Union "to defeat Germany decisively . . . without great amounts of material and considerable numbers of first-rate troops from the U.S. and Britain."[40]

Stalin rejected troops but accepted materiel. Lend-Lease aid became substantial the same year that Germany effectively lost the war in the East. Stalingrad did not destroy the German armies, but in destroying one of them, and depriving the Nazis of the initiative, it did allow the Soviet Union to further build its military-industrial plant, stockpile supplies, and reorganize its forces. Lend-Lease alone did not enable the Soviet Union to launch Operation Uranus, nor would its absence have prevented the attack. On the other hand, although the direct contribution to Soviet operations seems modest, aid arrived at a time when the Soviet margin of military superiority was thin or nonexistent, stockpiles of food and petrol were barely adequate, and transport, communications, and coordination of large forces were handicapped by lack of equipment. In this environment of scarcity, Lend-Lease certainly aided in the buildup of the Soviet forces and, perhaps, their offensive success.

NOTES

1. John Erickson, *The Road to Stalingrad* (London: Harper & Row, 1975); idem, *The Road to Berlin: Continuing the History of Stalin's War with Germany* (Boulder, CO: Westview Press, 1983).

2. Georgii K. Zhukov, *The Memoirs of Marshal Zhukov* (New York: Delacorte Press, 1972), 391.

3. *Great Soviet Encyclopedia*, vol. 14 (New York: Macmillan, 1980), 351. The reference to the late start of production in the Urals is a bit misleading, as Soviet industry had begun its expansion there well before the war, and a good deal of industry had already been shifted eastward.

4. Regarding the change in the Red Army's fortunes, see A. M. Nikolaieff, "The Red Army in the Second World War," *Russian Review* 1 (Autumn 1947), 49.

5. U.S. President, *Reports to Congress on Lend-Lease Operations*, nos. 13, 15, 16, 18, and 19 (Washington, DC: Government Printing Office, 1943-45), no. 13, 13; no. 15, 50; no. 16, 31; no. 18, 15; no. 19, 12.

6. U.S. Department of State, Protocol and Area Information Staff of the U.S.S.R. Branch of the Division of Research and Reports, "Report on War Aid Furnished by the United States to the U.S.S.R." (Foreign Economic Section, Office of Foreign Liquidation, November 28, 1945), 9.

7. Ibid., 11, 12, 13.

8. Wesley Frank Craven and James Lea Cate, eds., *The Army Air Forces in World War II*, vol. 7, *Services around the World* (Chicago: University of Chicago Press, 1958), 159.

9. U.S. President, *Reports to Congress on Lend-Lease Operations*, no. 14 (1944), 32.

10. Winston Churchill, *The Hinge of Fate* (New York: Bantam Books, 1974 [Boston: Houghton Mifflin, 1953]), 241.

11. U.S. President, *Reports to Congress on Lend-Lease Operations*, no. 15 (1944), 19.

12. Robert Huhn Jones, *The Roads to Russia: United States Lend-Lease to the Soviet Union* (Norman: University of Oklahoma Press, 1969), 272.

13. *Records of the Joint Chiefs of Staff: Part 1, 1942-1945: The Soviet Union* (Frederick, MD: University Publications of America, n.d.), "Russian Combat Estimate" (April 1, 1942), 115; Robin Higham and Jacob W. Kipp, eds., *Soviet Aviation and Air Power: A Historical Review* (Boulder, CO: Westview Press, 1977), 80.

14. "History of the U.S. Military Mission to Moscow," Modern Military Records Division, R.G. 165, Box 146, OPD 336TS, N.A., 352; Jones, *Roads to Russia,* 43.

15. "History of the U.S. Military Mission," 352-53; U.S. Civilian Production Administration, *Historical Reports on War Administration: War Production Board, Documentary Publication No. 3: Minutes of the Supply Priorities and*

Allocations Board, September 2, 1941-January 15, 1942 (Washington, DC: Government Printing Office, 1946), 18.

16. N. Dunaeva, "Lend-Liz: Fakty i vymysly," *Voenno-Istoricheskii Zhurnal* (No. 3, 1977), 103-4; U.S. Army, Assistant Chief of Staff (Intelligence), "History of the War in Eastern Europe, 1941-1945" (Synopsis) (1953), U.S. Army Military History Institute, Carlisle Barracks, Pa, 125.

17. Jones, *Roads to Russia,* 272; *History of the Great Patriotic War of the Soviet Union 1941-1945* (Moscow: Voenizdat, 1960; OCMH translation), 2:520, 523.

18. *O.S.S./State Department Intelligence and Research Reports, Part 6: The Soviet Union, 1941-1949* (Frederick, MD: University Publications of America, 1977), "Losses of Russian Industrial Production Resulting from the Eastward Movement of the War Front: General Geographic Distribution of Russian Industry" (September 19, 1941), 1.

19. U.S. Army, Assistant Chiefs of Staff (Intelligence), "History of the War in Eastern Europe," 77.

20. *Joint Chiefs of Staff,* "Russian Combat Estimate" (April 1, 1942), 46; Kenneth Macksey and John H. Batchelor, *Tank: A History of the Armoured Fighting Vehicle* (New York: Charles Scribner's Sons, 1970), 105.

21. Macksey and Batchelor, *Tank,* 92-113 passim.

22. Dunaeva, "Lend-Liz," 104. Total tank production was higher, but Soviet authors frequently cite only T-34 and KV production in this period, arguing that the remainder were obsolete. This may have been true, but it also puts the performance of the Red Army in a better light. Soviet writers have revised downward the size of both the Soviet tank park and the Nazi armored force, for which the official Soviet history (1960) cited a figure of 30,000.

23. Stephen B. Patrick et al., *War in the East: The Russo-German War, 1941-1945* (New York: Simulations Publications, 1977), 111, 112, 116, 117, 120-21.

24. Concerning improvements in the performance of Soviet armor, see *World War II German Military Studies: A Collection of 213 Special Reports on the Second World War Prepared by Former Officers of the Wehrmacht for the United States Army,* 24 vols. (New York: Garland Publishing, 1974), 16:VII(C)1, 293.

25. U.S. President, *Reports to Congress on Lend-Lease Operations*, no. 14, 32.

26. William H. Standley and Arthur A. Ageton, *Admiral Ambassador to Russia* (Chicago: Henry Regnery, 1955), 67, 68.

27. *History of the Great Patriotic War,* 1:532; *Joint Chiefs of Staff,* "Russian Combat Estimate" (April 1, 1942), 64.

28. U.S. President, *Reports to Congress on Lend-Lease Operations,* no. 14, 32.

29. George C. Herring, Jr., *Aid to Russia, 1941-1946: Strategy, Diplomacy, and the Origins of the Cold War* (New York: Columbia University Press, 1973), 66.

30. U.S.S.R. Ministry of Foreign Affairs, *Correspondence between the Chairman of the Council of Ministers of the U.S.S.R. and the Presidents of the*

U.S.A. and the Prime Ministers of Great Britain during the Great Patriotic War of 1941-1945 (London: Lawrence & Wishart, 1958), 2:14-15; *Joint Chiefs of Staff,* "Memorandum for Information: Russian Capabilities: Military Materiel and Manpower" (June 20, 1942), 1-2; Hessel Duncan Hall, *North American Supply* (London: Her Majesty's Stationery Office, 1955), 339.

31. *O.S.S.,* "Military Potential of the Soviet Union, Part VI: Munitions" (November 11, 1942), 1-2; *History of the Great Patriotic War,* 2:361, 510; Dunaeva, "Lend-Liz," 104; *Joint Chiefs of Staff,* "Memorandum for Information: Russian Capabilities: Military Materiel and Manpower" (June 20, 1942), 1-2. The Soviet tank park in mid-1942 was estimated at 11,000 machines, including 1,400 from the West.

32. Macksey and Batchelor, *Tank,* 92-113 passim.

33. *Correspondence,* 2:14-15; *Joint Chiefs of Staff,* ""Memorandum for Information: Russian Capabilities: Military Materiel and Manpower" (June 20, 1942), 1-2; Hall, *North American Supply,* 339.

34. Richard C. Lukas, *Eagles East: The Army Air Forces and the Soviet Union, 1941-1945* (Tallahassee: Florida State University Press, 1970), 166.

35. *O.S.S.,* "Military Potential of the Soviet Union, Part VI: Munitions" (November 11, 1942), 1-2; *History of the Great Patriotic War,* 2:361, 510; Dunaeva, "Lend-Liz," 104; *Joint Chiefs of Staff,* "Memorandum for Information: Russian Capabilities: Military Materiel and Manpower" (June 20, 1942), 1-2.

36. Hall, *North American Supply,* 339; *Joint Chiefs of Staff,* "Memorandum for Information: Russian Capabilities: Military Materiel and Manpower" (June 20, 1942), 1-2; *History of the Great Patriotic War,* 2:361. The Soviet artillery was estimated at about 25,000 pieces, with monthly production of 2,000 (as well as 18,000 mortars). By May 1, 1942, the United States had sent 282 guns.

37. *O.S.S.,* "Losses of Russian Industrial Production Resulting from the Eastward Movement of the War Front: General Geographic Distribution of Russian Industry," (September 19, 1941), 6; Ibid., "The Effect of Territorial Losses on Russia's Petroleum Position" (May 20, 1942), 5.

38. John Frederick Gardner, "The Lend-Lease Program of World War II: Analysis and Appraisal" (Ph.D. dissertation, University of Pittsburgh, 1946), 128-29; "History of the U.S. Military Mission."

39. Robert E. Sherwood, *Roosevelt and Hopkins*, vol. 2, *From Pearl Harbor to Victory* (New York: Bantam Books, 1950 [Harper & Brothers, 1948]), 126.

40. *Joint Chiefs of Staff,* "Russian Combat Estimate" (April 1, 1942), 162-63.

5

Lend-Lease and the Road
to Berlin

THE END OF THE ROAD FOR HITLER: 1943

In 1943 the Wehrmacht still retained enough freedom of movement to maintain some initiative in the East. The psyche of its leadership, however, had not escaped unscathed from Stalingrad. Its superiority in skill deteriorated as the casualty lists grew. The ability of the Soviet forces to execute complex, deep-penetration offensives would soon force the Germans into an ultimately hopeless defensive position. The leadership, impatiently seeking to reverse the flow of the war in one gigantic stroke, and fearing that time was against Germany, threw away the armored cutting edge of its military machine at Kursk. If all this were not enough, the Soviet forces gained superiority in tanks and aircraft in 1943, partly due to more efficient tactics, and partly because of growing production.

The increasing material wealth of the Soviet forces coincided with the explosive growth of the Lend-Lease program. The opening of the Persian corridor rapidly increased deliveries to the Soviet Union. Shipments included 920 tanks, over 5,000 aircraft, and almost 145,000 motor vehicles, nearly five times as many as in 1942.[1] By the end of 1943 the Soviet Union had received 173,000 vehicles and 4,300 tanks from the United States.[2] Gross tonnage almost doubled, and the Soviet share of all Lend-Lease grew to 27 percent (estimated dollar value of American aid is shown in table 26). Machinery and parts increased the most, to half a billion dollars, absorbing almost one-third of all Lend-Lease in 1943. Deliveries became less erratic. By the end of the year the Soviet Union was receiving supplies near the agreed-upon pace (see table 27).

How much of this was actually available for use by the Soviet Union in 1943? Generally speaking, anything shipped by the middle of the year would arrive soon enough for actual use within the year. The value of shipments (table 28), the tonnage (table 29), and the cumulative total of supplies sent by the summer of 1943 (table 30) are important not only because they indicate supply availability, but also because they reflect changing Soviet priorities. Besides machinery, food grew the most from 1942 to 1943, except for naval equipment, statistically insignificant in 1942. Ammunition and clothing were also popular, and 6 million pairs of army boots (designed to Soviet specifications) were shipped by 1944.[3] The low number of tanks reflects increasing Soviet production, inadaptability of Allied armored vehicles to the Eastern Front, and difficulty of shipping tanks. Of over 6,000 aircraft sent by August 1943, about 70 percent arrived, 1,300 were still en route at year's end, and over 500 were diverted or lost in transit.[4]

The tonnage figures in table 29 reflect Soviet priorities. In comparison with the previous twelve-month period, food shipments rose from 24 to 33 percent and metal declined from 33 to 25 percent, while motor vehicles showed a modest decline, from 17 to 15 percent. All three increased in absolute terms, with agricultural products alone increasing at a much faster rate than the total. Petroleum shipments also grew rapidly, but British and Canadian supplies fell from almost 150,000 tons to less than 60,000 per year. Cumulative totals of aid sent (table 30) should be reduced by about 13 percent for losses, which were as high as 25 percent in some categories.

What did it all mean? The turning point in the war came in 1943, beginning with the surrender of the German Sixth Army at Stalingrad on February 2. The Germans fell back from the Caucasus, where their armies had threatened the Soviet oil fields and the Lend-Lease import route through Grozny and Astrakhan. The Red Army smashed the German armored forces at Kursk, after which there was no realistic hope of victory for the Nazis. By year's end the First Ukrainian Front had reached the prewar Soviet-Polish border. The year 1943 is viewed as a turning point by Soviet authors who, in keeping with Soviet thinking on force rations, norms, and the laws of armed combat, note that the U.S.S.R. "surpassed the numerical superiority of the Germans in tanks and aircraft."[5]

If German defeat was a virtual certainty after 1943, given the combination of Soviet victories, defeat in North Africa, and the increasing air bombardments, were those Soviet victories in 1943 also inevitable? Soviet and some German sources agree that this was not so, arguing that to see Kursk as a "logical, an inescapable Russian victory" is "based on ideology or propaganda."[6] The Red Army did enjoy a numerical superiority in 1943, having grown to some 6 million soldiers supported by 9,000 aircraft and 46 tank brigades.[7] Soviet estimates placed Nazi forces at 4.9 million troops (700,000 from satellite states), 3,000 aircraft, and more than 5,000 tanks. The actual totals, according to German documents, were closer to 3 million, 2,500, and 2,000, respectively.[8] Yet the increasing size of the Red Army, which eventually peaked at around 7 million (according to some estimates, 13 million), meant that supply requirements grew on a matching scale. The consumption of ammunition in 1943 (3 million tons) was double that of 1942, while fuel needs (3.3 million tons) had gone up by almost one-quarter. During major engagements consumption was much higher.[9] All this translated into a vast increase in the demand on the transport net.

The Soviet command won many of its 1943 victories by being able to move, concentrate, coordinate, and sustain large forces. The value of Lend-Lease motor vehicles and communications equipment in these operations is evident in many respects. While Soviet writers rarely mention domestic motor vehicle production (quite low), motor transport is described as "generally improved," handling almost twice as much as in 1942.[10] This was in large part due to foreign aid. It is noteworthy that Soviet references to Lend-Lease almost invariably mention motor vehicles.

In some categories, however, Lend-Lease became less important as Soviet industrial production recovered (see table 31). The Soviet Union cancelled orders for antitank, antiaircraft and machine guns, and tanks.[11] The tanks were not cancelled simply because of their unpopularity. Monthly Soviet AFV (armored fighting vehicle) production had soared to almost 2,000.[12] Foreign tanks amounted to about 10 percent of the Soviet armored force in 1943, a proportion which declined thereafter.[13]

The situation was somewhat different in the air. While Soviet aircraft production has been estimated as high as 35,000 for calendar year 1943, foreign aircraft still amounted to about 15 percent of the Soviet air force, certainly a significant number.[14] Stalin apparently thought so. On January 5, 1943, Stalin told Roosevelt that the "arrival of airplanes, without fliers (we have enough fliers of our own) at the Southwestern or the Central front would play an enormous role on the most important sectors of struggle against Hitler."[15]

Perhaps the most important categories are those that are unfortunately the most difficult to evaluate, either chronologically or qualitatively. These are raw materials, machinery, and agricultural products. Soviet agricultural production made a very slow recovery, hitting bottom in 1943, when many other sectors of the economy were already recovering.[16] The Soviet government showed no inclination to reduce food imports. The same was true of industrial supplies, although its interest in some items may have been stimulated by postwar considerations rather than wartime exigencies.[17]

That the Soviet Union was less concerned about survival in 1943 than in 1942 is reflected in the greater reserve shown by Soviet officials in evaluating Lend-Lease for this period. Zhukov, for example, conceded that relationships between the Soviet Union and her allies improved in 1943, noting that the U.S.S.R. received "somewhat greater material aid from the United States than in 1942."[18] The American leadership, perhaps anxious to 'sell' Lend-Lease to Congress and the public, proclaimed Lend-Lease as a major factor in the Soviet fall 1943 offensive. Both viewpoints are correct. By then the Soviet Union's survival seemed assured and the initiative was firmly hers.[19] Driving the Nazis out of the country, however, required tremendous improvements in logistics and communications, not to mention increasing sophistication in technology and industry. Lend-Lease provided both in 1943.

THE LAST ACT, 1944-1945

In the last fourteen months of the war, almost 11.1 million tons of Lend-Lease supplies were sent to the Soviet Union. Shipments in 1944 were almost 30 percent greater than in 1943. The dollar value of aid during the twelve months ending in June 1944 (see table 32) exceeded that of the previous twelve months by 81 percent. U.S. deliveries finally caught up with treaty commitments. The United States had fallen almost 1.1 million tons short of meeting the commitments stated in the Second Protocol, which covered Lend-Lease during the twelve months ending June 30, 1943. As of March 1, 1944, however, Lend-Lease deliveries were already 1 million tons ahead of the requirements under the Third Protocol, which covered the twelve months beginning in July 1943 (see table 33). When the Third Protocol period expired on June 30, 1944, Lend-Lease had met or exceeded every treaty commitment except for aircraft.[20] Aid in the first eleven months of 1944 totalled $3.16 billion and included 144,000 motor vehicles.[21]

The Fourth Protocol treaty covered Lend-Lease during the year beginning in July 1944 but was abruptly terminated when Germany surrendered. During the ten months of the Fourth Protocol period, the United States, Britain, and Canada furnished 6.6 million tons of supplies (table 34). On May 12, 1945, President Harry S. Truman issued a directive extending Lend-Lease to the Soviet Union for the war against Japan. Although aid to the Soviet Union was officially terminated as soon as Japan capitulated, some shipments reached the Soviet Union even after the official Japanese surrender on September 2, 1945.[22] Deliveries between the time of the surrender of the two major Axis powers totalled about one and three-quarter million tons (table 35).

Even with the opening of new routes, extensive experience, and relative security for the vessels plying the Northern route, the aid flow was not completely smooth. In August 1944 tight shipping caused a drop in truck deliveries, which fell from a monthly average of 10,000 to less than 7,700 (half of the maximum), to the distress of the Soviet government.[23] February and March shipments were slightly below those planned. During the eight months ending in February 1944, however, the United States shipped 4 million tons, almost a third more than projected.[24] Fourth Protocol commitments would probably have been exceeded had it not been terminated early.

Changing Soviet priorities were reflected in tonnage allocated to the various types of supplies. While food, metals, and vehicles predominated in the Third Protocol, as they did in the Second and Fourth (table 36), food increased by three-quarters from the Second to the Third, motor vehicles by two-thirds, and metals by over one-third. Petroleum supplies and machinery almost tripled, while chemicals and explosives rose by a factor of two and a half. The similarity of the Third Protocol to actual Soviet requests, as well as the need to make best use of shipping space, indicates that these figures give a close approximation of Soviet priorities. The Fourth Protocol reflects an increasing Soviet demand for petroleum products, which had become the second-largest category. This was partly due to Soviet need, and also to the (relative) ease with which oil could be pumped to the U.S.S.R. from the Abadan refineries, which contributed one-third of the total (table 34).

This phase of the war saw the Soviet Union expel the invader from its soil, albeit at immense human and material costs. This was no small achievement, even considering the Red Army's growing numerical and material superiority. The Soviet command had to mass substantial forces, requiring (as mentioned earlier) spectacular feats of coordination, logistics, and communications. Unfortunately, this had to be accomplished with a transport net which was in an abominable state. The Red Army had to advance through areas where the retreating Nazis had systematically destroyed the bridges and railways, for which even the intensive reconstruction program could not compensate. Given the destruction of the railways, the Soviet forces were heavily dependent on imported motor vehicles. Domestic vehicle production in 1945 was still less than Lend-Lease imports, although greater than before the war.[25] In the last year of the war monthly truck imports averaged 11,500, enough to equip the operational units of either 2 tank or 9 infantry armies. The monthly import figure may be compared to the use of trucks in Operation Bagration, the summer 1944 offensive, which required 12,000 trucks just for the immediate needs of operational units.[26]

Vehicle imports were never excessive. The Soviet government cannot be suspected of ordering them to build up a postwar stockpile. In the words of John Erickson, "Every armored formation needed more lorries than it could muster."[27] A British observer believed that "the successes achieved by the Red army artillery in the later stages of the war could never have been achieved without adequate transport" and noted that of all Lend-Lease aid, "the most valuable was probably the vast number of trucks."[28] An American official report claimed that Lend-Lease trucks carried "half of the highway-borne supplies for the advancing Soviet armies in the great offensives on this [1944] spring and summer on the eastern front."[29]

Western aid helped Soviet transport in several other ways. Over a thousand locomotives and a quarter of a million tons of steel rails were shipped in the last year and a half of the war, not to mention all the communications gear useful for coordinating the vast transport net. The United States also supplied huge quantities of tires and an entire Ford tire plant with an annual capacity of 1 million tires, but it did not go into production until late 1944, and possibly not even until after the war.[30] Certainly American aid "served to alleviate difficulties in restoring the transport system."[31]

There is quantitative proof that Lend-Lease helped. A comparison of freight carried in the last half of 1943 to the first half of 1944 shows a motor transport increase of 23 percent, from 1,400 million ton-kilometers to 1,724. No other transport mode (air, river, maritime, or rail) showed anything near this improvement. It is doubtful that one could explain as coincidence that the greatest improvement was precisely in that area where so much aid was given. As for the rail net, its capacity hardly improved at all before the arrival of most foreign equipment.[32]

However much the increasing flow of petroleum products and refinery equipment improved ground transportation, its effect may have been even greater on aviation, since the Soviet Union did not have the capability to produce first-rate aviation gas. Lend-Lease production equipment had the capacity to raise Soviet aviation fuel output from 110,000 metric tons in 1941 to 1.67 million metric tons in 1944.[33] This figure was probably not reached, however, because some equipment was apparently damaged in transit, lost, or sent to the wrong sites once inside the Soviet Union, and some plants may have been unfinished even in 1945.[34] Even so, Lend-Lease's impact on aviation fuels production must have been substantial.

Aircraft were an important part of both American and British aid to the Soviet Union, and this remained the case during the last phase of the war. Monthly Lend-Lease shipments in 1944-45 averaged 500 planes, slightly below the 1943 rate. By October 1944 the Soviet Union had received 8,734 U.S. and 6,015 British aircraft.[35] Soviet production had grown prodigiously, however. American analysts pegged the production rate at 2,200 per month in mid-1944 and at 3,500 in 1945.[36] Soviet sources since have claimed an almost continuous 3,300-3,500 monthly production rate in 1944-45.[37] Losses were estimated at 1,500 aircraft per month. The size of the Soviet air force, including rear-area and training machines, exceeded 20,000 (the occasionally cited figure of 50,000 seems doubtful). Of the 17,000 fighters and 9,500 bomber/ground-attack aircraft in the Voenno-Vozdushnye Sily at war's end, 1,600 (9.4 percent) of the former and 1,500 (15.8 percent) of the latter were Lend-Lease planes.[38] If these wartime government estimates are correct, and an allowance is made for British aircraft, about 17-18 percent of the Soviet air force at war's end would have been composed of foreign aircraft.

As for staples such as food and raw materials, Lend-Lease here was still important, but perhaps not as vital as in 1943. Although serious shortages continued, Soviet food production (table 37) and industrial materiel (table 38) were recovering, more notably in some areas than in others. Aluminum, for example, was still shipped but was not nearly as significant as it had been in 1942 and 1943. By the summer of 1944 aluminum production reached 90 percent of estimated minimum requirements.[39] More important in 1944-45 were the several synthetic-rubber-production plants shipped during the war, which more than doubled Soviet rubber capacity. Rubber produced in the Lend-Lease facilities was also twice the tensile strength of the Soviet product.[40] Food remained an important item throughout the war, since Soviet production had not yet recovered completely. American analysts feared that food shortages would impair Soviet military performance, believing that by "the summer of 1944, the present stringencies in food and manpower will probably produce, in turn, a considerable reduction of Russia's military capabilities."[41] This did not come to pass, partly due to the stringent Soviet rationing system, which heavily favored the army and essential industrial workers, and substantial drafts of farm labor, which might not have been possible without food imports.

Despite continuing problems, the Soviet economy continued to expand in 1944-45, growing in every major category except petroleum, which declined slightly. Ordnance production did not change much from 1944 to 1945, but there was no military reason why a major increase in production would have been sought after the jump in production in 1944. Instead, qualitative improvements were emphasized, such as a shift to significantly heavier battle tanks.[42]

This economic machine was adequate to support the growing field forces. By December 1944 the Red Army maintained 6.5 million men on the Eastern Front, supported by 13,000 tanks, 15,000 aircraft, and 100,000 guns and mortars. In early 1945 this force had grown by about 600,000 troops, 2,000 tanks, and 15,000 guns and mortars, not counting the presence of some 300,000 Allied troops. The assault on Berlin involved no less than 2.5 million troops, 41,600 guns and mortars, 6,250 tanks, and 7,500 aircraft.[43] As overwhelming as the Red Army at times appeared to the retreating Wehrmacht, it was not disproportionately large in relation to the Soviet Union's population, economy, or military requirements. As will be discussed in more detail later, the Soviet Union had to maintain a careful balance between the manpower requirements of the economy and the army, which could not afford to disturb this balance by drafting too many soldiers.

It is tempting to suggest that Lend-Lease was not truly significant in 1944-45 due to the Soviet economic recovery. Survival was not a major concern after Kursk. By mid-1944 the Soviet diplomatic focus had already shifted to the postwar era and (more immediately) the defeat of Japan. On June 24, 1944, the Military Mission reported that 40 percent of supplies coming through Vladivostok were staying in the eastern U.S.S.R. for a "Siberian Army."[44] A report filed three days earlier mentions efforts by the Soviet government to generate public hostility toward Japan among the people.[45] Apparently Soviet officers and officials (or Stalin, at least) by this time saw both victory in the West and war in the East as inevitable.[46]

Lend-Lease, however, was not extended to the Soviet Union to ensure Soviet survival; rather, it was designed with Nazi defeat in mind. Adding to existing Soviet advantages, which is precisely what it did in 1944-45, fit quite well with the aid program's goals. In transport, for example, the improvements that the Soviet Union made with Lend-Lease assistance significantly accelerated the pace of the Soviet offensives. This in turn prevented Nazi Germany from shifting large forces to other theatres of war, where they might have been used to inflict major defeats and give Hitler some extra breathing room.

By the end of the war, the Western Allies delivered 19.6 million tons of materiel to the Soviet Union, including almost half a million vehicles, 19,000 aircraft, and 5.5 million tons of foodstuffs.[47] Soviet industrial production was dramatically enhanced by shipments of chemicals, machine tools, specialized metals, complicated blending agents, and entire plants. Food and finished products could be put to use as fast as logistics allowed, while other items required a greater lead time. At the very beginning of the war the impact of Lend-Lease was mainly psychological, while at the very end it was no longer essential to the survival of the Soviet Union. During much of the war, however, it was important to the maintenance of the pace of the 1943-45 offensives, an important part of the complex system of command, control, and communications which the VgK-Stavka battle-management teams used to coordinate the vast Soviet forces.

Even contemporaries disagreed among themselves about the value of Lend-Lease to the Soviet Union during the various phases of the war. In the latter part of the war Soviet officials hardly seemed desperate for aid, refusing to cooperate with Harriman and Deane, failing to allow the repair of U.S. aircraft behind

Soviet lines, grounding and cancelling orders of some types of unwanted American aircraft, and recommending an end to deliveries of those types.[48] On the other hand, George Marshall, once a critic of the Soviet aid program because of the drain that it represented on the U.S. Army's stockpiles, reported to President Roosevelt on March 1, 1944, that if "Russia suddenly lost Lend-Lease, the Nazis could probably still defeat her."[49] This seems unlikely, but it is also doubtful that the Soviet Union could have conducted its immense offensives without some foreign aid. The assistance to transport and communications systems gave Soviet commanders a special advantage in massing their forces quickly, sustaining them during the "buildup" phase of an attack, and supporting them during offensives which ranged 300-400 miles in depth. In addition, assemblage, movement, equipping, and coordination of the Red Army's strategic reserve were areas in which the Lend-Lease "shipment of raw materials played an important part."[50] Without Western aid in this phase of the war the Soviet Union would still have survived and probably eventually would have won. But without Lend-Lease victory would have been postponed, and the Soviet share of victory and presence in eastern and central Europe reduced.

NOTES

1. U.S. President, *Reports to Congress on Lend-Lease Operations,* no. 14 (Washington, DC: Government Printing Office, 1944), 32.

2. U.S. President, *Reports to Congress on Lend-Lease Operations,* no. 13 (Washington, DC: Government Printing Office, 1944), 16; no. 14, 32..

3. Ibid., no. 13, 19; no. 14, 31-33.

4. Memorandum, "Status of Aircraft Deliveries to U.S.S.R. as of August 31, 1943," Modern Military Records Division, R.G. 334, Box 13, Subject File October 1943-October 1945, Folder September 1943 through 31 July 1944, N.A.

5. "The Armored and Mechanized Troops of the Soviet Armed Forces" (n.d.) (U.S. Army Intelligence translation), U.S. Army Military History Institute, Carlisle Barracks, PA, 9.

6. Paul Carell, *Scorched Earth: The Russian-German War, 1943-1944* (Boston: Little, Brown, 1970), 95.

7. John Erickson, *The Road to Berlin: Continuing the History of Stalin's War with Germany* (Boulder, CO: Westview Press, 1983), 65-66.

8. Erickson, *Road to Berlin,* 145-46, 668-69. One Soviet source placed the German striking force at Kursk at 5,000 tanks. "Armored and Mechanized Troops," 74.

9. I. V. Plotnikov and I. N. Chaban, "Tyl sovetskikh vooruzhennykh sil v gody velikoi otechestvennoi voiny," *Istoriia SSSR* (No. 1, 1975), 10.

10. Ibid, 11.

11. Robert Huhn Jones, *The Roads to Russia: United States Lend-Lease to the Soviet Union* (Norman: University of Oklahoma Press, 1969), 122.

12. N. Dunaeva, "Lend-Liz: Fakty i vymysly," *Voenno-Istoricheskii Zhurnal* (No. 3, 1977), 104; Erickson, *Road to Berlin,* 66, 405; *Istoriia Vtoroi Mirovoi Voiny, 1939-1945,* vol. 8 (Moscow: Voenizdat, 1977), 355, 357, Appendix; "Armored and Mechanized Troops," 59.   The latter mentions an annual production of 30,000 but includes "automotive vehicles" in that figure. Armored cars may be included in the highest production figures.

13. Dunaeva, "Lend-Liz," 104.

14. *History of the Great Patriotic War of the Soviet Union 1941-1945* (Moscow: Voenizdat, 1960; OCMH translation), 3:165; *Istoriia Vtoroi Mirovoi Voiny,* 357; Erickson, *Road to Berlin,* 66, 405; Dunaeva, "Lend-Liz," 104.

15. *Records of the Joint Chiefs of Staff: Part 1, 1942-1945: The Soviet Union* (Frederick, MD: University Publications of America, n.d.), "Bradley Mission: Bombers for the Far East" (January 11, 1943), 1.

16. See *History of the Great Patriotic War,* 2:523.

17. Even the Germans suspected that later Lend-Lease was intended for postwar use. German Army, "Fuehrung, Kampf, und Kraftquellen der Roten Armee," lecture prepared by Foreign Armies East, January 15, 1945 (translated as "Leadership in the Red Army and the Sources of Power and Combat," U.S. Army Intelligence translation), 23.

18. Georgii K. Zhukov, *The Memoirs of Marshal Zhukov* (New York: Delacorte Press, 1972), 391.

19. U.S. President, *Reports to Congress on Lend-Lease Operations,* no. 18 (Washington, DC: Government Printing Office, 1945), 15, 19-21; Erich von Manstein, *Lost Victories* (London: Methuen, 1958), 368.

20. Douglas to Harriman, March 14, 1944, Modern Military Records Division, R.G. 334, Box 13, Subject File October 1943-October 1945, Folder September 1943 through 31 July 1944, N.A.; Robert W. Coakley and Richard M. Leighton, *Global Logistics and Strategy, 1943-1945* (Washington, DC: Office of the Chief of Military History, 1968), 674-75.

21. U.S. President, *Reports to Congress on Lend-Lease Operations,* no. 18, 15, 19-21.

22. U.S. Department of State, Protocol and Area Information Staff of the U.S.S.R. Branch of the Division of Research and Reports, "Report on War Aid Furnished by the United States to the U.S.S.R." (Foreign Economic Section, Office of Foreign Liquidation, November 28, 1945), 5, 6.

23. Harriman to Hopkins, July 31, 1944, Modern Military Records Division, R.G. 334, Box 13, Subject File October 1943-October 1945, Folder September 1943 through 31 July 1944, N.A.

24. "Monthly Summary--Lend-Lease," AGWAR to Spalding, May 14, 1944; "Shipments--Monthly Summary," AGWAR to Harriman, April 16, 1944; Harriman to Douglas, March 14, 1944, Modern Military Records Division, R.G. 334, Box 13, Subject File October 1943-October 1945, Folder September 1943 through 31 July 1944, N.A.

25. *Joint Chiefs of Staff,* "Postwar Economic Policies and Capabilities of the U.S.S.R." (November 1, 1945), 18; *O.S.S./State Department Intelligence and*

Research Reports, Part 6: The Soviet Union, 1941-1949 (Frederick, MD: University Publications of America, 1977), "Relative Capabilities on the Eastern Front" (May 1, 1944), 10. Domestic production averaged 8,000 per month, while imports averaged 11,500.

26. Each 'front' controlled a 1,275-vehicle truck brigade. Infantry armies had 1,200 vehicles, including an independent regiment of 348 trucks. A tank army possessed about 5,340 motor vehicles. All these numbers represent planned strengths, meaning that the actual numbers during operations were probably less. William Henry Chamberlin, "American-Russian Cooperation," *Russian Review* 3 (Autumn 1943), 7; Stephen B. Patrick et al., *War in the East: The Russo-German War, 1941-1945* (New York: Simulations Publications, 1977), 117-25.

27. Erickson, *Road to Berlin,* 81.

28. F. Noel Mason, "Observing the Russians at War," *Military Review* 28 (May 1948), 101.

29. U.S. President, *Report on Operations of the Foreign Economic Administration* (Washington, DC: Government Printing Office, 1944), 29-30. See also U.S. Army, Assistant Chief of Staff (Intelligence), "History of the War in Eastern Europe 1941-1945" (Synopsis) (1953), U.S. Army Military History Institute, Carlisle Barracks, PA, 156.

30. Antony C. Sutton, *Western Technology and Soviet Economic Development, 1930 to 1945* (Stanford: Hoover Institution Press, 1971), 88.

31. Erickson, *Road to Berlin,* 405.

32. *Istoriia Vtoroi Mirovoi Voiny,* 357-87.

33. Sutton, *Western Technology and Soviet Economic Development, 1930 to 1945,* 88.

34. "History of the U.S. Military Mission to Moscow," Modern Military Records Division, R.G. 165, Box 146, OPD 336TS, N.A., 368.

35. Walter Schwabedissen, *The Russian Air Force in the Eyes of German Commanders* (New York: Arno Press, 1960), 385.

36. *Joint Chiefs of Staff,* "Soviet Forces in Far East at 1 January 1945: Report by the Joint Intelligence Staff" (June 6, 1944), 3; Ibid., "Air Capabilities and Intentions of the USSR in the Post-War Period: Report by the Joint Intelligence Staff" (October 19, 1945), 3-4, 9.

37. *Istoriia Vtoroi Mirovoi Voiny,* 357; Dunaeva, "Lend-Liz," 104; see also Erickson, *Road to Berlin,* 405.

38. *Joint Chiefs of Staff,* "Air Capabilities and Intentions," 3-4, 9.

39. *O.S.S.,* "Russian Capabilities and Prospects: Basic Industries" (July 11, 1944), 27-30. The aluminum situation may have been worse. See *Istoriia Vtoroi Mirovoi Voiny,* 355.

40. Sutton, *Western Technology and Soviet Economic Development, 1930 to 1945,* 125-26. Totals do include several Dow Chemical plants.

41. *Joint Chiefs of Staff,* "Memorandum for Information No. 121: Strategy and Policy: Can America and Russia Cooperate?" (August 22, 1943), 6.

42. *Istoriia Vtoroi Mirovoi Voiny,* 355, 357, Appendix; Dunaeva, "Lend-Liz," 104; Erickson, *Road to Berlin,* 405.

43. Erickson, *Road to Berlin,* 429; V. A. Matsulenko, "Velikaia pobeda sovetskogo naroda i ego vooruzhennykh sil," *Voprosy Istorii KPSS* (No. 9, 1963), 112, 113.

44. Spalding to Arnold, June 24, 1944, Modern Military Records Division, R.G.334, Box 13, Subject File October 1943-October 1945, Folder September 1943 through 31 July 1944, N.A. If there was indeed such a force, it might have been present in the Far East for a variety of reasons other than an expected war against Japan. For example, dispersal of forces would have reduced some of the strain on the logistics network.

45. Spalding and Deane to Joint Chiefs of Staff, June 21, 1944, Modern Military Records Division, R.G. 334, Box 13, Subject File October 1943-October 1945, Folder September 1943 through 31 July 1944, N.A.

46. "Report of Trip to USSR by General Connolly," Modern Military Records Division, R.G. 334, Box 5, Subject File October 1943-October 1945, N.A.

47. Albert Seaton, *The Russo-German War, 1941-1945* (New York: Praeger, 1972), 588.

48. *Joint Chiefs of Staff,* "Arrangements with the Soviets" (April 3, 1945), 1.

49. Jones, *Roads to Russia,* 175.

50. Erickson, *Road to Berlin,* 405.

6

Overall Impact

In general, what impact did Lend-Lease have on the Eastern Front? Did it affect the length of the war in that theatre? To answer this question requires a two-step process: first, estimating the percentage of Soviet wartime needs fulfilled by Lend-Lease, and second, a consideration of qualitative factors. The first step, which will be the focus of this chapter, requires an examination of the three obvious units of measurement: tonnage, value, and number of items. Unfortunately, all three have shortcomings.

Tonnage figures tell little about relative military value in the algebra of war. Radar sets and communications gear, for example, had far greater impact than their low tonnage figures reflect. The time of arrival in a given setting could have psychological and physical effects well beyond whatever numerical norms might be used at a distance or in hindsight. In a parallel vein, much of the food shipped to the Soviet Union was in dehydrated form: only by considering its value in terms of protein, vitamins, carbohydrates, and expansibility could its usefulness be measured. Nor do total tonnage figures reflect changes in the composition of aid shipments as new routes were opened or came under attack. For a variety of reasons, most large items had to go via the Northern route. Vladivostok could not be used for finished military equipment, and the Persian Corridor was not equipped to handle any large equipment (such as presses, cranes, or locomotives).[1] Thus the frequent interruptions of the vulnerable Northern route, which might only have a small statistical effect on the aid program, deprived the Soviet Union of a higher percentage of finished products.

Although dollar figures better indicate the value of finished products, they inevitably reflect American wartime price regulation policies and a distortion of the market system in several dimensions. Conversion of these figures into Russian currency would be a useless exercise, since the ruble's exchange value and Soviet prices were (and are) set by government decree, which means that conversion would yield only a hypothetical figure. Because both prices and wages in the Soviet Union were lower than in the United States, dollar-based conversions would overstate the value of Lend-Lease.

Simply counting the number of items works well in some individual categories. The number of field telephones, for example, is more meaningful than the slight tonnage and relatively low cost that these represented. On the whole, however, simple counting of items has a limited utility for estimating the value of Lend-Lease because there are so many different types of items, and adding them together would produce a large set of meaningless numbers.

None of these strictures means that the overall impact of Lend-Lease cannot be evaluated. Used carefully, such measures as those discussed here can be useful. The dollar value of the program to the Soviet economy, for example, can yield a broad estimate of the incremental value of American aid. Other means for estimating the importance of Lend-Lease also exist. Views of the participants (in this context, the Soviet Union, the United States, and Nazi Germany) can be useful. In the strictly military domain, consumption estimates lead to a general sense of how Lend-Lease supplies benefitted the Red Army and whether its command-and-control-augmenting component played a role in the army's ability to inflict losses on the Wehrmacht.[2]

The largest issue, the effect of Lend-Lease on the Soviet economy as a whole, is not a simple one to address, because not all authorities agree on Soviet production figures, making it difficult to calculate the percentage that Lend-Lease represents. Nor does economic effect translate directly into military result. Aid shipments may have had a specific impact on the Soviet economy without this effect being directly felt at the front. At the same time, the two are too closely interrelated to make statistical division of Lend-Lease into military and economic supplies meaningful. Finally, to express Lend-Lease as a simple percentage of Soviet production ignores the incremental aspect which economists express in terms of 'marginal' calculations. The aid program must be evaluated both as a total percentage of Soviet production and as an increment; in other words, what the effect of its absence would have been.

Percentage estimates of the value of Lend-Lease in relation to domestic Soviet production vary according to the source. Soviet authors usually estimate Lend-Lease aid as equivalent to 4 percent of domestic production,[3] a figure accepted by at least one Western authority.[4] Most non-Soviet sources place the percentage at a somewhat higher level, possibly as much as 10-11 percent.[5]

Any debate over the exact figure, moreover, should not leave out of consideration that victory in war may be obtained by small incremental advantages in the military-economic infrastructure or in particular performance capacities. For example, the Allied fighter edge of 10-15 mph is considered by some as crucial in the 1943-45 air war. Calculating the percentage of French and German national income devoted to armored force development would provide no clear understanding of *panzer* successes in 1940. In other words, small differences in organization, doctrine, or weapons performance can create the conditions for decisive victory. Using gross percentage figures to evaluate Lend-Lease does not allow a clear view of whether Lend-Lease merely provided additional increments to materiel the soviets were already manufacturing, or which aid items were shipped which they could or did not make. Thus American shipments of specialized chemicals, metals, and industrial machinery may have had a disproportionate effect on Soviet production. The Soviet use of gross percentage figures (in keeping with their providing as little specific information as possible) is aimed at showing that Lend-Lease cannot be credited with the economic or military survival of the Soviet Union. In this limited sense it may be true that "comparisons between Lend-Lease shipments and Russian production serve no useful purpose."[6]

To American officials, Lend-Lease was as much political, designed to keep the Soviet Union in the war, as military or economic. As already noted, shipments were sent even when American officials were sure that the Soviet Union would perish. Roosevelt feared that Stalin might seek a separate peace if he were not given substantial material aid.[7] Even the ill-starred placement of American bases in the Ukraine in 1944 was a political act, designed to cement the Soviet-American relationship, although Stalin's obvious reluctance about the project guaranteed that friendship would not be one of its results.[8] Soviet collapse or withdrawal from the war would have increased the need for American aid to Britain and the entire empire. Even in mid-1944 American analysts still believed that the U.S.S.R. faced exhaustion and stalemate, if not capitulation. While it seems doubtful that the Soviet Union would have left the war in the absence of foreign aid, it would have been foolish for Britain and America to risk her withdrawal, as well as to have the Soviet Union win through on her own, having been denied all assistance. In this sense, both America and Russia may have viewed Lend-Lease with postwar considerations in mind.

The public statements of the wartime U.S. government were aimed at building political support for Soviet aid and hence tended to be quite optimistic about what aid was actually doing. Soviet Lend-Lease was described as an "essential component" in the Soviet offensives.[9] Similar statements appeared in the media, in Hollywood films and comic strips. The secret conclusions of the Joint Intelligence Staff, however, were somewhat more conservative, attributing the Soviet ability to maintain fighting strength to the mobilization of Soviet industry, "aided by the critical marginal imports under Lend-Lease."[10] The Joint Intelligence Committee (J.I.C.) believed that Lend-Lease aid made up deficiencies in food, raw materials, manufactured goods, and machinery.[11]

Soviet commentary varied. Stalin stated at the Teheran conference that the war would have been lost without American aid and referred to it as an "absolute necessity."[12] Writing many years after the event, Marshal Zhukov conceded that there "can be no denial that the supplies of gunpowder, high octane petrol, some grades of steel, and motor vehicles were of certain help," but he reminded his readers that aid came "in much smaller quantities than promised," and its "proportion was insignificant against the overall requirements of our country." Zhukov did "not wish completely to deny its value," but concluded that Lend-Lease "did not amount to much and hence cannot be considered of much significance."[13]

Nor did Soviet wartime behavior do much to clarify the picture. On the one hand, the demand for aid was constant and unrelenting, and as has been related earlier, proposals to reduce it were denounced with vehemence. On the other hand, requests for convoy-route protection were frequently ignored, although current Soviet sources stress the important role of the Northern Fleet in distracting the enemy from operations against the convoys.[14] In September 1944 the Soviet government agreed to close one of the Persian routes because of its relatively limited capacity (17,000 tons per month).[15] Only two weeks later, however, the Soviet government informed the U.S. Military Mission that the opening of the Black Sea route was a matter of great importance.[16]

The Nazis did not ignore foreign aid to the Soviet Union. Walter Schellenberg, head of German foreign intelligence, was very interested in the comprehensive list of Lend-Lease shipments supplied by his spy at the British embassy in Turkey.[17] A 1945 German army study conceded that Allied aid "amounted to only 15% of the total Russian production," but argued that the deliveries of food, machine tools, and motor vehicles "constitute one of the principal explanations for the strengthened resistance shown by the Russians during the critical period."[18] In the summer of 1942 almost the entire German surface fleet, along with submarines and Luftwaffe detachments, was used to inflict heavy shipping losses on Allied convoys, assaults which only ended when Allied escorts inflicted unacceptable losses on the Nazi attackers.[19] In 1944 American analysts worried about the possibility that German forces in the Aegean, some 70 planes, 3 submarines, and 125 small surface craft, might harass the Black Sea route, opened in January of 1945 after Turkey declared war on Germany.[20] The attacks did not materialize, but this was not due to any lack of interest in Lend-Lease on the part of the Germans. In fact, all the evidence indicates that they took it quite seriously. Information on its impact was spotty, however, because German intelligence had far too many tasks to complete in the East to focus much attention on foreign aid, and perhaps also because some elements within German intelligence displayed little interest in economic factors.[21]

The Germans were fairly well informed about another Soviet weakness, however, a weakness that might seem surprising, and one that is very important to consider when evaluating Lend-Lease. The Soviet Union suffered from a labor shortage. Given the perennial image of Russian/Soviet military victories being the result of the expending of immense quantities of lives, this may seem strange. But it was the Germans, the supposed victims of these 'mass' attacks, who were the first to note this problem. General Reinhard Gehlen's Foreign Armies East intelligence organization concluded in 1942 that the Soviet Union could not meet the combined needs of front, reserve, agriculture, and industry.[22] This view deserves serious consideration for two reasons. Gehlen's staff had a good track record in evaluating the actual and potential size of the Soviet military throughout the war, having captured an enormous quantity of documents in the invasion. More importantly, American analysts reached the same conclusions, fearing that severe labor and material shortages would hamper the Soviet economy in 1943 and anticipating that by 1944 the combined shortages in food and manpower would lead to "a considerable reduction of Russia's military capabilities."[23]

The American analysts based this view on an overly conservative estimate of Soviet casualties; the situation may have been even worse than they thought. Americans stationed in the Soviet Union believed that the manpower situation was dire. The N.K.V.D. guards attached to the American military attache were transferred at war's outbreak and not replaced for quite some time.[24] The U.S. Military Mission in Moscow attributed visible construction delays to the labor shortage and noted that both military and political prisoners were pressed into service.[25] This was not new, of course, but had not been previously observed by embassy staff. Allied materials sometimes languished in Soviet depots because Soviet transportation officials could not send enough people to unload them.[26] The Soviet government favored opening the Black Sea route in part because it would reduce the number of people needed to transport Lend-Lease goods.[27]

The manpower problem was equally visible in the Soviet military. Soviet divisions usually fought at about 70 percent of their authorized strength.[28] Many infantry units, especially those in secondary theatres, consisted of local conscripts with little training, recruited as the Red Army advanced.[29] After the battle of Kursk, the battered Soviet First Tank Army scoured rear-area hospitals, using lightly wounded men for tank crews.[30]

Part of the shortage was caused by the invasion itself. The occupied territories contained about 40 percent of the Soviet population.[31] In 1941 the total nonagricultural work force fell from 31.5 million to 18.5 million.[32] The number of industrial workers declined from 11 million to just over 7 million.[33] By 1945 the labor force still had not regained the prewar level.[34] Heavy industry and mining suffered disproportionately, the heavy machine-tool industry losing over two-thirds of its workers.[35]

The Soviet Union thus lost much of its labor force in 1941, while at the same time it had to draw more men into the army and increase industrial production. Some of the labor demand could be met by recruiting among refugees, who may have numbered as many as 21 million.[36] These, however, had to be fed, and much of the country's richest farmlands had been overrun. Although this meant that more would have to be produced in the rest of the country, the Red Army had systematically stripped many farms of their tractors, making agriculture even more labor-intensive. There was no labor surplus to bring to the farms, and food shortages existed throughout the war. Rationing did not end until 1947.[37] In effect, the Soviet Union faced a proverbial Hobson's choice in its labor policies. It could concentrate on feeding the masses adequately, thereby losing the war due to inadequate military manpower or industrial output, or it could meet all the manpower and equipment needs of the front and starve. The only real solution was to accept serious inadequacies in all areas.

During the most critical phases of the war, the army was given precedence: *vce dlia fronta,* "all for the front." Workers in threatened cities were formed into military units and sent to the front. Some defense-related industries lost as many as two-thirds of their workers in 1941.[38] Much of the Communist party's membership joined the ranks, causing the party's civilian organizations to decline by 40 percent as the membership joined the army. By 1943 over half the party was in uniform, reflecting both mobilization and easier admission standards for soldiers.[39] As many as three-quarters of all the able-bodied, military-age men may have seen service at some point during the war.[40] Even with looming food shortages, skilled farm workers were taken into the Red Army.[41]

The tight labor situation was not just the result of invasion losses and competing demands. The Red Army's offensive tactics were often costly. The "echelon" attack was designed to build up overwhelming force and penetrate entire defensive zones. Artillery and mortar units pounded the German lines for about half an hour. Screened by second-rate troops, a first echelon of infantry battalions supported by air and artillery units would penetrate a weak sector of the enemy defenses. A second echelon of armored, motorized, and infantry units would attack through the breach into rear areas, toward reserves, command and control centers, and logistic support areas.[42]

While this might sound like an effective method (and it often worked) the cost in lives of Soviet tactics could be appalling. By Western standards Soviet losses seemed excessive. Early in the war large masses of men (possibly penal units) were used to penetrate German minefields.[43] This tactic was later justified by Zhukov as a life-saving measure, as it gave the enemy less time to prepare than did the traditional, methodical approach to clearing minefields. A frequent method of attack was to cease artillery fire along a corridor not over a hundred yards wide, through which infantry would (gingerly) advance. If the defenders' fire forced the attackers out of their corridor, however, the result could be devastating even by Russian standards.[44] As the echeloned Soviet units often attacked in close-packed array, Nazi counterfire (if not suppressed) often inflicted terrible losses.[45]

Yet costly as these attacks seemed, they were not without purpose. The German defenders could expect no respite from Red Army attacks until the latter either achieved its goals or expended all forces allocated to the attack, as the Soviet command was committed to the principle of uninterrupted execution.[46] At the very least it required great 'fire-discipline' to survive these onslaughts by (sometimes drunken) Soviet infantrymen, backed up by formidable artillery and tank forces.[47] The massive nature of the Soviet attack, costly as it was, was based on early war experience which showed that narrow breakthroughs did not lead to decisive victories.[48]

Even if the Red Army's methods were rational, the cost in lives was still high, rising unnecessarily because of frightful mistakes committed by tactical commanders. The first Soviet counterattacks were all too often uncoordinated, poorly planned, and inflexible, leading to the wholesale destruction of units.[49] Mishandling of tank units and infantry fear of enemy tanks (tankboyazn) were especially serious problems.[50] The leadership of some service branches, such as the airborne force, had not yet recovered from the purge.[51] Excessive losses meant a greater need for recruits, further draining the manpower pool.

It is, however, important not to exaggerate battlefield problems, severe as they were. If the Red Army had consistently performed as ineptly as its foreign detractors claimed, the Soviet Union would not have survived, despite its numerical advantages. Soviet tactics improved throughout the war, but the army was hampered by casualties among trained personnel in battle and by the losses of capable personnel in the 1938 purge and in the encirclements of July-October 1941. The purge had not encouraged Soviet officers to question orders, take the initiative, or be innovative, and the use of centralized planning and battle management by teams from VgK-Stavka maintained the doctrine of *edinonachalniye*, one-man control.

Mass assaults became less prevalent as the war progressed, partly because of increasing skill, and probably partly due to declining reserves.[52] Many of the bloodier attacks were made with units of marginal quality, which composed the first echelon of attack even late in the war, presumably to avoid the loss of trained specialists.[53] Heavy losses of unskilled workers were not necessarily a great drain for a nation with serious food shortages, especially when unskilled farm labor requirements were being reduced by large shipments of food from its allies.

There were practical reasons for the Red Army to continue the costly mass attacks even with the drain they imposed on the labor pool. They pinned down the less numerous German defenders and prevented them from moving reserves around. The enemy force was smaller and had to function as an elite army, however much it actually was, dependent on mobility, quick reflexes, and innovative tactics. The Germans relied on maneuver skills to counter the more numerous Soviet forces, but their advantage in that realm could be nullified if they were forced to join the less mobile frontline troops in countering mass attacks. Nor did the Wehrmacht enjoy quite the qualitative edge often attributed to it. N.K.V.D., Cossack, and some Guards divisions were as good as any in the German army. Thus the relentless Soviet attacks, costly as they were, reduced the quality and the numbers of their foes. By the last year of the war new German divisions arriving at the front had little more training than their Soviet counterparts. Furthermore, losses in attack had to be balanced against losses during retreats, and the latter, as the Red Army had learned, could be far greater.

Concern over the high level of losses permeated the Soviet Union both during and after the war. The scars of the losses of World War II have not all healed and are everywhere to be seen in the U.S.S.R. The Red Army did what it could to reduce losses. Surrounded Soviet formations usually tried to break out en masse, but if that failed, small units would infiltrate the encirclement to bring out selected personnel, who would then form the core of new formations.[54] The prevention of encirclement had even occupied the General Staff before the war. Faced with the actual event again and again in 1941, the Red Army began organizing breakouts as early as July, and by 1943 trapped Soviet formations were able to avoid disorganization, thereby at least constituting a threat to the surrounding German forces.[55]

The effort to fight more efficiently and reduce casualties took a number of forms, one of which was an increased emphasis on small-unit infiltration of the German lines.[56] Small-unit operations were frequently used, although hampered by a lack of initiative and by control and communications problems.[57] Soviet units would penetrate the thin, extended German lines at night and dig in, sometimes undiscovered for days, feints would be made to distract attention from the operation, and reinforcements would move up quickly so that the bridgehead could be used as a jumping-off point for an offensive. The Germans concluded that the Soviets had an "unparalleled genius" for infiltration. In 1942, for example, Soviet units near Kursk quietly slipped behind the front and bested the Germans in a series of mobile engagements.[58]

Nor was infiltration the only way in which the Red Army proved to be resourceful and methodical. The Germans marveled at the quickness with which the Soviet command derived basic lessons from German tactical methods.[59] Reconnaissance, minefield clearing, and artillery tactics had become reasonably scientific by the end of the war. The Soviet artillery, for example, would sometimes fire a preparatory bombardment to locate German batteries, shift fire to rear positions while simulating an infantry attack, and then open fire on the German troops as they returned to the frontline trenches.[60]

Against the overstated image of reckless attack and needless losses there must be balanced the clear evidence of the inherent strength and ability of the Red Army. Even in 1941 the Red Army demonstrated its ability to function with little in the way of materiel by attacking and destroying a German tank unit with mounted Cossack troops, armed only with small arms and Molotov cocktails.[61] Early efforts to penetrate the German rear and capture weaponry were sometimes spectacularly successful.[62] The Red Army also demonstrated an astonishing ability to function in the worst imaginable weather and to fight at night and in all types of terrain, as exemplified by river-crossing operations made in full view of German forces.[63] In these conditions the 'backwardness' of the peasant soldiers, combined with the paucity of supplies and equipment, could actually be an advantage.[64] All this the Red Army combined with extraordinary talents for camouflage.[65]

The Soviet command was not willing, however, to rely on these innate advantages and took steps to eliminate the needless loss of troops at the front. The General Staff published and circulated detailed studies to teach its officers 'correct' solutions to almost every conceivable tactical problem. In 1941 the General Staff established a Section for the Utilization of Combat Experience which communicated information and conclusions to lower-echelon commanders and wrote a variety of instructions, orders, and regulations. The section began publishing *A Miscellany of Materials for Studying Combat Experience* in the fall of 1942, later superseded by the *Information Bulletin* and *Tactical Methods Miscellany*. Subjects included the destruction of surrounded enemy formations, the correct employment of tanks, amphibious operations, defense against tanks and aircraft, operational war games, problems of studying combat operations, reconnaissance, order of battle, methods of command control, forcing rivers, and descriptions of interesting small-unit engagements.[66]

The results were rewarding. In many engagements the Red Army proved adept at combining many methods, such as mass, mobility, camouflage and deception, and skillfully orchestrated initiation, for the attack.[67] Not only did the Soviet forces inflict devastating casualties, but they frequently destroyed German divisions which had acquitted themselves well elsewhere.[68]

The Soviet Union then did attempt to reduce casualties, probably in part because of its labor shortage. Did Lend-Lease assist this effort to lower losses? At the immediate tactical level, probably not to any significant degree. It must be kept in mind that the Red Army was by far the most important arm, with air and naval forces functioning mostly in a supporting role.[69] The United States did not furnish that much combat equipment to the ground forces. Foreign observers were not permitted to view the Red Army in action, but the Germans, who saw it all too often, rarely noted the presence of either American or British tanks.[70] Lend-Lease did include over 4,000 amphibious vehicles, undoubtedly useful for the many river-crossing operations, but most were small, and nothing is known about their use.[71]

In the artillery arm Lend-Lease did have some impact, but in a very indirect way. The Red Army relied heavily on the power of its artillery, which even in 1941 proved capable of repelling German attacks and effectively bombarding rear areas.[72] German officers described the Soviet artillery as "good" and "unpleasantly effective."[73] As the war progressed, the Red Army's gunnery grew both more skillful and massive, and capable of surprise artillery attacks.[74] During the Soviet breakout from the Kitska bridgehead in Romania, for example, the Germans were subjected to a 90-minute bombardment by 4,000 guns and mortars.[75] Soviet offensives were spearheaded by artillery concentrations of 200 guns and mortars per half-mile of front, plus 150-300 rocket batteries. Not surprisingly, the resulting bombardments were described as "veritable drumfires of destruction."[76]

The artillery helped save Soviet lives during both offensive and defensive operations. Heavy shelling suppressed German fire, demoralized enemy troops, sometimes disorienting their entire defense, and covered retreats that otherwise might have become costly routs. To this vital arm the contribution of Lend-Lease was highly indirect. Very few artillery guns and little ammunition was shipped, as little was requested. Where American aid does become important to the artillery arm has more to do with improved communications and transport (chapter 7) and ammunition quality through imports of explosives and chemicals (chapter 8).

Increased firepower and better command and control of forces allowed the Red Army to make better use of its manpower. If its losses had been even greater than the estimated 7-8 million military deaths, it would have had to use a defensive strategy oriented to reducing losses at the expense of allowing the Germans to remain on Soviet soil. This does not mean that defeat would have ensued. According to the German commanders, its defensive skills were great, especially in designing ambushes, erecting field fortifications, defending cities, and holding positions regardless of the odds.[77] During retreats equipment was not often abandoned intact.[78] German offensives in 1943, 1944, and 1945 were blunted by carefully designed defensive zones up to 40 kilometer deep with interlocking defense and closely linked fire-points. These defenses were based on hidden gun emplacements, dummy installations to confuse attackers, minefields, anti-tank ditches, and alternate defensive positions. Mobile obstacle-setting units were available in case of a German breakthrough. These defenses were flexible, designed to take the sting out of the German attack rather than to stop it.[79] Not only did this defense system cost the attacker heavily, it also reduced the defender's losses.

The Soviet government did not, however, contemplate a completely defensive war; to do so would have surrendered the initiative to the Nazis. An offensive strategy, however, required more manpower. This necessitated draining personnel from many tasks to replace the army's losses and establish new combat formations. The Tyl (Rear Services) absorbed about one-fifth of the field strength (a low figure by foreign standards), the Main Military Roads Administration alone requiring some 125,000 workers to maintain vehicles and roads.[80] The secret police, which fielded some combat units, was estimated at 3 million.[81] While many office workers were recruited for farm or military duty, the war required intensified administrative work in the military, transport, and industrial sectors. Before the war there were approximately 1.2 million administrators in industry and 600,000 on the farms (not including some 3.5 million clerical workers).[82] These made tempting targets for recruitment, but wartime administration is hardly simpler than the same work in peacetime, and the shift of any workers from one sector of the economy to another spelt a loss of performance in the former sector.

The shortage went beyond numbers. Skilled workers were at a premium, especially as the ranks of industry were filled with women and youths with little training.[83] The situation was most critical in the early part of the war but was never completely resolved.[84]

The number of available male workers (15-65) declined from 56.4 million in 1941 to 33.6 million in 1943.[85] Other than the very old and very young, the most logical source for additional labor was obviously women. The Soviet Union, however, lacked a large pool of nonworking women to draw upon. Female farm labor was extensive before the war, and the recruitment of male farm workers made the labor of women even more important. Mobilization of women alone could not make up for existing labor shortages.[86] In addition to their role on the farms, women constituted half of all workers in large-scale industry, a majority in textiles and clothing, and a substantial share of the heavy-industry work force.[87] The high presence of women in the workplace was partly due to Soviet views on equality but was also caused by the toll which World War I, the Civil War, and the purges had taken of the male population.

Nevertheless, civilian and some military mobilization of women, combined with large-scale military mobilization of men, saw an increased 'feminization' of the Soviet labor force. The percentage of the work force that was composed of women grew from 40 percent in 1940 to 53 percent in 1942.[88] By 1942 women comprised 70-80 percent of all workers in light industry and 38-45 percent of the heavy-industry labor force, over half of the laborers in the Ural machine-tool factories, and most of the work force in the R.S.F.S.R. and the Ukraine.[89] Women worked one-half of all the workdays in the Soviet Union during the war, as opposed to one-fourth by working-age men and less than one-tenth by minors, the balance being pensioners and part-time workers.[90] Americans noted the almost total absence of men from the Moscow labor force.[91] Wendell Willkie visited a collective farm and saw only a single adult male on the entire work force: the manager.[92] Nor were women limited to the civilian sector, as over a million served in the Red Army, many in the combat ranks.[93]

The young were also called into civilian and military service. They contributed 8.5 percent of wartime workdays, comprising about 40 percent of the Moscow work force and 15-30 percent of the workers in the Urals.[94] Their presence in the military was immediate (2 million Komsomol members joined the army in the first year after the invasion) and became more pronounced toward the end of the war.[95]

Proof of a labor shortage in the Soviet Union does not depend on Western interpretations. Soviet writers concede that the problem was real. "The national economy was faced with an unusually critical problem of finding and rationally employing additional labor resources."[96] The decline of the labor force and its recruitment into the military led to an increase in acreage per farm laborer (and per "unit of draft power," showing the requisitioning of farm tractors and animals into the army), a remarkable statistic given the amount of Soviet land overrun by the Nazis.[97] The massive number of labor-related decrees in 1946-50 indicates the severity of the situation.[98] Soviet authors also emphasize the successful resolution of the crisis. The number of workdays actually increased in 1940-42.[99] "The extreme shortage of manpower was compensated for by the widespread drawing of women and young people into industry and well-organized training of reinforcements."[100]

Interestingly enough, the severity of the labor shortage did not lead the Soviet Union to accept Allied troops. As noted earlier, Anglo-American suggestions to that effect were refused, except very early in the war when Stalin himself proposed sending an Allied army to the U.S.S.R. The Soviet government rejected proposals for the basing of foreign air units in the Caucasus, the stationing of a British squadron at Murmansk (to protect convoys), and the establishment of American bases in Siberia. The latter may have been viewed by the Soviet government as a potential provocation of Japan and, recalling the American military occupation of 1919-20, an attempt to take advantage of Soviet weaknesses.[101] American pilots were not welcome, and some aircraft orders were refused when the United States insisted on training the pilots in the Soviet Union.[102] A Soviet request in July 1944 for American bombsight instructors was followed six weeks later by notification that the Soviet bombardiers had mastered the instrument and that the Americans were no longer needed (although later the instructors were invited again).[103] American officials attributed the Soviet refusal of foreign technicians not to a lack of need, but to paranoia, pride, lack of accommodations, and fear that U.S. technicians' high standards might keep equipment inactive.[104]

Stalin did allow American bombers into the Ukraine, but their operations were restricted and their presence was more accepted than appreciated.[105] When the

American bomber force was devastated by a German raid on July 21, 1944, Soviet antiaircraft fire was energetic but ineffective, and no night fighters were available nearby, despite American requests. Controversy raged between American and Soviet authorities about whether night fighters had been sent up at all to defend the bases. American proposals to place U.S. night fighters and antiaircraft batteries at the Ukrainian bases (Poltava, Mirgorod, and Piryatin) were first delayed, then denied. The project was discontinued amidst an atmosphere of acrimony and mutual distrust, and much of the remaining U.S. equipment was either shipped out of the Soviet Union or destroyed on the spot by American personnel.[106]

The refusal of foreign personnel in no way suggests that a labor shortage did not exist, merely that the Soviet Union had passed the total desperation phase of the war. It is clear from both American and Soviet sources that whatever the causes, the Soviet margin of surplus labor was at best thin throughout the war. American and German analysts both believed the Soviet labor pool was nearing exhaustion toward the end of the war. Any easing of the Soviet labor difficulties would have been the single most important contribution which Lend-Lease could make. This is precisely what it achieved. Lend-Lease equipment made the Red Army substantially more efficient, with transportation and communications gear allowing the army to concentrate forces more rapidly, thereby allowing the use of surprise on a large scale. If the Soviet forces had not been able to concentrate or react as quickly as they did, the German army could have regrouped and redeployed to meet the threat, thereby increasing Soviet casualties and depriving them of the initiative. Without Lend-Lease transportation aid the Red Army could not have maintained the pace of its offensives. The Germans would have had more of a respite and a chance to move away or to counterattack with uncommitted reserves.

The heavy, rapid concentration of large forces in the offensive places an immense strain on logistics. Since Soviet offensives required great concentrations of force, the Red Army could not, without adequate transport, have been adequately supplied, and the tremendous confluences of men and firepower necessary for decisive breakthroughs would have been virtually impossible. If Soviet tactical methods often led to bloody and inconclusive results, the alternative of slow, ponderous advances in the style of World War I would have been their only option, other than armistice, a purely defensive position, or surrender. The choice would have been between more costly military options, or less costly methods adopted at the expense of Soviet territorial integrity or survival. The adoption of attrition warfare would not have denied the German mobility over time to the same extent that this was accomplished by the early time-and-space-buying Soviet counterattacks. Slow, wide advances could have pushed the Germans back, but without certainty of decisive success. In the end the Red Army might have run out of men before the Nazis were defeated or driven from Soviet soil.

Lend-Lease communications equipment made it far easier for Soviet commanders to control their forces.[107] This was especially important because the

Red Army had few intermediate commands, having no real equivalent, for example, to the Western "corps." Qualified commanders were scarce, and staffs thin, requiring headquarters to coordinate large numbers of units. Improved communications allowed the Red Army to use its resources more efficiently and take advantage of sudden weaknesses in the overstretched Nazi forces. Imported aircraft substantially increased the Red Army's firepower, taking some of the strain off the ground troops and therefore acting indirectly as a lifesaver.

Without Lend-Lease food shipments, Soviet agriculture would have had to produce more. There was certainly no food surplus during the war. How could Soviet farms have increased their harvest? With much of their mechanized equipment lost to the army and becoming increasingly labor-intensive as the male work force entered the army, the farms needed additional workers to increase production. From whence could they have come? On a smaller scale, the same is true of Lend-Lease raw materials, which slightly reduced the need for miners. If nothing else, Western aid in these categories enabled more men to enter the army. Finally, shipments of finished goods undoubtedly saved many man-hours in the skilled-labor sector.

If Lend-Lease released men from the civilian economy to enter the army and kept more alive once they were there, how many soldiers could it actually sustain in the field? A general estimate can be gleaned from the average consumption of supplies by the Soviet soldier calculated by the U.S. Military Mission to Moscow (table 39) (American consumption is listed for comparison). These numbers are designed to show the requirements of armies, not individual soldiers. An individual soldier, for example, does not consume "arctic fuel," but a field unit in the cold climes of Russia certainly will. The size of a unit is the simplest way of estimating its consumption. For example, the "rations" figure given for the Soviet soldier, .042, does not mean that each and every soldier will consume .042 long tons of rations each month. A division of 10,000 soldiers, however, will probably consume, if the estimate is accurate, about 420 long tons of rations.

The figures that are most important for our purposes are those listed at the bottom of table 39. The total required to keep an average Soviet soldier alive and supplied with necessities is .381 long tons, slightly more than 853 pounds (note that the American soldier, on the average, required .764 long tons, about 1,711 pounds). In gross terms, Lend-Lease supplies would have kept 675,000 men in the field throughout the war, about a tenth of the Soviet forces. If the data is applied to ground forces alone, the figure rises to 975,000. As much Lend-Lease was not intended directly for the Red Army, however, these are rough approximations at best. Lend-Lease foodstuffs could have fed several million soldiers for the duration. Petroleum shipments would have sufficed for about a quarter-million troops for the entire war. Most Lend-Lease petroleum consisted of specialized blending agents, however, some of which could not be produced domestically. Nor can the impact of all imported petroleum-production equipment be accurately gauged. The aviation fuel plants alone were capable of producing 1.9 million tons by 1944.

Can these numbers be translated into "division-days," that is, the number of Soviet units that Lend-Lease supplies could sustain? The World War II Soviet unit was complex. A single brigade, for example, might contain motorized, artillery, antiaircraft, and infantry elements, and its size and composition might vary during the war.[108] A few divisions had all their authorized equipment, while some had little more than rifles and small arms.[109] A division might be full strength (table 40) or have as few as 6,000 men. The Soviet division's "slice" (division strength plus all rear-service troops necessary to support the division) averaged about 25,000 men, as compared to 40,000 men in the U.S. Army.[110] Based on this data, Lend-Lease supplies sufficed to support 65-100 divisions from December 1941, to May 1945, not allowing for the fluctuating flow of supplies, which would have caused the number to rise and fall. In 1942, for example, Lend-Lease might have been enough for 35-45 divisions, while in 1944 the figure was closer to 85-110 divisions.[111] These figures should be read with the understanding that they represent a hypothetical index of the effect of Lend-Lease, as many Lend-Lease supplies were not directly useable by the Red Army. The nonmilitary supplies (for example, machine tools and raw materials) however, ultimately did translate into assistance for the army, certainly at least in proportion to their original tonnage.

Unfortunately, all such estimates are hampered by lack of knowledge of losses due to wastage. Equipment was often left to the mercy of the Russian climate, mishandled, poorly serviced and maintained, or pilfered for personal use, although one might assume that such factors affected all Red Army supply, not just Lend-Lease aid. The commander of the U.S. Military Mission in Moscow concluded that the "total amount of such diversion cannot even be roughly estimated."[112] He complained that more than 100 marine diesel engines (out of 150 shipped) were left rusting in open storage.[113] Such waste led Ambassador Harriman to demand detailed statistics in support of Soviet aid requests.[114] Soviet officials complained about defective equipment, losses due to poor packaging, and theft of goods in transit to the Soviet Union.[115]

On the other hand, when considering the overall role of Lend-Lease, it perhaps does not matter whether Lend-Lease was enough to supply 20 or 50 or 100 divisions, whether it could feed 3 million or 10 million soldiers, or whether it was equivalent to 4 or 7 or 10 percent of Soviet production. To focus on the exact quantitative conclusion misses the real point. The Soviet Union was in desperate shape during the Great Patriotic War: its industry was devastated, its farmlands were overrun, and its labor force could barely be stretched to service farm, factory, and army simultaneously. Lend-Lease may not have been a very large share of all the food, weaponry, and other goods required by the Soviet Union during the war, but given that the Soviet state had literally nothing to spare, be it people, food, or materiel, the increment provided by Lend-Lease could very well have been the vital difference between defensive and offensive warfare by the Red Army.

There is, in addition, the inevitable imponderable: morale. Did foreign aid bolster Soviet morale? It is impossible to give any numerical or quantitative answer to this question. Soviet writers note the "moral" as well as the "material" assistance provided. Soviet wartime governmental publicity about Lend-Lease was spotty, but its existence seems to have been widely known, at least based on the limited contacts that American observers had with Soviet citizens. Much of the aid was visible, including the trucks, jeeps, aircraft, and canned food. Morale and the psychology of war were a constant preoccupation of the regime, which may have contributed to its ambivalence about Lend-Lease. The program would be seen to bolster morale (good) but might suggest that the regime had not fully prepared for the war (bad). Consider the account given by Soviet emigre Mikhail Soloviev of his discovery that a foreign power was sending supplies to the Soviet Union. Late one night early in the war, he was awakened by his commander, Colonel Prokhorov.

> Prokhorov: Do you see this?
> Soloviev: Well you've been issued a can of food. So what?
> Prokhorov: Listen! Read what it says on the can, you idiot.
>   Soloviev took the can. It was heavy, weighing several pounds.
>   He saw on the label the words "Pork and meat" and, below
>   that, "Made in U.S.A." We had got used to the idea that we
>   were fighting all alone, but here was a can of food that came
>   like a greeting from another world. Prokhorov was even more
>   excited, proclaiming that he would like to raise a royal
>   monument.
> Prokhorov: Today, I was issued food from America. But tomorrow
>   I shall get tanks and airplanes from the Americans. The pork is
>   a kind of advance guard, but there's an army following up behind,
>   and sooner or later we'll see it.[116]

If he lived long enough, Colonel Prokhorov saw the planes and maybe a few tanks. The army never came; it was not invited. But if the colonel's reaction was typical, and about this we cannot be certain, then Lend-Lease meant a great deal indeed.

NOTES

1. *Records of the Joint Chiefs of Staff: Part 1, 1942-1945: The Soviet Union* (Frederick, MD: University Publications of America, n.d.), "Resumption of Northern Convoys to Russia" (May 24,1944), 3.

2. F. W. von Mellenthin, *Panzer Battles: A Study of the Employment of Armor in the Second World War* (Norman: University of Oklahoma Press, 1971), 283. The lion's share of German casualties were suffered on the Eastern Front (where most of their forces were).

3. Nikolai A. Voznesensky, *The Economy of the U.S.S.R. during World War II* (Washington, DC: Public Affairs Press, 1948), 43-44; Rolf Kieser, "Die

Kriegswirtschaft der Sowjetunion im Grossen Vaterlaendischen Krieg--Beweis fuer die Gesetzmaessigkeit der Militaeroekonomischen Ueberlegenheit des Sozialismus ueber den Imperialismus," *Zeitschrift fuer Militaergeschichte* 7 (1968), 91; Nikolai Yakovlev, "USSR-USA: 50 Years of Diplomatic Relations," *Soviet Life* (November 1983), 37.

4. James R. Millar, "Financing the Soviet War Effort in World War II," *Soviet Studies* 32 (January 1980), 123.

5. George C. Herring, Jr., *Aid to Russia, 1941-1946: Strategy, Diplomacy, and the Origins of the Cold War* (New York: Columbia University Press, 1973), 286.

6. Robert Huhn Jones, *The Roads to Russia: United States Lend-Lease to the Soviet Union* (Norman: University of Oklahoma Press, 1969), 224.

Herring, Aid to Russia, 21.

8. "Final Report," Robert L. Walsh Papers, U.S. Army Military History Institute, Carlisle Barracks, PA, Archives.

9. U.S. President, *Reports to Congress on Lend-Lease Operations,* no. 20 (Washington, DC: Government Printing Office, 1945), 7.

10. *Joint Chiefs of Staff,* "Postwar Economic Policies and Capabilities of the USSR" (November 1, 1945), 1.

11. Ibid., 12.

12. Edgar L. Erickson, Foreword to Jones, *Roads to Russia,* vii.

13. Georgii K. Zhukov, *The Memoirs of Marshal Zhukov* (New York: Delacorte Press, 1972), 392, 466.

14. V. Konovalov, "Iz opyta popol'neniia sostava severnogo flota v gody velikoi otechestvennoi voiny," *Voenno-Istoricheskii Zhurnal* (No. 8, 1978), 107.

15. *Joint Chiefs of Staff,* "Closing of the West Persian Route via Khanaquin for Transport of Supplies to Russia: Memorandum by the Representatives of the British Chiefs of Staff" (September 15, 1944), 1, 3.

16. *Joint Chiefs of Staff,* "Allied Communications to the U.S.S.R. via the Black Sea: Report by the Joint Staff Planners" (September 15, 1944), 1, 6.

17. Walther Schellenberg, *Hitler's Secret Service* (New York: Jove Publications, 1977), 333.

18. German Army, "Fuehrung, Kampf, und Kraftquellen der Roten Armee," lecture prepared by Foreign Armies East, 15 January 1945 (translated as "Leadership in the Red Army and the Sources of Power and Combat," U.S. Army Intelligence translation), U.S. Army Military History Institute, Carlisle Barracks, PA, 25.

19. Jones, *Roads to Russia,* 100-104.   German surface attacks on Allied convoys virtually ceased after December 26, 1943, when the *Scharnhorst* was sunk. Convoy losses were only 4 percent after this point.

20. *Joint Chiefs of Staff,* "Communications with the U.S.S.R. via the Black Sea: Report by the Joint Intelligence Committee" (October 16, 1944), 2-3.

21. Reinhard Gehlen, *The Service: The Memoirs of General Reinhard Gehlen* (New York: World Publishing, 1972), 32.

22. Ibid., 41-42.

23. *O.S.S./State Department Intelligence and Research Reports, Part 6: The Soviet Union, 1941-1949* (Frederick, MD: University Publications of America, 1977), "Russian Military Potential: Economic Prospects for 1943" (June 25, 1943), 1-2; *Joint Chiefs of Staff*, "Memorandum for Information No. 121: Strategy and Policy: Can American and Russia Cooperate?" (August 22, 1943), 6.

24. Memoirs, Ivan Downs Yeaton Papers, U.S. Army Military History Institute, Carlisle Barracks, PA, Archives, 29.

25. "History of the U.S. Military Mission to Moscow," Modern Military Records Division, R.G. 165, Box 146, OPD 336TS, N.A., 369.

26. Memoirs, Oleg Pantuhoff Papers, U.S. Army Military History Institute, Carlisle Barracks, PA, Archives, 506.

27. *Joint Chiefs of Staff*, "Allied Communications to the U.S.S.R. via the Black Sea: Report by the Joint Staff Planners" (November 8, 1944), 23.

28. U.S. Army, Assistant Chief of Staff (Intelligence), "Soviet Rear Services" (n.d.), U.S. Army Military History Institute, Carlisle Barracks, PA, 10.

29. John Erickson, *The Road to Berlin: Continuing the History of Stalin's War with Germany* (Boulder, CO: Westview Press, 1983), 412.

30. Ibid., 117.

31. J. Halperin, "L'economie sovietique pendant la guerre," *Revue d'Histoire de la Deuxieme Guerre Mondiale* 2 (April 1952), 18.

32. M. M. Kucherenko, "Podgotovka rabochego popol'neniia v gody velikoi otechestvennoi voiny," *Voprosy Istorii* (No. 5, 1979), 5. These figures have also been estimated at 31.2 million and 18.4 million. Rene Girault, "L'effort humain de l'arriere (1941-43)," *Revue d'Histoire de la Deuxieme Guerre Mondiale* 17 (October 1967), 24.

33. Girault, "Effort humain," 24.

34. Ibid., 24.

35. M. S. Zinich, "Iz istorii stankostroeniia i tiazhelogo mashinostroeniia v pervyi period velikoi otechestvennoi voiny," *Istoriia SSSR* (No. 6, 1971), 93; Girault, "Effort humain," 24-25.

36. *O.S.S.*, "Military Potential of the Soviet Union, Part IIb: The Food Problem under War Conditions" (November 30, 1942), 12.

37. Sheila Fitzpatrick, "New Perspectives on Stalinism," *Russian Review* 45 (October 1986), 363.

38. Girault, "Effort humain," 19-22.

39. Erickson, *Road to Berlin,* 401.

40. "Fuehrung, Kampf, und Kraftquellen," 20-22. According to the German estimates, Russia began the war with 50.4 million men of military age. After deducting for the unfit and service-exempt (15.45 million), normal deaths (1.5 million), and wartime losses (17.5 million), there remained 15.95 million available for duty. As 12.5 million were in uniformed service of some kind according to this analysis, 3.45 million could be mobilized into full-time reserve duty (note that population growth is not considered).

41. *O.S.S.,* "Military Potential of the Soviet Union, Part IIb: The Food Problem under War Conditions" (November 30, 1942), 10.

42. John G. Hines, "The Principles of Mass in Soviet Tactics Today," *Military Review* 62 (August 1982), 15; *The Great March of Liberation* (Moscow: Progress Publishers, 1972), 44, 97-98.

43. *World War II German Military Studies: A Collection of 213 Special Reports on the Second World War Prepared by Former Officers of the Wehrmacht for the United States Army,* 24 vols. (New York: Garland Publishing, 1974), 18:(VII)(D)(10), 25, 163.

44. Mellenthin, *Panzer Battles,* 301.

45. On the density of the Soviet attack, see Ivan Parotkin, ed., *The Battle of Kursk* (Moscow: Progress Publishers, 1974), 144, 163-64.

46. Graham D. Vernon, "Soviet Combat Operations in World War II: Lessons for Today?" *Military Review* 60 (April 1980), 46.

47. Mellenthin, *Panzer Battles,* 147; *Great March of Liberation,* 119; Eugene D. Betit, "The Soviet Manchurian Campaign, August 1945: Prototype for the Soviet Offensive," *Military Review* 56 (May 1976), 68; Gerald R. Kleinfeld and Lewis A. Tambs, *Hitler's Spanish Legion: The Blue Division in Russia* (Carbondale: Southern Illinois University Press, 1979), 90, 106, 134.

48. "Fuehrung, Kampf, und Kraftquellen," 9.

49. Consider, for example, the attacks launched in June and July 1941 by the Red Army at Yelnia and Khristishche. At Yelnia the Red Army launched 13 consecutive bloody, unsupported infantry attacks. At Khristishche 60 percent of a rifle regiment was mowed down by the Germans within minutes of the attack. Heinz Guderian, *Panzer Leader* (New York: E. P. Dutton, 1952), 185; *German Military Studies,* 18:(VII)(D)(16), 24-31.

50. *German Military Studies,* 18:(VII)(D)(11), 21; Erickson, *Road to Berlin,* 143, 153; Mellenthin, *Panzer Battles,* 101; Vernon, "Combat Operations," 296

51. For example, this was possibly a factor in the disastrous performance of the parachute forces at the Bukrin bridgehead. Graham H. Turbiville, "Paradrop at the Bukrin Bridgehead: An Account of the Soviet Dnieper Airborne Operation," *Military Review* 56 (December 1976), 26-40. Operations at Crete and Arnhem demonstrated that other combatants rarely mastered the intricate problems of executing, coordinating, and reinforcing parachute attacks.

52. Mellenthin, *Panzer Battles,* 265.

53. Ibid., 269, 282; *German Military Studies,* 18:(VII)(D)(10), 125; Vladimir Sevruk, ed., *Moscow 1941/1942 Stalingrad: Recollections, Stories, Reports* (Moscow: Progress Publishers, 1970), 12, 41; Alexander Werth, *Russia at War, 1941-1945* (New York: E. P. Dutton, 1964), 241. In general, the Russians believed that specialists required less training than the Americans thought necessary. "History of the U.S. Military Mission," 291.

54. *German Military Studies,* 16:(VII)(C)(1), 91; Mellenthin, *Panzer Battles,* 256.

55. Franz Halder, *The Halder Diaries: The Private War Journals of Colonel General Franz Halder* (Boulder, CO: Westview Press, 1976), 2:1065;

Mellenthin, *Panzer Battles,* 263; *German Military Studies,* 16:(VII)(C)(1), 91.B. D. Bobrov, "Combat of the Infantry Division under Conditions of Encirclement," *Military Review* 21 (January 1942; translated from *Voennaia Mysl,* January 1940), 14;

56. Kleinfeld and Tambs, *Hitler's Spanish Legion,* 249.

57. Ibid. The Waffen SS, for example, suffered disproportionate casualties on the Eastern Front. George H. Stein, *The Waffen SS: Hitler's Elite Guard at War, 1939-1945* (Ithaca: Cornell University Press, 1977), 134.

58. *German Military Studies,* 16:(VII)(C)(1), 64; Ibid., 18:(VII)(D)(10), 6, 103-6; Halder, *Halder Diaries,* 2:1352, 1369; Mellenthin, *Panzer Battles,* 185, 196.

59. Guderian, *Panzer Leader,* 234-35; *German Military Studies,* 18:(VII)(D)(10), 125.

60. *German Military Studies,* 18:(VII)(D)(10), 25, 68-73, 163; *Great March of Liberation,* 97; Vernon, "Soviet Combat Operations," 43.

61. Augustin L. Guillaume, *The German RussianWar* (London: War Office, 1956), 249.

62.*German Military Studies,* 18:(VII)(D)(10), 4; Halder, *Halder Diaries,* 2: 1009, 1013.

63. *German Military Studies,* 16:(VII)(C)(1), 75, 185; Ibid., 18: (VII)(D)(10), 39-40; Guillaume, *German Russian War,* 9; *Great March of Liberation,* 20; Kleinfeld and Tambs, *Hitler's Spanish Legion,* 112; Mellenthin, *Panzer Battles,* 196.

64. Halder, *Halder Diaries,* 2:1250; Mellenthin, *Panzer Battles,* 205.

65. Halder, *Halder Diaries,* 2:1079; Mellenthin, *Panzer Battles,* 219; Parotkin, 167.

66. S. M. Shtemenko, *The Last Six Months: Russia's Final Battles with Hitler's Armies in World War II* (Garden City, NY: Doubleday, 1977), 11-14.

67. "Fuehrung, Kampf, und Kraftquellen," 9.

68. Mellenthin, *Panzer Battles,* 283.

69. M. G. Saunders, *The Soviet Navy* (New York: Praeger, 1958), 74.

70. "Report of Trip to USSR by General Connolly," Modern Military Records Division, R.G. 334, Box 5, Subject File October 1943-October 1945, N.A.: Halder, *Halder Diaries,* 2:1386, 1441; Nikolai V. Sivachev and Nikolai N. Yakovlev, *Russia and the United States: U.S.-Soviet Relations from the Soviet Point of View* (Chicago: University of Chicago Press, 1979), 210.

71. Halder, *Halder Diaries,* 2:1156; Spalding to Protocol Committee (July 25, 1944), Modern Military Records Division, R.G. 334, Box 13, Subject File October 1943-October 1945, Folder September 1943 through 31 July 1944, N.A.; Mellenthin, *Panzer Battles,* 246; *Great March of Liberation,* 77; Jones, *Roads to Russia,* 280-82. Apparently the amphibians were popular, as the Soviet Union requested (but did not receive) 1,200 more.

72. John Erickson, *The Road to Stalingrad* (London: Harper & Row, 1975), 169; Kleinfeld and Tambs, *Hitler's Spanish Legion,* 221.

73. *German Military Studies,* 18:(VII)(D)(11), 19-20; Halder, *Halder Diaries,* 2:1145-46, 1150, 1166, 1188.

74. Parotkin, *Battle of Kursk,* 208; *Great March of Liberation,* 96.

75. *Great March of Liberation,* 96.

76. Mellenthin, *Panzer Battles,* 299-301.

77. *German Military Studies,* 18:(VII)(D)(10), 91-92; Mellenthin, *Panzer Battles,* 162, 205; *Great March of Liberation,* 20; "Report of Trip to USSR by General Connolly," 3-4.

78. *German Military Studies,* 18:(VII)(D)(10), 4; Halder, *Halder Diaries,* 2:1225; Guillaume, *German Russian War,* 4.

79. *German Military Studies,* 16:(VII)(C)(2), 37; Parotkin, *Battle of Kursk,* 162-63; *Great March of Liberation,* 192-240; Mellenthin, *Panzer Battles,* 229-30.

80. Erickson, *Road to Berlin,* 81-82.

81. "Lessons of ESCOM" (n.d.), Report of Major General Robert Walsh, Robert L. Walsh Papers, U.S. Army Military History Institute, Carlisle Barracks, PA, Archives, 8.

82. Gregory Bienstock, Solomon M. Schwarz, and Aaron Yugow, *Management in Russian Industry and Agriculture* (New York: Oxford University Press, 1944), xxvii.

83. Kucherenko, "Podgotovka rabochego popol'neniia," 3, 5.

84. Girault, "Effort humain," 22. The annual number of engineering graduates was less in 1939 than in 1935. Bienstock, Schwarz, and Yugow, *Management,* 110, Observers noted a tendency to do things exactly "by the book." David Kahn, *Hitler's Spies: German Military Intelligence in World War II* (New York: Macmillan, 1978), 133. Did this reflect a lack of initiative, or lack of skill?

85. Erich Klinkmueller, "Some Economic Reflections on the Great Patriotic War (1941-1952)," *Soviet Union* 4 (1977), 228.

86. *O.S.S.,* "Military Potential of the Soviet Union, Part IIb: The Food Problem under War Conditions" (November 30, 1942), 11.

87. M. S. Zinich, "Izuchenie trudovoi deiatel'nosti zhenshchin v gody velikoi otechestvennoi voiny (1941-1945)," *Istoricheskie Zapiski Akademii Nauk SSSR* 97 (1976), 237.

88. Kucherenko, "Podgotovka rabochego popol'neniia," 9.

89. Ibid., 9; Girault, "Effort humain," 26; William H. Standley and Arthur A. Ageton, *Admiral Ambassador to Russia* (Chicago: Henry Regnery, 1955), 435; Zinich, "Izuchenie trudovoi deiatel'nosti zhenshchin," 240-41. "R.S.F.S.R." stands for "Russian Soviet Federated Socialist Republic."

90. *History of the Great Patriotic War of the Soviet Union 1941-1945* (Moscow: Voenizdat, 1960: OCMH translation), 2:524.

91. Memoirs, Wellington Alexander Samouce Papers, U.S. Army Military History Institute, Carlisle Barracks, PA, Archives, 75.

92. Wendell L. Willkie, *One World* (New York: Simon and Schuster, 1943), 71.

93. The sniper Lt. Lyudmila Pavlichenko, for example, has been credited with several hundred 'kills.' Boris Skomorovsky and E. G. Morris, *The Siege of Leningrad* (New York: E. P. Dutton, 1944), 65, 76.

94. *History of the Great Patriotic War,* 2:524; Girault, "Effort humain," 26.

95. *History of the Great Patriotic War,* 2:175; Kahn, *Hitler's Spies,* 433.

96. *History of the Great Patriotic War,* 2:498.

97. G. Kumanev, "Soviet War Economy," in *The Great Patriotic War of the Soviet People and Our Times* (Moscow: USSR Academy of Sciences, 1985), 114; *History of the Great Patriotic War,* 2:524.

98. M. S. Rozofarov, *Trudovoye Rezervye SSSR, Sbornik Ofitsialnikh Materialov* (Moscow: Gosudarsvennoe Izdatelstvo, 1950; U.S. Army Intelligence translation).

99. *History of the Great Patriotic War,* 2:524.

100. Kumanev, "Soviet War Economy," 114.

101. Robert E. Sherwood, *Roosevelt and Hopkins,* vol. 2, *From Pearl Harbor to Victory* (New York: Bantam Books, 1950 [Harper & Brothers, 1948]), 237; Marc Ferro, "Une histoire Russe de la deuxieme guerre mondiale," *Revue d'Histoire de la Deuxieme Guerre Mondiale* 11 (January 1961), 31; Standley and Ageton, *Admiral Ambassador to Russia,* 196; Patrick Beesly, *Very Special Intelligence: The Story of the Admiralty's Operational Intelligence Centre, 1939-1945* (London: Sphere Books, 1978), 175.

102. Maurice Matloff and Edwin M. Snell, *Strategic Planning for Coalition Warfare, 1941-42* (Washington, DC: Office of the Chief of Military History, 1953), 336-37; Standley and Ageton, Admiral *Ambassador to Russia,* 66; *Joint Chiefs of Staff,* "Bradley Mission: Bombers for the Far East" (January 11, 1943), 1-2; Project brief, "Giving B-24s to Soviets" (n.d.), Walsh Papers.

103. Project brief, "Bombsight Training Project" (n.d.), and Col. C. R. Bond to Walsh, "Memorandum for General Walsh" (October 18, 1944), Walsh Papers.

104. John Daniel Langer, "The 'Red General:' Phillip R. Faymonville and the Soviet Union, 1917-1952," *Prologue* 8 (Winter 1976), 217-18.

105. Richard C. Lukas, *Eagles East: The Army Air Forces and the Soviet Union, 1941-1945* (Tallahassee: Florida State University Press, 1970), 166; "Final Report" (n.d.), Walsh Papers, 2.

106. Kessler to USSTAF, June 25, 1944; Report of Proceedings of Board of Officers, August 2, 1944; Deane to USSTAF, June 27, 1944; Walsh to USSTAF, August 2, 1944; Walsh to USSTAF, July 10,1944; "Lessons of ESCOM" (n.d.), 16: Spaatz, to Walsh October 1, 1944, Walsh Papers; Memoirs, Pantuhoff Papers, 697; Memoirs, Samouce Papers, 90.

107. Marshal Konev described his HF communication system as a "godsend." I. Konev, *Year of Victory* (Moscow: Progress Publishers, 1984, 105.

108. Halder, *Halder Diaries,* 2:1340, 1353.

109. *Joint Chiefs of Staff,* "Russian Combat Estimate" (April 1, 1942), 26-27.

110. Ibid., 30.

111. The commanding general of the Persian Gulf Command estimated that Persian Gulf supplies could (at their height) suffice for 60 Soviet divisions. T.

H. Vail Motter, *The Persian Corridor and Aid to Russia* (Washington, DC: Office of the Chief of Military History, 1952), 6.

112. "History of the U.S. Military Mission," 369.

113. Deane to AGWAR, "Lend-Lease to Soviets" (January 6, 1944), Modern Military Records Division, R.G. 334, Box 13, Subject File October 1943-October 1945, Folder September 1943 through 31 July 1944, N.A., 2.

114. John Daniel Langer, "The Formulation of American Aid Policy toward the Soviet Union, 1940-1943: The Hopkins Shop and the Department of State" (Ph.D. dissertation, Yale University, 1975), 199.

115. Saunders, *Soviet Navy,* 76. See "Synopsis of Conference with Director of Kazvin Soviet Transport" (March 29, 1943), Sidney Gruneck Papers, U.S. Army Military History Institute, Carlisle Barracks, PA, Archives.

116. Mikhail Soloviev, *My Nine Lives in the Red Army* (New York: David McKay, 1955), 259-60.

7

Command and Control

In the movie *Patton,* the General is quoted as saying that "beside war, all man's other endeavors shrink into insignificance." This statement seems to reflect unabashed militarism and no doubt sent shivers of horror down many a pacifist spine. Yet no matter the intent behind the statement, it does, intentionally or otherwise, point out the incredible complexity involved in the conduct of war. To some extent this has always been the case. War has never been simple. In a sense all the participants are amateurs, because every situation is in some way different from the others. The lessons learned in one conflict may not apply in another. More importantly, the magnitude of the tasks of preparing and waging war have often strained not only the physical resources of a society, but its organizational capacity as well.

In general, the organizational problems have grown over time, not only in terms of planning, but also in relation to the actual conduct of war. Battle management has become increasingly complex as war has expanded in time and space. Armies have grown from a few thousand in the Middle Ages to the millions employed in the twentieth century. This growth was due to the development of the modern state, increasing economic resources, population growth, and innovations in transport that made it possible to support larger forces. Because of technological changes, the tempo of battle has also accelerated. While these changes have made it possible to conduct war on a larger and faster scale, they have also generated enormous problems. Military forces in the twentieth century have to be substantial enough to concentrate the firepower necessary for victory, but at the same time they must be able to react quickly, and simultaneously increasing size of forces and speed of response is no easy thing.

This increase in the scale of warfare took place even in World War II itself. This was obviously the case for the Nazis. While Poland and France were not small , the time and space problems encountered during the invasions there were much less than was the case during Barbarossa. The "failure" of the *blitzkrieg* during that operation has often been attributed to geographical factors. It is easy to forget, however, that the Red Army had to operate in exactly the same environment, and its most recent operations, such as the fighting against Japan along the Khalkin-Gol river and the invasion of Finland, represented vastly smaller theatres of war than would be the case during the fighting against the Nazis. Both combatants had to solve the problems of command, control, and transport of forces over immense areas against opposition capable of well-timed counterstrikes in the event of carelessness or errors. Victory would belong to the army which arrived at the best solution to these problems.

The solution lay partly in skill but also required resources. In this respect both armies in the East faced certain disadvantages. The German army's transport was not adequate, much of it still horse-drawn. The Red Army suffered from a whole series of shortcomings, ranging from too few vehicles to initial dependency on a wholly antiquated telephone network. The losses of equipment in the early months of the war seriously aggravated the problem.

In no area was Lend-Lease more important than in command, control, and transport. The modern army, because of its size, can succeed in battle only if it is well supplied and effectively coordinated. The tendency to view military success as no more than the result of the brilliance of an individual commander simply ignores reality. As justly famous as Soviet Marshal Georgii K. Zhukov became, he could not have succeeded if the Soviet logistical system had been unable to move forces quickly enough, build up supplies for large troop concentrations, and keep the umbilical supply cord connected to his advancing armies. Nor would Zhukov or any of the other galaxy of marshals have achieved success if they had been unable to communicate with their subordinate units. Orders would have come too late, and information would have moved too slowly.

The time that a single commander had his entire force within sight has long been over, at least since the Napoleonic era, but this vision of warfare persists. Influenced by war games, histories, and some treatises, a few twentieth-century military leaders have even attempted to command in the style appropriate to their seventeenth-century counterparts, with rather limited success. Armies are far too large, and their needs much too complex, to live off the land, but the dry and unglamorous problems of logistics are not the stuff of which exciting military histories are made.

The importance of Lend-Lease communications equipment is clear when one considers the extent to which warfare has degenerated into an extended series of small engagements commanded by junior and noncommissioned officers. On paper these units in the aggregate may be an immensely imposing force, but in the absence of effective coordination their strength is wasted. Isolated forces can function well if defending a geographical obstacle, as was demonstrated in 1941 at the Pripet Marshes. Much Soviet geography, however, did not lend itself easily to static defense, and hence good communications were a necessity for success, if not survival.

Geography was also a major reason why Lend-Lease transportation equipment was so important. The very size of the Soviet Union complicated military supply and movements. The Red Army was stretched along a front sometimes almost two thousand miles long. At the beginning of the war, was the Soviet transport net in any condition to adequately supply military forces over such a vast terrain without foreign assistance?

In terms of motor vehicles, essential in areas where railroads did not run, it was not. The Soviet Union only had some 800,000 vehicles, including 228,000 farm trucks, most of which could carry only small payloads. Many were lost in the first months of the war, and production was inadequate. The Red Army could also use the 684,000 tractors controlled by the *kolkhoz* machine-tractor stations and in fact did requisition half of them, but could not take them all, as to do so would have effectively disabled the farms.[1]

The Soviet Union, then, was obviously in need of imported vehicles. The reasons for the relatively low number of vehicles are not too difficult to determine. Motor vehicles were simply not the basic method of transport. Before the war 82.1 percent of all goods were shipped via the 58,500-kilometer rail net, as compared to 8.5 percent by river and coastal shipping and 7.5 percent by vehicle.[2] Rail use actually grew, both before and during the war.[3] By 1943-44, 82 percent of all shipments (measured in ton-kilometers) went by rail, in comparison to 1 percent by vehicle.[4] Apparently almost all long-distance transport, such as from the Ural factories to the front, was by rail, while vehicles were used in frontline areas where rail lines were nonexistent or destroyed. This meant that the Red Army's offensive operations were heavily dependent on imported vehicles.

Lend-Lease aid to Soviet transportation was vital because the system was barely adequate even with foreign help. The official Soviet history of the war concedes that the "communications of the Soviet Armed Forces were poorly developed."[5] Soviet sources often describe the transport situation as "difficult," beset by overcrowding at rail off-loading points and by inadequate roads, and "not equal to the task of providing uninterrupted flows of supplies to the troops in winter conditions when the troops [had advanced]."[6]

At the risk of exaggerating the effect of Lend-Lease, one wonders how Soviet transport would have functioned without it. Soviet transport even had trouble coping with Lend-Lease shipments. Persian Gulf Command shipments piled up for extended periods due to lack of Soviet transport. Although the situation supposedly eased in late 1943, reports of this bottleneck continued to surface in 1944. Even so, the U.S.S.R. refused the United States permission to build a railroad all the way to the Caspian Sea. Supplies were off-loaded at the Soviet zone, then picked up by the Russians and sent on their way.[7]

The problem was most noticeable in the postinvasion chaos of 1941, before any meaningful Lend-Lease aid arrived. During the embassies' evacuation to Kuibishev in 1941, for example, the U.S. military attache saw "miles and miles of flatcars on siding loaded with uncovered machinery, rusting in the snow. At many places the machinery had been dumped off onto the ground because of a shortage of freight cars."[8] Lend-Lease could hardly solve problems on this scale. Even in later years Americans noted problems in obtaining transport and in finding someone with authority to order rail cars (for the U.S. air units in the Ukraine), and the heavy reliance on horse-drawn wagons.[9] The Military Mission noted the absence of traffic-control procedures and concluded that these were apparently "never considered...a serious matter." On this last point the report was in error (traffic control was taken quite seriously), but it indicates the impression that the condition of the transport net made on the Americans.[10]

Foreign aid was necessary because the transport system was both slow and unreliable. Great difficulties were encountered in transporting food from areas with a surplus to regions where shortages existed.[11] East of Moscow the transportation system was very thin. Large aircraft, for example, could not land at the airfield at Magnitogorsk.[12] It took at least three months for American equipment to reach the front, a delay aggravated by port congestion, especially in the Far East.[13] Unfortunately, the value of U.S. observations is limited because the Soviet Union did not permit unrestricted travel. Trips taken by U.S. officers, which formed the basis for such reports, were all "guided tours."

The Americans, however, were not alone in noticing Soviet transport problems. German generals believed that Soviet reliance on "staggered" rather than simultaneous offensives at Stalingrad was partly due to the Soviet inability to supply all armies at once.[14] It seemed that the Red Army would not (or could not) decide whether to devote the bulk of its resources to destroying the encircled Sixth Army or driving away the German front. The successful Russian battles "did not here result in clear-cut decision," but "ended in one of their compromises that became so familiar."[15] This may have reflected either transportation or communication/control problems, or both. As late as 1945 the Germans saw Soviet transportation as "struggling with great difficulties," unable to deliver enough fuel to the forces in the field.[16]

The Red Army did its best to untangle the transport mess. After Stalingrad the Red Army established supply norms for its various division types, such as ammunition issues (*boekomplekty*) for rifle divisions, and fuel fills (*zapravki*) for armored divisions. These norms could not always be met. Trains failed to appear, unloading areas were too far back (troops were sometimes unloaded 100 miles behind the front to conceal their movements), and infantrymen and horse-drawn columns had to carry supplies forward. Despite heavy imports there never were enough trucks, and the pace of the advance was frequently slowed as supplies ran out, although this was not a uniquely Soviet problem.[17]

Nor were the U.S.S.R.'s problems limited to a lack of vehicles and rolling stock. The road network was minimal.[18] Only the "very thin" rail net's main lines were "up to European expectations," and trains often moved at a "pitifully slow pace." [19] Nor did the railways recover quickly from the 1941 disasters.[20] The lines were too few to adequately supply the army and were frequently bombed by the Germans.[21]

Amid all the disasters, the Soviets kept the system going. The rail net was rebuilt as the front moved westward. Field Marshal von Manstein observed that "the Russians were masters at reconstruction of railways," thereby explaining the mobility and depth of Soviet attacks.[22] American observers shared this view. Special railway-reconstruction troops rebuilt the thoroughly destroyed lines at a rate of six kilometers per day (sometimes much faster).[23] By dint of increasing rail production and tearing out the second track on interior lines and transferring the rails westward, the Soviets were able to reconstruct between 30,000 and 43,000 kilometers of rail lines in 1943-44.[24] In general, the Soviet ability to bring supplies through destroyed, recaptured areas amazed the Germans.[25]

That the system functioned at all was partly due to the immense and complex administration established to run it. Stalin centralized control of all rear services in a Main Directorate, which included the Directorate of Military Communications, responsible for railroads and waterways (vehicles and roads each had their own directorates, also subordinate to the Main Directorate).[26] The Rear Services' functions extended to security, organization, administration, service, and evacuation.[27] He also created a 'supply forces' command, whose officers were attached to the army's operational units.[28] Some branches (armor, artillery, engineering, aviation) had separate supply units.[29] After the 1943 reorganization most subordinate units received supplies from the parent unit, but mechanized and tank units usually picked up their own.[30]

The Red Army naturally kept a close watch on all transport. The Rear Services were attached to the Ministry of the Armed Forces and the commander-in-chief (Stalin), not to the General Staff.[31] The latter, however, had a large truck pool at its disposal and controlled railway operations. An officer was placed in charge of every rail junction, with control of all movements in the area.[32] Each front commander controlled movements in his area through his chief of rear services and had a railway-reconstruction unit at his disposal.[33] Despite the complex bureaucratic system, however, supply administration was reasonably flexible.[34]

The biggest problem for Soviet transport was simply the sheer size of the requirements it had to meet. The first major problem was the size of the army, which by the end of the war fielded over 500 divisions, divided among 70 field armies (60 infantry, 5 shock, and 5 tank), in addition to reserve formations. Supply for the infantry armies was complicated, as they contained their own artillery, antitank, and antiaircraft elements. The war effort directly absorbed over 12 million men in uniform, including both combat and rear-service troops.[35]

Aggregate size of the armed forces was not, however, the greatest problem. The Red Army was actually smaller than the U.S. armed forces. By far the greater headache was the supply problem posed by the army's immense concentrations assembled for the offensives. The Red Army achieved its successes through rapid concentration and frequent shifting of the axis of attack.[36] This meant that huge quantities of materiel had to be moved into relatively small areas, often served by a single, inadequate rail line, supplemented by atrocious roads. Concentrations were sometimes spectacular; for the battle of Kursk, for example, the Red Army assembled about 40 percent of all its rifle formations.[37]

Supply problems did not end with the Soviet victory at Kursk but became even greater as immense forces were marshalled for offensives conducted over distances of unprecedented length. For Operation Bagration, the 1944 summer offensives which resulted in the destruction of the German Army Group "Center," the Soviet command used 1.25 million men for attack and another 416,000 for flank protection, supported by more than 4,000 armored vehicles, 6,000 aircraft, and 26,000 guns. Almost 100 trains per day moved supplies to pickup points for trucks as the system struggled to meet the daily 50,000-ton requirement of the fronts involved in the attack. The Warsaw-Berlin push was even greater, employing 2.5 million troops. The buildup for the final attack on Berlin, the largest concentration of ground forces in World War II, called for 1,200 trainloads and 920,000 truckloads of supplies. Each of the two fronts in this operation required 25,000 tons per day (actually somewhat less than an equivalent-sized U.S. force required in World War II); so strained was the system that an extra meatless day had to be imposed.[38]

Magnitudes of firepower and distance further complicated supply. The Red Army's volume of fire was immense.[39] While this was necessary to produce decisive breakthroughs, much of the ammunition supply would be consumed in the initial attack. The first day of operations sometimes consumed as much as the ensuing two weeks.[40] Nor was this an isolated problem, as ammunition was less than one-tenth of the army's required tonnage. In 1943 deliveries to the fronts totalled 1.2 million railroad wagon loads, including 3.2 million tons of fuel. By 1944 these figures had risen to 1.5 million and 4 million, respectively. The depth of offensive operations, which rose to 750 miles in the fall of 1944, further complicated supply.[41] If all this were not enough to create chaos, the rail net had to devote 50-80 percent of its movements to troop movements during offensives, versus a normal 80-85 percent for supply functions.[42]

It was, then, into this overstretched system that Lend-Lease poured huge quantities of railroad equipment, motor vehicles, and petroleum. These shipments were themselves phased and routed in such a way as to minimize strain on the Soviet transport net. Lend-Lease furnished half a million miles of rails, which accounted for one-half of all Soviet wartime construction, automatic signal equipment for 3,000 kilometers of rail lines, and almost 2,000 locomotives and over 11,000 rail cars, which "placed the Soviets in a better position by 1943-44 than before the German invasion."[43] Some were received with limited enthusiasm (in late 1944 the Soviet Union complained about some defects in flatcars), but, in general, railroad equipment was high on the Soviet shopping list.[44]

Much additional useful equipment found its way to the U.S.S.R. Knowing that the Soviets suffered from a "severe deficiency in automobile tires," the United States sent tires, rubber, rubber-manufacturing plants, and a complete tire plant (possibly incomplete at war's end).[45] America gave Russia 708 twin-engined transports, as well as 862 medium bombers which might have been used for transport in a pinch, since air transport was fairly tight during the war.[46] The 1,530 field repair trucks may have helped maintain the speed of offensives, especially given the (universally) high breakdown rate of armored units.[47]

More significant were the shipments of petroleum, which exceeded a total of 3 million tons, supplemented by a variety of refining equipment.[48] Fuel was in perpetually short supply during the war. The shortage led to American aircraft being shipped by rail from Siberia to the front, rather than being flown.[49] The scarcity of petroleum may, however, have been caused by transport problems, not only by low production.[50]

No Lend-Lease item, however, transport-related or otherwise, has received as much attention as the trucks. The United States sent 362,288 '6 x 6' trucks during the war, as well as 47,238 jeeps and several thousand other motor vehicles of various types.[51] So strongly did the Soviet government request trucks that the U.S. devoted over one-sixth of all shipping tonnage to these machines. Except for a brief drop in mid-1942, the rate of U.S. vehicle shipments remained almost constant throughout the war.[52]

The trucks were vital because, as mentioned earlier, Soviet production was "very inadequate." Soviet truck production was cut in half during the war, to barely a hundred thousand per year. When American trucks flooded into the Soviet Union, Soviet production was scaled back even further, thus making production capacity available for other purposes. The Soviet Union imported more trucks than it built, and most in service (especially new models) were American.[53] Soviet authors seeking to downplay Lend-Lease are noticeably reticent about Soviet truck production. A 1977 Soviet analysis of Lend-Lease, for example, gives 1942 import and domestic production statistics for aircraft and tanks, but lists only the import total for trucks.[54]

Barely one-sixth of the American trucks had arrived before the battle of Stalingrad. Even so, that was still more trucks than the Red Army used at Stalingrad, suggesting that the imported vehicles may have allowed the Red Army to supply far greater concentrations of force than might otherwise have been the case.[55] Beyond that, little is known of the early use of Lend-Lease trucks.

The American trucks were far more important in the Soviet offensives of 1943-45. Red Army attacks in 1942 and early 1943 had suffered from the lack of transport, but the situation certainly got better by mid-1943, by which time the United States had delivered 183,000 vehicles.[56] As many trucks as the Red Army got, however, it still needed more. The invasion of Germany alone, for example, called for 100,000 two-and-one-half-ton truckloads to assemble supplies. The offensive on Berlin required over 1 million truckloads; the first Byelorussian front overhauled 22,000 trucks to keep up with its needs. Zhukov called for 4,000 trucks just to move up artillery ammunition for the attack. The first Ukrainian front used 15,000 American machines in this operation.[57]

Western observers knew more about the importance of Lend-Lease vehicles than any other item. General Deane, observing that the Soviet forces did not have enough of any one kind of vehicle (other than imported) to set up convoys, was certain in 1944 that "the superior mobility of the Red Army is due in considerable part to American motor transport and has placed the Germans at a serious disadvantage."[58] Deane's views were echoed by many other observers.[59] The U.S. Military Mission concluded that the trucks had contributed "immeasurably," and the public Lend-Lease reports stated that "one-half of the highway-borne supplies for the advancing Soviet armies [in 1944] were carried in American trucks," a "vital factor in maintaining supply services for the 2,000 mile Russian front."[60] British officers agreed that Lend-Lease vehicles were important to the Red Army's successes.[61]

Western reports alone do not prove much, because travel in the U.S.S.R. was severely restricted. More telling is the extent to which Soviet views, as shown in wartime actions as well as postwar publications, parallel the Western opinions. Soviet demand for trucks never slackened, and Red Army officers openly admitted their need for the trucks.[62] So important were the trucks that the Soviet Union maintained a separate bureaucracy to coordinate motor vehicle imports.[63] Soviet wartime literature specifically refers to "Studebaker trucks" in describing training exercises.[64] After the war, Zhukov complimented the American vehicles; the *Great Soviet Encyclopedia* conceded that "the deliveries of motor vehicles were of great importance"; and Khrushchev suggested that the Stalingrad-Berlin advance would have been impossible without U.S. trucks.[65]

The American trucks were especially important in frontline areas where railroads did not exist and were seen near the front more often than elsewhere. Trains could carry much materiel in the interior, but even given track-reconstruction efforts, could not supply the advancing armies. Rail reconstruction units could not build or repair the 10 kilometers of track per day along every rail line needed to keep up with the advance in the summer of 1944. Many areas were devoid of tracks, and important rail centers were held by besieged German units (Hitler's "hedgehogs"). The speed of the advance indicates that the Red Army's fronts and armies, all of which had their own truck regiment, were not dependent on railroads.[66] Assuming American estimates were correct, there were enough Lend-Lease vehicles to carry most of the Red Army.[67] The four- and six-wheeled trucks enabled the Soviet troops to move cross-country, placing the more road-bound German army at a distinct disadvantage.[68] Clearly the pace of the Soviet offensives would have been impossible without American trucks.

Better transport meant quicker movement of large reserve forces. The central, or VgK, reserve was perhaps the most important component of the Red Army, giving the Soviet offensive an edge in numbers and firepower that the Germans could not deal with.[69] Organized early in the war, the VgK reserve consisted of 1.5 million troops by late 1942, divided among 10 armies. Strategy, logistics, and the (remote) possibility of a Japanese attack dictated the deployment of much of the Red Army's reserve east of Lake Baikal throughout the war.[70]

The reserve, according to Stalin, was the biggest factor in Soviet victories.[71] The Soviet command could achieve overwhelming superiorities at crucial points, against which the Germans could not mount effective defense (especially if bridgeheads could not be immediately eradicated).[72] This was so even though German intelligence knew the size of the Russian reserve (and would claim after the war that the Soviet offensive at Stalingrad came as no surprise).[73] In addition to transport, the American contribution to the reserve apparently included most Lend-Lease military supplies.[74]

Lend-Lease communications supplies were perhaps as important as transport equipment, but their effect is even harder to calculate. Coordinating the large and increasingly mobile Red Army was a complicated task. Cooperation among the various arms was so poor that the General Staff in 1942 tabbed it as a major reason for the lack of clear victories up to that point.[75] All too often, combat units were not informed about arrangements for coordination among artillery, tanks, and aircraft, these details being the province of higher command staffs.[76] Transport movements also were difficult to control.[77] In response to these problems, the Red Army took several steps to avoid major failures on the battlefield. Artillery was distributed to the troop commands. The "Fedorenko order" of June 1942, on the other hand, forbade the splitting up of tank armies or subordinating them to infantry operations (an order both praised and regretted by German commanders).[78] Finally, detailed planning was encouraged to make up for a lack of trained commanders and problems with communications.

Typically the Soviet unit received a detailed plan designed to eliminate potential control problems. Soviet histories and memoirs are replete with phrases such as "nothing was uncertain or improvised about the attack and the plan of campaign had been worked out to the most minute detail."[79] Initiative, even at the planning level, was not encouraged (although its absence was criticized). When the General Staff published two artillery manuals after a laborious process of study and criticism, its authors received such a dressing-down from Stalin for having failed to obtain his approval that General S. M. Shtemenko wrote, "Like everyone else affected by it, I remembered the lesson always."[80]

The purpose of detailed planning might seem quite simple: the establishment of centralized control. A more subtle purpose is to achieve better coordination when the communications system at lower levels is inadequate for well-timed combined arms operations. Centralization was achieved by making all major operational decisions, including those regarding objectives, timing, coordination, reserves, and control of air units, in Moscow.[81] Lower-level unit commanders had little latitude and rarely disobeyed orders, even when faced by a changing situation and heavy losses.[82] Battlefield control was intense, and close coordination was sought constantly.[83] The results were uneven. At Stalingrad, for example, the Red Army succeeded brilliantly in coordinating the combat arms during the fight for the "corridor" but proved unable to duplicate that performance in an attack on Kergachi Hill.[84]

As suggested before, popular histories emphasize the most notorious failures and resulting casualties to impute ineptitude to the Red Army. There was incompetence in the Red Army, as in most armies, which was precisely the reason to establish closer control of the actions of lower-level commanders and perhaps contributed to the decision to use special teams of VgK command specialists to control major operations.[85] Unfortunately, strict control did not encourage junior officers to make decisions. Lack of initiative, whether due to unimaginative orders, incompetence, or fear of retribution for failure to carry out an order, was a chronic problem, recognized in *Voennaia Mysl* even before the war.[86] Certainly the loss of many capable officers in the prewar purges and in the first four months of the German invasion impaired the army's performance.

Yet despite its mistakes the Red Army won through, proving sufficiently mobile and coordinated to frustrate Hitler's goal that the Soviet forces be "destroyed," with "no units . . . permitted to remain intact and retreat into the wide Russian spaces."[87] This failure, along with many others, is usually attributed to German errors, or the harsh winter, or the fall *rasputitsa,* ignoring real Soviet successes and improvements. The Red Army improved its methods, allocated supplies and reserves to the most crucial sectors, and managed to cut through the red tape when really important decisions had to be made.[88] Lower-quality forces, often encouraged to go into action by N.K.V.D. units deployed to their rear, were used in an effort to crush rather than outmaneuver the German army.[89] This was done for two reasons: first, it neutralized the German army's own maneuvering skills, and second, it simplified many command and control problems.

The importance of Lend-Lease communications equipment did not lie solely in the inherent control requirements of the vast Soviet offensives of 1943-45. More significant was the decrepit condition of the Red Army's communications. In 1941 the army relied mostly on the civilian telephone network, but calls between administrative areas (even if adjacent) had to be routed via the central exchange in Moscow. Many main lines paralleled important rail lines and roads and were destroyed in Luftwaffe bombing raids.[90] Retreating units could not warn their neighbors that their flanks were exposed. The rapid collapse of the front in 1941 so overtaxed the mediocre communications net that Red Army general staff officers had to go forward by automobile in search of the frontline positions.[91]

At times the army's situation was such a nightmare that one wonders how it could have functioned without imported assistance. The invasion destroyed 40 percent of the Soviet Union's telegraph sets, and in 1941-42 telephone sets and cable were in such short supply that two or three battalions often shared a single line.[92] The absence of radios in most tanks hampered battle control and coordination and led some units to receive attack orders after the offensive was already under way.[93] The shortage of field telephones forced some commanders to send out signals in the clear, risking German interception. The Soviet General Staff's doctrine of redundancy in communications channels, including liaison officers, was rarely achieved before mid-1943.[94]

Although the Red Army became more methodical in its approach to communications, it probably could not have equipped its communications units without some imported supplies. Ideally, each infantry battalion's 10-man signal platoon was equipped with 6 miles of wire and about 8 telephones, and each regiment had a 50-man signal company. Artillery units had their own communications net; radio was the mainstay of mechanized units, while infantry relied on field telephones. Soviet commanders' aversion to radio use early in the war, for fear of revealing their positions, led Stalin to issue an order in 1943 pointing to the necessity of radio communications.[95]

Enhancement and reorganization without resources, however, would have availed little. Russian distances strained the system even during relatively quiet phases. In the 1944-45 offensives the operational depth of a division was normally 25-60 kilometers, of an army, 50-100 kilometers, and that of a front almost 300 kilometers. In the fall of 1944 the army's communications net at one point stretched 750 kilometers westward.[96] Some of these problems could be circumvented by the travelling VgK command teams, but certainly not all.

To help the Red Army maintain its cohesion, the United States provided over 40,000 radios, some 380,135 field telephones, a million and a quarter miles of wire, and a miscellany of other communications gear. About four-fifths of these supplies had arrived by the end of 1944.[97] This equipment obviously bolstered the Red Army's weak communications net, established better control and coordination of units, and increased the flow of information. Furthermore, the Red Army's lateral communications links, almost nonexistent at war's beginning, grew as the war progressed, again partly as a function of Lend-Lease supplies. Lend-Lease also supplied 348 locators and 750 direction finders, useful no doubt for the Red Army's highly successful radio-electronic battalions.[98]

The credit for most of the improvements in Soviet command and control must go to the Soviet military leadership, which reorganized the system in the midst of chaos and continually trained and educated its officers to improve coordination and operational skill. Yet American gear undoubtedly made up for shortages and the heavy equipment losses of 1941. Here again is the question of qualitative appraisal, of the effect of certain types of Lend-Lease equipment which the U.S.S.R. chose not to make or could not provide for itself. In this respect, Lend-Lease gave the Soviet Union something just as valuable as equipment: knowledge. While the Soviet Union did not lack scientific know-how, it was deficient in the ability to design and produce sophisticated electronic gear. During the war the Soviet Union requested and received small quantities of various sophisticated electronic devices. As Soviet engineers had shown a marked ability before the war in adapting and copying imported equipment, it seems safe to assume that they continued doing so under the pressures of war.

Would the Red Army have survived without Lend-Lease transport and communications equipment? Probably, but it is not likely that the Soviet Union would have been able to defeat Nazi Germany by May 1945. The road to Berlin was a hard road and took almost two years to travel after Kursk, notwithstanding the Red Army's size, firepower, and skill. Remove any of the Red Army's advantages, especially ones as closely linked to its ability to wage offensive war as transport and communications, and it would have been slowed, if not crippled. The precise numbers are, in a sense, not important. Lend-Lease was a vital increment in the offensive capacity of the Red Army.

NOTES

1. *History of the Great Patriotic War of the Soviet Union 1941-1945* (Moscow: Voenizdat, 1960; OCMH translation), 1:532, 537-538; Gregory Bienstock, Solomon M. Schwarz, and Aaron Yugow, *Management in Russian Industry and Agriculture* (New York: Oxford University Press, 1944), 135; *O.S.S./State Department Intelligence and Research Reports, Part 6: The Soviet Union, 1941-1949* (Frederick, MD: University Publications of America, 1977), "Military

Potential of the Soviet Union, Part IIb: The Food Problem under War Conditions" (November 30, 1942), 7-8.

2. *History of the Great Patriotic War,* 1:531; U.S. Army, Assistant Chief of Staff (Intelligence), "Soviet Rear Services" (n.d.) U.S. Army Military History Institute, Carlisle Barracks, PA, 4.

3. In 1939 average daily loading increased by one-quarter. G. A. Kumanev, "Zheleznodoroznyi transport SSSR nakanune velikoi otechestvennoi voiny," *Istoriia SSSR* (No. 1, 1975), 112.

4. *Istoriia Vtoroi Mirovoi Voiny, 1939-1945,* vol. 8 (Moscow: Voenizdat, 1977), 359.

5. *History of the Great Patriotic War,* 1:625.

6. U.S.S.R. Red Army, General Staff, *Collection of Materials for the Study of the War Experience* (Moscow: Voenizdat, 1942; U.S. Army Intelligence translation), 84; Col. V. Gorskii, "Concerning the Rear of an Army in a Defensive Operation," *Voennaia Mysl* (No. 7, 1949; U.S. Army Intelligence translation), 12-13; U.S.S.R. Red Army General Staff, *Collection of Materials for the Study of War Experience No. 2* (Moscow: Voenizdat, 1942; U.S. Army Intelligence translation), 5-6; Col. K. Lavrov, "The Army Group Rear in Offensive Operations," *Voennii Vestnik* (No. 6, 1946; U.S. Army Intelligence translation), 2.

7. Col. C. R. Bond to Walsh, "ESCOM Logistical Notes with Respect to Russia" (17 August 1944), Robert L. Walsh Papers, U.S. Army Military History Institute, Carlisle Barracks, PA, Archives; Memoirs, Oleg Pantuhoff Papers, U.S. Army Military History Institute, Carlisle Barracks, PA, Archives, 491-92, 513; Memoirs, Wellington Alexander Samouce Papers, U.S. Army Military History Institute, Carlisle Barracks, PA, 20.

8. Memoirs, Ivan Downs Yeaton Papers, U.S. Army Military History Institute, Carlisle Barracks, PA, 45. The same thing happened in ports (due to a lack of warehouse space). "History of the U.S. Military Mission to Moscow," Modern Military Records Division, R.G. 165, Box 146, OPD 336TS, N.A., 368.

9. Kessler to Walsh (September 19 and 22, 1944), Walsh Papers; File, "Copies of Photographs to Be Placed within Memoirs," Samouce Papers. In 1941, two-thirds of the German army's transport was still horse-drawn.

10. Deane to AGWAR, "Order of Battle" (August 11, 1944), Modern Military Records Division, R.G. 334, Box 1, Subject File October 1943 to October 1945, Folder "Air Intelligence," N.A. The Red Army had rear-service units specifically for this purpose.

11. "Report of Trip to USSR by General Connolly," Modern Military Records Division, R.G. 334, Box 5, Subject File October 1943-October 1945, N.A.

12. Col. Alfred A. Kessler, "Report on Russian Trip" (December 2, 1943), Modern Military Records Division, R.G. 18, Box 1045, File "Report on Russian Trip," Folder 333.1, N.A.

13. Harriman to Hopkins (July 31, 1944), and McPherson to Spalding (May 14, 1944), Modern Military Records Division, R.G. 334, Box 13, Subject File October 1943-October 1945, Folder September 1943 through 31 July 1944, N.A.

14. Erich von Manstein, *Lost Victories* (London: Methuen, 1958), 439.

15. Frido von Senger und Etterlin, *Neither Fear Nor Hope: The Wartime Career of General Frido von Senger und Etterlin, Defender of Cassino* (New York: E. P. Dutton, 1964), 77, 86.

16. German Army, "Fuehrung, Kampf, und Kraftquellen der Roten Armee," lecture prepared by Foreign Armies East, 15 January 1945 (translated as "Leadership in the Red Army and the Sources of Power and Combat," U.S. Army Intelligence translation), 23, 24.

17. John Erickson, *The Road to Berlin: Continuing the History of Stalin's War with Germany* (Boulder, CO: Westview Press, 1983), 82, 208, 244, 524; David Kahn, *Hitler's Spies: German Military Intelligence in World War II* (New York: Macmillan, 1978), 132.

18. Memoirs, Samouce Papers, 84.

19. German Army, "Experiences Gained in the Supply Services for the Commitments of Motorized and Armored Divisions in the Region of Courland Extending to the Don River and Eastward to within 200 Kilometers from Moscow" (n.d.) (U.S. Army Intelligence translation), 4; Bond to Walsh, "ESCOM Logistical Notes with Respect to Russia" (August 17, 1944), Walsh Papers. Things were even worse in winter. Deane and Spalding to AGWAR, "Soviet Far East" (June 21, 1944), Modern Military Records Division, R.G. 334, Box 13, Subject File October 1943-October 1945, Folder September 1943 through 31 July 1944, N.A.

20. In the first year and a half of the war, loadings dropped by 59 percent, while turnaround time more than doubled. *History of the Great Patriotic War,* 2:525. Soviet trains could barely cope with the 1942-43 offensives and were still stretched to the limit in the 1944 operations. Erickson, *Road to Berlin,* 81, 204. Soviet demands for railroad equipment were constant. See, for example, Memoirs, Pantuhoff Papers, 495.

21. *Collection of Materials for the Study of War Experience No. 1,* 7; Otto Heilbrunn, *The Soviet Secret Services* (Westport CT: Greenwood Press, 1981), 96-98; "Report of Trip to USSR by General Connolly," 11-12. The German side of the equation was not neglected. In 1943, for example, partisans carried out over 10,000 attempts to disrupt the German rail net, mostly with mines. They destroyed 293 locomotives and 846 wagons.

22. von Manstein, *Lost Victories,* 411.

23. "Report of Trip to USSR by General Connolly," 10, 13-14. The prescribed timetable suggested 5 kilometers in 24 hours, 8 in 36, and 12 in 48. O. M. Kuznetsov, "Railway Stations of Army Group Lines of Communications" (n.d.) (U.S. Army Intelligence translation), U.S. Army Military History Institute, Carlisle Barracks, PA.

24. "Fuehrung, Kampf, und Kraftquellen," 23, 24; G. Buehlmann, *The Supply Services of Foreign Armies (Economic Principles, Organization and Supplies, Transportation and Problems of the Supply Services)* (Frauenfeld, CH: Huber & Co., 1949; U.S. Army Intelligence translation), 43 (30,000 kilometers. in 1943-44); J. Halperin, "L'economie sovietique pendant la guerre," *Revue d'Histoire de*

la Deuxieme Guerre Mondiale 2 (April 1952), 20 <(43,000 kilometers. in 1943-44).

25. Buehlmann, *Supply Services,* 64.

26. "General Organization of the Rear Service" (n.d.) (U.S. Army Intelligence translation from "Vooruzhennye Sili, Sluzhba Syla: Manuscript by a Displaced Person"), 1, 2.

27. "General Organization of the Rear Service," 1; Lt. Gen. M. Zagyv, "Some Problems of the 'Rear,'" *Voennaia Mysl* (No. 9, 1946; U.S. Army Intelligence translation), 1-2, 4-5.

28. Gen. Istvan Beleznay, "The Logistical Service of the Soviet Army," *Honved* (December 1949; U.S. Army Intelligence translation and abstract), 1; "General Organization of the Rear Service," 2-3.

29. "Soviet Rear Services" (n.d.), 5.

30. Beleznay, "Logistical Services," 1; "Soviet Rear Services," 3.

31. U.S.S.R., "Tetrad' Po Voennoi Administratsii" (1947) (U.S. Army Intelligence translation), 1.

32. "Notes on Archangel-Murmansk Trip of General Spalding by Captain Ware" (n.d.), Modern Military Records Division, R.G. 334, Box 13, Subject File October 1943-October 1945, Folder September 1943 through 31 July 1944, N.A.

33. "Report of Trip to USSR by General Connolly," 8-10, 16-17.

34. "Soviet Rear Services," 6. Normally, supplies were shipped from the factory to a central storage depot, then to a front depot, and finally to an army depot, which distributed them directly to the divisions. In emergencies, which occurred frequently, the system could be short-circuited and supplies moved directly from factory to division.

35. "Fuehrung, Kampf, und Kraftquellen," 4, 10-14; Erickson, *Road to Berlin,* 146.

36. This method was used to drive the Germans away from Stalingrad. "Lesson of ESCOM" (n.d.), Walsh Papers, 11.

37. Erickson, *Road to Berlin,* 65-66.

38. Ibid., 214, 447. For example, the 15-division, 770,000-man force planned for Normandy required 26,500 tons per day. Roland G. Ruppenthal, *Logistical Support of the Armies,* vol. 1, *May 1941-September 1944* (Washington, DC: Office of the Chief of Military History, 1953). Each of the two fronts in the Berlin attack was larger.

39. See, for example, *Brief Tactical-Technical Manual, 2nd, ed.* (Moscow: Voenizdat, 1945; U.S. Army Intelligence translation), 41. The Southwest front fired more than 900,000 artillery rounds in its breakthrough north of Stalingrad, November 1942. *Collection of Materials for the Study of War Experience No. 1,"* 214. Most ammunition consumption during the Stalingrad counteroffensive was below expectations. Ibid., 228. The crossing of the Volga (November 20-December 12, 1942) absorbed 12,000 tons of ammunition. Ibid., 279. Before an offensive, ammunition would be about equally divided between combat units and depots. Ibid., 204.

40. Lavrov, "Army Group Rear," 3. At Stalingrad, however, the ratio was a bit more conservative: first-day use equalled that of days two to five. *Collection of Materials for the Study of War Experience No. 1,* 205. None of these consumption figures are out of the ordinary.

41. Erickson, *Road to Berlin,* 423.

42. I. V. Kovalev, *Transport v Velikoi Otechestvennoi Voine (1941-1945)* (Moscow: Izdatel'stvo Nauka, 1981), 250.

43. U.S. President, *Reports to Congress on Lend-Lease Operations,* no. 19 (Washington, DC: Government Printing Office, 1945), 16; Robert Huhn Jones, *The Roads to Russia: United States Lend-Lease to the Soviet Union* (Norman: University of Oklahoma Press, 1969), 227; *Records of the Joint Chiefs of Staff: Part 1, 1942-1945: The Soviet Union* (Frederick, MD: University Publications of America, n.d.), "Resumption of Northern Convoys to Russia: Report of the Joint Logistics Committee" (May 24, 1944), 2, 6, and "Allied Communications to the U.S.S.R. via the Black Sea: Report by the Joint Staff Planners" (November 8, 1944), 23; "History of the U.S. Military Mission," 354; Antony C. Sutton, *Western Technology and Soviet Economic Development, 1930 to 1945* (Stanford: Hoover Institution Press, 1971), 199, 202, 206.

44. *Joint Chiefs of Staff,* "Memorandum for the United States Chiefs of Staff: Present Relations between the USMM, Moscow, and the Soviet Military Authorities: Memorandum by the Commanding General, Moscow" (January 22, 1945). Rails were the preferred item. "Report of Trip to USSR by General Connolly," 10.

45. Maj. Gen. Semichastnov to Deane (December 30, 1944), Modern Military Records Division, R.G. 334, Box 13, Subject File October 1943 to October 1945, Folder 1 August 1944 through 31 December 1944, N.A.; "History of the U.S. Military Mission," 375-76.

46. U.S. Department of State, Protocol and Area Information Staff of the U.S.S.R. Branch of the Division of Research and Reports, "Report on War Aid Furnished by the United States to the U.S.S.R." (Foreign Economic Section, Office of Foreign Liquidation, November 28, 1945), 18; *Joint Chiefs of Staff,* "Memorandum for Information: Note on Conference of Russian Mission with Executives, Munitions Assignment Board" (April 19, 1942), 1.

47. Jones, *Roads to Russia,* 280-82.

48. "History of the U.S. Military Mission," 355.

49. *O.S.S.,* "Military Potential of the Soviet Union, Part III: Basic Industries" (November 25, 1942), 15.

50. Kessler, "Report on Russian Trip," 14.

51. "Report on War Aid," 19; "History of the U.S. Military Mission," 353.

52. Jones, *Roads to Russia,* 49, 60-62, 272-73; "Report on War Aid," 11.

53. *Joint Chiefs of Staff,* "Postwar Economic Policies and Capabilities of the USSR" (November 1, 1945), 10; "Allied Communications to the U.S.S.R. via the Black Sea: Report by the Joint Staff Planners" (November 8, 1944), 15; "Russian Combat Estimate" (April 1, 1942), 64; "Postwar Economic Capabilities of the U.S.S.R." (November 1, 1945), 18; *O.S.S.,* "Relative Capabilities on the

Eastern Front, 1 May 1944" (March 20, 1944), 30; Roger Munting, "Lend-Lease and the Soviet War Effort," *Journal of Contemporary History* 19 (1984), 500; Erickson, *Road to Berlin,* ix.

54. N. Dunaeva, "Lend-Liz: Fakty i vymysly," *Voenno-Istoricheskii Zhurnal* (No. 3, 1977), 104.   The author agrees, however, that vehicle deliveries "considerably increased" the Soviet vehicle park and "positively affected" transport of military cargoes. Dunaeva, "Lend-Liz," 105.

55. Jones, *Roads to Russia,* 138, 232-33. Not all the U.S. trucks shipped would be in service, as a certain percentage must have been lost to mechanical breakdown, enemy fire, and other causes.

56. Erickson, *Road to Berlin,* 81.

57. I. I. Volkotrubenko, "Boepripasy i artsnabzhenie v velikoi otechestvennoi voine," *Voprosy Istorii* (No. 11, 1972), 90; Erickson, *Road to Berlin,* 453-521, 539, 558.

58. Harriman to Hopkins (July 31, 1944), Modern Military Records Division, R.G. 334, Box 13, Subject File October 1943-October 1945, Folder September 1943 through 31 July 1944, N.A. Deane was quoting Harriman. John R. Deane, *The Strange Alliance: The Story of Our Efforts at Wartime Cooperation with Russia* (New York: Viking Press, 1947), 93-94.

59. For example, see William H. Standley and Arthur A. Ageton, *Admiral Ambassador to Russia* (Chicago: Henry Regnery, 1955), 167; "Rebellion" file, A. E. Schanze Papers, U.S. Army Military History Institute, Carlisle Barracks, PA, Archives; Memoirs, Samouce Papers, 182. The trucks were seen often after the war as well.

60. U.S. President, *Reports to Congress on Lend-Lease Operations,* no. 16 (Washington, DC: Government Printing Office, 1944), 28; ibid., no. 13, 16; U.S. President, *Report on Operations of the Foreign Economic Administration* (Washington, DC: Government Printing Office, 1944), 29-30. The "one-half" estimate is probably correct, as over half of all motor vehicles in Soviet service at the end of the war were American. Albert Seaton, *The Russo-German War 1941-1945* (New York: Praeger, 1972), 588-89; Deane, *Strange Alliance,* 93-94. Not all sources agree with this estimate. U.S. President, *Reports to Congress on Lend-Lease Operations,* no. 21, 25; John Frederick Gardner, "The Lend-Lease Program of World War II: Analysis and Appraisal" (Ph.D. dissertation, University of Pittsburgh, 1946), 180-81. The lower estimate, however, was based on the visual observations of a single American officer. The estimates contained in secret U.S. reports were just as general as those in public materials. *Joint Chiefs of Staff,* "Postwar Economic Policies and Capabilities of the U.S.S.R." (November 1, 1945), 15.

61. F. Noel Mason, "Observing the Russians at War," *Military Review* 28 (May 1948), 101.

62. Harriman to Hopkins (July 31, 1944); Spalding to Protocol Committee (July 25, 1944), Modern Military Records Division, R.G. 334, Box 13, Subject File October 1943-October 1945, Folder September 1943-July 31, 1944, N.A.

63. Memoirs, Pantuhoff Papers, 506.

64. "Report of Trip to USSR by General Connolly," 7.

65. Deane, *Strange Alliance,* 93-94; Georgii K. Zhukov, *The Memoirs of Marshal Zhukov* (New York: Delacorte Press, 1972), 428 (apparently the marshal used a jeep for his personal travels); George C. Herring, Jr., *Aid to to Russia, 1941-1946: Strategy, Diplomacy, and the Origins of the Cold War* (New York: Columbia University Press, 1973), 286; *Great Soviet Encyclopedia,* vol. 14 (New York: Macmillan, 1980), 352; Munting, "Lend-Lease and the Soviet War Effort," 500. Soviet eagerness for trucks and jeeps continued throughout the war. See Erickson, *Road to Berlin,* 84.

66. Charles G. FitzGerald, "Operation Bagration," *Military Review* 44 (May 1964), 70; "Tetrad' Po Voennoi Administratsii," 11, 27. The front regiment was allocated 1,200-1,300 trucks, while the army regiment had 348. These are TOE, not actual, figures.

67. One thousand trucks could move two divisions, according to the Persian Gulf Command. T. H. Vail Motter, *The Persian Corridor and Aid to Russia* (Washington, DC: Office of the Chief of Military History, 1952), 73.

68. Seaton, *Russo-German War,* 352, 421.

69. "Foreign Military Digests: New Aspects of the War in the West," *Military Review* 22 (October 1941; condensed and translated from *Krasnaia Zvezda* [No. 4, 1940]), 60. According to *Krasnaia Zvezda,* "The army that possessed strong strategical reserves . . . and has mastered the art of strategical defense, may well parry the assaults and liquidate the penetrations of the enemy in modern warfare." The French experience of 1940 had certainly shown the need for a powerful reserve, which was useless, however, without the ability to transport and control its units.

70. Walter Kerr, *The Secret of Stalingrad* (Chicago: Playboy Press, 1978), 36; *Joint Chiefs of Staff,* "Specific Action to Be Taken under Revised Policy with Russia--memo, CGUSMMUSSR" (April 16, 1945), 26; Spalding and Deane to Arnold (June 24, 1944), and Spalding and Deane to Joint Chiefs of Staff (June 21, 1944), Modern Military Records Division, R.G. 334, Box 13, Subject File October 1943-October 1945, Folder September 1943 through July 31, 1944, N.A.

71. Seaton, *Russo-German War,* 588-89.

72. Senger und Etterlin, *Neither Fear Nor Hope,* 161; F. W. von Mellenthin, *Panzer Battles: A Study of the Employment of Armor in the Second World War* (Norman: University of Oklahoma Press, 1971), 185-86; *World War II German Military Studies: A Collection of 213 Special Reports on the Second World War Prepared by Former Officers of the Wehrmacht for the United States Army,* 24 vols. (New York: Garland Publishing, 1974), 18: VII(D)(10), 117-18; V. I. Chuikov, *The End of the Third Reich* (Moscow: Progress Publishers, 1978), 48, 50, 52.

73. *The German Army High Command, 1938-1945* (Arlington, VA: University Publications of America, 1975), "Intelligence on Foreign Armies: Military Foreign Service of OKH from 1938 to 1945," 13.

74. *Joint Chiefs of Staff,* "Memorandum for Information No. 45: Remarks by Lt. Col. Richard Park, Jr., USA, Former American Military Attache in Russia" (January 31, 1943), 1-2, 4; Spalding to Protocol Committee (July 25, 1944), Modern Military Records Division, R.G. 334, Box 13, Subject File October 1943-October 1945, Folder September 1943 through 31July 1944, N.A.

75. *Collection of Materials for the Study of War Experience No. 2,* 2, 5, 9.

76. *German Military Studies* 18:VII (D)(10), 6.

77. Erickson, *Road to Berlin,* 85.

78. See "Fuehrhung, Kampf, und Kraftquellen,," 16; *German Military Studies,* 18:VII (D)(10), 106-9. Fedorenko was Chief Marshal of Tanks and Mechanized Forces and Deputy Commissar of Defense.

79. Boris Skomorovsky and E. G. Morris, *The Siege of Leningrad* (New York: E. P. Dutton, 1944), 183.

80. S. M. Shtemenko, *The Last Six Months: Russia's Final Battles with Hitler's Armies in World War II* (Garden City, NY: Doubleday, 1977), 15, 16-17. Stalin became chairman of the newly organized State Defense Committee (GKO) on June 30, 1941. As of July 10, he was also chairman of the Stavka of the VgK and became People's Commissar of Defense on July 19. Harriett Fast Scott and William F. Scott, *The Armed Forces of the U.S.S.R.* (Boulder, CO: Westview Press, 1979), 23. He received the title of "Generalissimo" on June 26, 1945. Isaac Deutscher, *Stalin: A Political Biography* (London: Pelican, 1966), 534. In addition, Stalin was chairman of the Revision Commission, of the Secretariat of the Central Committee of the Party, of the Politburo, of the Organization Bureau, of the Supreme Naval Council, and of the Control Bureau. He was also Prime Minister. See *Joint Chiefs of Staff,* "Russian Combat Estimate" (April 1, 1942), 4.

81. Jeffrey Arthur Kern, "Soviet Command and Control in an Historical Context" (M.A. thesis, Naval Postgraduate School, Monterrey, CA, 1981), 21; *Joint Chiefs of Staff,* "Memorandum for the United States Chiefs of Staff: Present Relations between the USMM, Moscow, and the Soviet Military Authorities: Memorandum by the Commanding General, USMM, Moscow" (January 22, 1945), 5.

82. Shtemenko, *Last Six Months,* 11; Mellenthin, *Panzer Battles,* 234.

83. *German Military Studies,* 16:VII(C)(3), 46.

84. Graham D. Vernon, "Soviet Combat Operations in World War II: Lessons for Today?" *Military Review* 60 (April 1980), 45; Mellenthin, *Panzer Battles,* 195, 300; *German Military Studies,* 18:VII(D)(10), 55-58. Comments about Kursk are based on Lonnie O. Ratley, III, "Air Power at Kursk: A Lesson for Today," *Military Review* 58 (April 1978), 54-62; Ivan Parotkin, ed., *The Battle of Kursk* (Moscow: Progress Publishers, 1974), 172; *The Great March of Liberation* (Moscow: Progress Publishers, 1972), 45; Cajus Bekker, *The Luftwaffe War Diaries* (Garden City, NY: Doubleday, 1968).

85. *German Military Studies,* 16:VII(C)(1), 231, 295.

86. B. D. Bobrow, "Combat of the Infantry Division under Conditions of Encirclement," *Military Review* 21 (January 1942; translated from *Voennaia Mysl,* April 1940), 13; *German Military Studies,* 16:VII(C)(1), 297.

87. *German Military Studies,* 5: Annex 8, 3.

88. See Harriet Fast Scott and William F. Scott, *The Soviet Art of War: Doctrine, Strategy, and Tactics* (Boulder, CO: Westview Press, 1982); Kern, "Soviet Command and Control," 100; "History of the U.S. Military Mission," 33-34.

89. Vernon, "Soviet Combat Operations," 34, 45, 46; Mellenthin, *Panzer Battles,* 269; Franz Halder, *the Halder Diaries: The Private War Journals of Colonel General Franz Halder* (Boulder, CO: Westview Press, 1976), 2:971; Parotkin, *Battle of Kursk,* 208; *Great March of Liberation,* 96, 106-7. The official task of the N.K.V.D. (People's Commissariat for Internal Affairs) was "maintaining public order in the country, of guarding socialist property, and of control over the registration of births, marriages, and deaths, etc." K. Meretskov, *City Invincible* (Moscow: Progress Publishers, 1970), 26n. The use of security troops to dispose of retreating soldiers was not unique to the Soviet Union nor to World War II. Toward the end of the war, SS officers sometimes executed German army officers found in the rear without proper orders. Whether or not because of the "law of the revolver," the Red Army did improve, mauling German divisions transferred from other theatres. Thomas A. Wilson, "Soviet Combat Operations in World War II: Lessons for Today?" *Military Review* 60 (March 1980), 32.

90. Wartime lines were built away from major arteries. Kern, "Soviet Command and Control,"80-81, 123.

91. S. M. Shtemenko, *The Soviet General Staff at War, 1941-1945* (Moscow: Progress Publishers, 1975), 35.

92. *History of the Great Patriotic War,* 2:175; U.S. Army, Intelligence, "Organization of the Signal Communications in the Soviet Army," U.S. Army Military History Institute, Carlisle Barracks, PA, 10, 22; Col. A. Mokov, "Planning of Signal Communications in a Tank Group in Offensive Battle," *Zhurnal Avtobronetankovykh Voisk* (Nos. 2-3, 1943; U.S. Army Intelligence translation), 1.

93. Erickson, *Road to Berlin,* 82; *History of the Great Patriotic War,* 2:11.

94. "Organization of the Signal Communications," 1, 3, 5-6; *Collection of Materials for the Study of War Experience No. 2,* 50; Lt. Col. I. Marshkov, "Liaison Officers' Service" (n.d.) (U.S. Army Intelligence translation), 1, 2.

95. "Organization of the Signal Communications," 2-3, 9-10, 19-20; Col. Bela Berczeli, "The Spine of Command of the Stalinian Army, the Communication Troops of the Soviet," *Honved* (December 1949; U.S. Army Intelligence translation and abstract), 7-8. Stalin on occasion issued the order, "I demand more. This is my last warning." "'More' usually materialized." Erickson, *Road to Berlin,* x.

96. "General Organization of the Rear Service," 2-3; Erickson, *Road to Berlin,* 423; Maj. Gen. S. Bronevskii, "Concerning the Operational Pursuit," *Voennaia*

Mysl (No. 5, 1946: U.S. Army Intelligence translation), 5; V. Larionov et al., *World War II: Decisive Battles of the Soviet Army* (Moscow: Progress Publishers, 1984), 272, 278; FitzGerald, "Operation Bagration,"70.

97. "Report on War Aid," 20, 23, 24.

98. "Report on War Aid," 20; "History of the U.S. Military Mission," 354. Thirty-two of the locators were for marine use. See also David R. Beachley, "Soviet Radio-Electronic Combat in World War II," *Military Review* 61 (March 1981), 67-69. The radio-electronic battalions, established in 1943, engaged in interception, jamming, and spreading of disinformation. Radio interception allowed the Red Army to locate German artillery units, communications posts, and command centers. Jamming was aimed at higher commands, while intercept techniques were practiced on tanks and air units. All these methods were tested at Stalingrad. The 394th Sectional Radio Battalion managed to communicate with the trapped German Sixth Army and received 86 messages from various German units. The radio-electronic battalions were equipped with vehicle-mounted jammers, receivers, directional finders, and captured German radios. According to Soviet sources, jamming at Kursk blocked 70 percent of German radiograms. The Germans thought the Soviets quite skillful in their electronic endeavors.

8

Technical Aspects

Lend-Lease consisted of a veritable cornucopia of products, ranging from mundane cans of food to sophisticated radar sets, and supplied in quantities ranging from single items into the millions. Analyzing the effect of any single item can be tricky. Comparing aid shipments with Soviet production does not tell the whole story. Much American aid was in the form of highly specialized items (for example, chemicals, fuel blending agents, electronic equipment) which were more important than indicated by weight or numbers alone. In addition, Soviet production figures are hard to verify. More useful is to examine areas in which Lend-Lease may have provided crucial marginal supplies in those areas where the U.S.S.R. suffered the most severe shortages. Where did these shortages exist? Lend-Lease itself provides the answer because aid shipments more or less reflected Soviet requests, and it is not unreasonable to conclude that the Soviet Union would place the largest orders to resolve its own shortages. Some orders, especially those for single items, may have been presented for a less prosaic reason: information. Lend-Lease gave the Soviet Union much technical knowledge. This effect is difficult, if not impossible, to quantify. A sophisticated radar set constituted a technology transfer with a value far greater than can be measured by the number of items sent. Some items of capital equipment, such as machine tools, had a long-run 'multiplier' effect by increasing production, but the effect can only be estimated.

As far as weapons go, aircraft were by far the most important. Not only did British and American planes constitute a significant part of the Soviet air force, but they added some technical sophistication as well. The Anglo-American aircraft total exceeded 20,000, accounting for about 13 percent of planes in service during the war. Three quarters were pursuit planes (table 41), although a number of types were supplied.[1] Half of all Lend-Lease aircraft were flown from Alaska to Siberia to conserve shipping space, about 85 percent arriving after 1942, when the Soviet air force's recovery was well under way.[2] Soviet monthly aircraft production by the end of the war has been estimated as high as 3,500, as against monthly losses of about 1,500, and the total number of machines may have been as high as 50,000, with 20,000 in tactical units. Yak fighters and

Shturmovik ground attack-aircraft were each produced at a rate of 300-400 per month in the last year of the war, at which time 500 American aircraft were arriving each month.[3]

Aircraft represent one item where the marginal significance of Allied aid was quite high. For one thing, German production was close to that of the Soviet Union (although the Germans could not use all their planes in the East). According to a recent Soviet estimate, the Soviet Union produced about 33,200 aircraft in 1944, compared to 32,900 German planes.[4] At crucial points in the war, the arrival of any number of aircraft was important. The arrival of each plane was awaited with "impatient anticipation," and 40 aircraft were described as "not a joke, but a formidable force."[5]

Raw numbers aside, how important were the Allied planes? In general, Soviet officials were enthusiastic about Western aircraft, and Stalin even endorsed requests for more machines with the statement that they would play an "enormous role."[6] Opinions about individual plane types, however, varied. Not all Russian pilots were enthused by one of the most common imported planes, the Bell P-39 Airacobra. Armed with a 37-mm cannon, two .50 calibre machine guns and two .30-calibre machine guns, and carrying up to 500 pounds of bombs, it did prove an excellent ground-attack aircraft. This was fortunate, because it had not performed well in the fighter role for which it was intended. Its unusual rear-mounted engine, connected to the propeller with a long shaft running forward between the pilot's legs, made it highly maneuverable but also vibration-prone and uncomfortable to fly. Neither the USAAF nor the Royal Air Force liked the plane, and they parted with it rather willingly (although General Chuck Yeager does remember the plane fondly). Its poor high-altitude performance made it an inferior fighter, but this fault was not especially important as it was not used in this role. This accounts for the widely differing views about the plane. Western air forces considered the plane as "approaching obsolescence" despite having come out on the eve of the war. The Soviet air force rated it highly, always requesting more and criticizing only the limited number supplied (over 4,700). Its inability to operate from crude airfields, however, made it difficult for Airacobra-equipped formations to keep up with advancing Soviet forces.[7] Apparently the plane was tricky to fly, and a number of experienced Soviet pilots were killed in accidents.[8]

The Curtiss P-40 in its various versions was considered an adequate if not exceptional aircraft in the United States and Britain, but was well received in the Soviet Union, where it was usually referred to by the British Tomahawk and Kittyhawk designations. Despite some reservations (Stalin preferred the Airacobra) the Soviet air force apparently liked its 2,400 P-40s, especially the later, faster models beginning with the Merlin-engined P-40D.[9]

Far more controversial was the final progeny of the Airacobra line, the P-63 Kingcobra. This aircraft was far more powerful, but the machine did not handle the greater engine power gracefully. The USAAF never had more than 339, the 2,400 sent to the Soviet Union representing more than two-thirds of the total produced. According to Soviet officials, the tail had the disconcerting habit of separating from the fuselage, and the planes were often withdrawn from service for structural modifications. Details of the problem and the solution, however, were never supplied. Until April 1945 the Soviet Union continued to accept the machine, which had a longer range than domestic fighters, but Soviet inspectors were even more rigorous than usual in their examinations.[10]

Other than about 200 P-47 Thunderbolts, the bulk of the other pursuit/ground-attack aircraft consisted of almost 3,000 Hurricanes and 1,300 Spitfires from Britain. The latter being faster and more maneuverable, were preferred to the former, but the Hurricanes were good ground-attack aircraft, and shipments were never refused. Postwar Soviet criticism focuses on the Hurricane's obsolescence as a fighter but does not comment on its antitank use.[11]

Most other Lend-Lease planes were light and medium bombers, such as the Douglas A-20 Havoc and the North American B-25 Mitchell. More than one-third of all Havocs built were sent to the U.S.S.R., but little is known of their actual use. The Soviet air force alternately complimented and criticized the plane, indicating that modifications were made, but no details were provided. Even less information is available about the role of the Mitchells. The Soviet Union produced relatively few medium and heavy bombers, but Lend-Lease did not add many, suggesting limited Soviet interest in these planes.[12]

How much did Western aircraft aid in Soviet operations? While Western aircraft were glimpsed in many places in the Soviet Union, itself evidence of widespread use, again, overall impact is hard to appraise. Several squadrons of Hurricanes were stationed at Murmansk and Moscow in 1941-42, apparently for air defense. U.S. aircraft defended Leningrad and attacked German shipping. In 1942 American World War I ace Eddie Rickenbacker saw over a hundred Airacobras at a single Moscow air base. Airacobras and A-20s were present at Kursk, albeit in a secondary role, and Kingcobras were used as fighters in the Ukraine in 1944.[13]

When the Nazis first encountered Western aircraft on the Finland front, they concluded that the Soviet pilots' "performance did not improve." Although believing that American planes "did not enable Russian pilots to achieve materially higher standards of flying performance," German commanders also judged that Allied aid "contributed materially" to the Soviet air force. The American commander of the ill-fated 'shuttle-bombing' operation agreed that Soviet air operations were deficient but concluded that Lend-Lease was a significant factor in the Soviet numerical air superiority.[14]

Tanks, as noted earlier, were less important. At first glance, however, the numbers look impressive; 14,000 combat vehicles were sent by Britain and America. British tanks arrived first. Some 1,000 Valentines and Matildas were shipped in 1941, many of the former being rearmed with heavier guns after arrival.[15] In general, the Russians thought the imported tanks inferior in a number of respects, the most important being vulnerability. Stalin complained to Roosevelt that "U.S. tanks catch fire very easily when hit" because "the high-grade gasoline used forms inside the tanks a thick layer of highly inflammable fumes."[16] Later American tanks used lower-grade gasolines, but the machines were judged dangerous (and not only on the Eastern Front). Soviet officers also considered the tracks on Western machines too narrow, and the official Soviet history of the war dismisses the mostly light and medium foreign tanks as "considerably inferior to Soviet tanks in quality."[17]

Although the Red Army was "not overly impressed" with the performance of foreign tanks, the machines were nevertheless in great demand early in the war, when tank losses were horrendous, replacements arrived slowly, and any armored fighting vehicle (AFV) was better than none. Even as late as 1943, with 8,500 tanks at active fronts and 4,700 in reserve, Western tanks remained on the Soviet shopping list, if not at the top. British and American tanks were certainly equal to early German models. It should not be forgotten that although the Red Army did have some of the KV-1 and T-34 tanks in 1941 (supposedly "created in consequence of the direct participation and instruction of Comrade Stalin"), most machines were obsolete and in poor repair.[18]

Soviet sources conclude that foreign armor "did not play any sort of significant role in the combat operations by Soviet tank forces" because, in addition to their qualitative shortcomings, they "constituted only an insignificant proportion of the total number of tanks in the active army."[19] Is this true? Soviet tank production is not easy to calculate. Annual production may have reached 30,000-40,000 by the end of the war, although such estimates sometimes include "automotive vehicles" and "armored cars" as well as tanks.[20] Certainly Soviet production outstripped that of Nazi Germany. One Soviet author gives a production figure of 29,000 in 1944, of which 21,800 are described as heavy, as compared to German production of 17,000 machines (although the Soviet figures do not distinguish between tanks and self-propelled guns).[21] Foreign tanks accounted for slightly over one-tenth of Soviet tank strength, a little more in the pivotal year of 1942. As for actual use, the Russians did have a few formations equipped with American machines, but most were apparently used in the rear, perhaps for training, and few were ever seen by the Germans.[22]

Except for planes and tanks, Lend-Lease included little weaponry. American aid had little direct impact on Soviet artillery, often considered the Red Army's most important arm. "From time immemorial, Russian artillery has ranked among the highest in all European armies." The Red Army began the war with over 45,000 artillery pieces and by 1945 had received almost 100,000 guns of 75 millimeters or greater, as well as almost 350,000 mortars. The gun park by the end of the war exceeded 70,000. To this Lend-Lease added only 7,544 guns (excluding naval ordnance), most of which were antiaircraft batteries, 30 mortars, and about 3,000 rocket launchers.[23]

The small weapons shipments reflected Soviet priorities, since Stalin was willing to forego weapons (except airplanes) to obtain other supplies, such as trucks, aluminum, explosives, and food.[24] The Soviet Union outproduced Nazi Germany in the production of every weapon, including tanks, artillery, mortars, and small arms, and approximately equalled Germany in aircraft production.[25]

In contrast, American naval deliveries look more important because the Soviet navy was so small. America furnished 424 ships, mostly small, several thousand engines, naval guns, miscellaneous naval gear, and shipbuilding equipment.[26] Some of these vessels were transferred outside Lend-Lease for security reasons.[27] Despite aid and technical assistance, foreign observers rated the Soviet fleet "ineffective" and "disappointing." In 1976 Admiral S. G. Gorshkov claimed that Lend-Lease had no practical influence on the Soviet navy, but this view seems peculiar given that Lend-Lease ships almost exactly equalled wartime losses.[28] American vessels are better remembered for the lengthy postwar wrangle over their disposition and the shabby condition in which they were returned than their wartime service.

If the Soviets could afford to fight without much in the way of imported combat machinery, the same was not true of food, industrial materiel, and certain raw materials. As explained earlier, the food situation verged on desperate. Production fell precipitously after the war began.[29] Any offsetting loss of mouths to feed was largely nullified by the eastward movement of some 20 million refugees. Per capita grain production, for example, fell to the level of the post-Civil War famine of 1921.[30] The decline of production continued well into 1943 (table 42), as the Red Army requisitioned almost all farm trucks and a third of all farm tractors.[31]

Food shortages were clearly visible and not denied by Soviet sources, then or later. Strict rationing gave priority to the army and production workers, with nonproducers receiving the absolute minimum necessary for survival. The problem was qualitative as well as quantitative, as rations were short on proteins, fats, and (in cities) calories. The official history concedes that improvements in 1942 "could not replace the tremendous losses in cultivated area, manpower, and the materiel-technical base." Soviet requests for food for the "underfed and drastically overworked population" only tapered off if a real military crisis threatened. The 'black market' offered little to the hungry Russian; in 1944, for example, a roast goose in Moscow went for about $150.[32]

Much of the Lend-Lease food tonnage consisted of dehydrated goods (see table 11), so that ultimate tonnage consumed well exceeded the total indicated. It has been suggested that most American food was used for the army, but this is not certain. American food could have provided one pound of concentrated ration per day for 6 million soldiers, virtually the whole army, for the entire war. Moreover, such relief would have avoided substantial reduction in civilian supplies.[33] The aggregate effect of American food was low in some ways (allegedly Allied grain totalled less than 3 percent of the total consumed, and the U.S.S.R. even exported a little in 1943) but not in others. O.S.S. analysts estimated that Lend-Lease food increased the per capita availability of sugar and vegetables by half, meat by a fifth, and more than doubled the amount of animal fats.[34] Without Lend-Lease average civilian calorie consumption might have declined by a third.[35]

The overall decline affected Soviet clothing as well; 1945 cotton production, for example, was about half that of 1940, and flax fibre suffered almost as badly. It is difficult to estimate the impact of Lend-Lease fabric and clothing (see table 11).

It has been suggested that American shipments sufficed for the entire Red Army.[36]

Given all the foregoing, Lend-Lease probably fed the Red Army and helped clothe it, but did not arm it, at least directly. Ultimately the fate of the Soviet Union hinged on its ability to maintain and increase industrial production, a factor mentioned in most Soviet interpretations of the victory. Whether or not one accepts the Soviet contention that victory was evidence of the superiority of the socialist system, the resurgence and, for that matter, the survival of Soviet industry must be considered a great achievement. The invasion cost the Soviet Union half of its industrial capacity and most of its coal, steel, cast iron, and aluminum. Output of the heavy machine-tool industry fell by more than two-thirds, while electricity generation declined by almost 40 percent.[37]

The wartime recovery was impressive (table 43). Much of the successful rebuilding of Soviet industry was achieved through evacuation of plants from threatened territory and the tripling of production in the Urals and western Siberia (table 44). Organized evacuation began two days after the invasion.[38] As a result of great efforts, the aggregate value of industrial production reached about 90 percent of the 1940 level. Electricity generation regained the 1940 level in 1945, and in almost all areas production had recovered from the 1942 trough. Coal and steel production alone rose almost one-third from 1943 to 1944, but steel only attained two-thirds of its prewar production level in 1945.[39]

Highest among Soviet import demands were industrial machinery, chemicals, and raw materials, which comprised about a third of all tonnage (see tables 13, 14, and 15). These items were considered far more important than military supplies. Machine-tool production did not decline precipitously but was simply inadequate to keep pace with wartime needs. Virtually no data exist to estimate the effect of imported machine tools, but the Soviet Union depended almost completely on imports for complex tools and ball and roller bearings.[40]

In addition to smaller machine tools, in 1944-45 the United States also sent an aluminum rolling mill, several small, specialized metalworking plants, and steel-making equipment capable of increasing annual Soviet capacity by 2.5 million tons. This would have represented almost a quarter of Soviet output, but as the steel equipment was shipped in stages, its impact must have been substantially less. American rubber manufacturing-gear, however, more than doubled Soviet capacity. The electricity-generating plants only provided a small percentage of Soviet output, but as a number of these were portable, their value was greater than their capacity would suggest.[41]

It is easier to estimate the importance of imported raw materials and chemicals. Before the war the Soviet Union was already heavily dependent on imports of certain materials, especially aluminum. The invasion cost the U.S.S.R. most of its iron, steel, and aluminum, and steel production did not recover completely during the war. Even Lend-Lease could not make up differences between existing supplies and requirements in all areas (table 45). The United States and Britain did, however, supply the Soviet Union with 40 to 50 percent of its aluminum, three-quarters of its copper, and about one-tenth of its steel. Explosives shipments were also important, as after 1941 Soviet factories were compelled to use inferior ammonium nitrates in shells, apparently due to the loss of two-thirds of the country's coke works in the summer of 1941.[42]

For immediate operational needs, however, nothing outranked fuels in importance. In terms of total requirements, the Soviet situation was not too bad. Except for an anxious moment in late 1942 when the Nazis overran part of the vital oil fields near the Caspian Sea, the Soviet Union did not have a major petroleum shortage. Occasional regional shortages due to stringent Red Army allocations stemmed from transport problems. A greater problem than quantity was quality. Much Soviet refinery equipment was antiquated. Little high-octane aviation gas was produced, and much of the imported fuel consisted of aviation fuels and highly specialized blending agents designed to raise octane ratings or otherwise improve fuel quality. While Soviet writers say little about imported oil, one-quarter of all aviation gas in the Soviet Union was imported.[43]

American refining equipment may have been even more important to the Soviet Union than the oil. Standard Oil of New Jersey furnished designs and pilot plants for production of 100-octane gas, lubrication oils, and various specialized procedures. In 1943 and 1944, four complete refineries supplied by the United States had capacity equal to 8 percent of known Soviet production. Lend-Lease equipment could have increased aviation-gas production from 120,000 tons in 1941 to 1.85 million tons in 1944, with American plants representing about 5 percent of the crude and 20 percent of the 'cracking' capacity of Soviet refineries.[44] Two of the four refineries were shipped too late for full completion during the war, however, leading a puzzled Military Mission to speculate that the plants might have been "an extremely valuable bargaining point, in exchange for some Soviet concession or operation not known here."[45]

As suggested, the Soviet Union got one thing that was valuable both during and after war: technical knowledge. Soviet science was not inherently backward, although Stalinism and the terror did adversely affect scientific research.[46] In the transition from village-oriented peasant culture to industrial society, Soviet managers and engineers solved many technical problems. Lacking a solid base of trained workers and engineers, however, the Soviet state imported technology. In the 1920s and 1930s the Soviet government purchased machinery abroad and then redesigned it to fit Soviet requirements. Foreign companies built entire communications systems and factories inside the U.S.S.R., and many of their engineers remained for years as consultants.

The war offered the Soviet Union unprecedented opportunities for acquiring foreign technology. The United States eagerly shared technical information, sent sophisticated equipment, and gave Soviet emissaries access to industrial facilities in the United States. Failure of the Soviet Union to reciprocate led the Military Mission to urge the Joint Chiefs of Staff to withhold some items until the Soviet government became more cooperative. The Mission's views had some effect, and the U.S. government refused some Soviet requests toward the end of the war. The Military Mission proposed that American technicians be allowed to examine Soviet equipment in return for advanced American equipment, but these exchanges were rarely agreed to and almost never productive.[47] The British were generally more cautious than the Americans when it came to sharing information with Soviet representatives.

Despite their irritation, American officials realized that the United States needed the Soviet Union more than the Soviet Union needed the United States. A few even sympathized with the Soviet argument that its sacrifices were at least a quid pro quo. Whatever the American motivations, the visible technological shortcomings of the Soviet military led to the sending of an abundance of electronic hardware (see table 10), meeting most Soviet requests, even those made near war's end. The gear was badly needed. U.S. observers reported Soviet electronic equipment production as inadequate and noted the Soviet air force's inadequate navigation, photography, and precision bombing. Although Soviet officials claimed to have a "complete radar service," the Soviet Union asked for and got almost every type of British and American radar. The Soviet navy was more interested in communications, sonar, and detection equipment than in ships.[48]

Electronic gear was only a small part of the wartime flow of information to the Soviet Union. Soviet industry copied imported items both before and during the war.[49] The multiplicity of Lend-Lease items resulted from Soviet orders, not American arbitrariness. In the last two years of the war the Soviet shopping list grew longer and longer, leading one analyst to conclude that "American Lend-Lease after 1943 gave a massive injection of modern technology which carried the Soviet economy well into the 1950s."[50]

Whatever uses American technology or supplies had later, during the war they were most necessary. No item discussed in this chapter was essential to the Soviet Union's survival, and the Red Army would have fought on without them. But in some respects, Lend-Lease supplies were vital. Without Lend-Lease aviation fuel, aluminum, and planes, the Soviet air arm would not have been nearly as powerful as it became. Without U.S. ground-attack aircraft, precisely the type most used by the Soviet forces, air force support of the army would have been far weaker.

Primarily, however, the Soviet services depended on industrial production. The flow of tanks, planes, and shells from Soviet factories was vital, and would have been far less a torrent without Lend-Lease. Many of the Soviet Union's largest enterprises were built with American assistance.[51] Without Lend-Lease raw materials and industrial equipment, the Soviet command would have had to fight a much more conservative war, delaying offensives until adequate stockpiles had been assembled. The Soviet leadership would have continued the war; but its ability to expel the Nazi forces and overrun most of eastern Germany by May of 1945 must be called into question.

NOTES

1. *Great Soviet Encyclopedia,* vol. 14 (New York: Macmillan, 1980), 35; Robin Higham and Jacob W. Kipp, eds., *Soviet Aviation and Air Power: A Historical Review* (Boulder, CO: Westview Press, 1977), 128; U.S. Department of State, Protocol and Area Information Staff of the U.S.S.R. Branch of the Division of Research and Reports, "Report on War Aid Furnished by the United States to the U.S.S.R." (Foreign Economic Section, Office of Foreign Liquidation, November 28, 1945), 9; "History of the U.S. Military Mission to Moscow," Modern Military Records Division, R.G. 165, Box 146, OPD 336TS, N.A., 353; *Records of the Joint Chiefs of Staff: Part 1, 1942-1945: The Soviet Union* (Frederick, MD: University Publications of America, n.d.), "Air Capabilities of the USSR Generally and by Areas" (October 31, 1945), 5; Richard C. Lukas, *Eagles East: The Army Air Forces and the Soviet Union, 1941-1945* (Tallahassee: Florida State University Press, 1970), 233-35; Antony C. Sutton, *Western Technology and Soviet Economic Development, 1945 to 1965* (Stanford: Hoover Institution Press, 1973), 11-12.

2. Wesley Frank Craven and James Lea Cate, eds., *The Army Air Forces in World War II,* vol. 7, *Services around the World* (Chicago: University of Chicago Press, 1958), 165; Lukas, *Eagles East,* 166, 233-35; Higham and Kipp, *Soviet Aviation and Air Power,* 80.

3. Col. Alfred A. Kessler, "Report on Russian Trip" (December 2, 1943), 6, 13, Modern Military Records Division, R.G. 18, Box 1045, Folder 333.1, N.A.; *Joint Chiefs of Staff,* "Air Capabilities and Intentions of the USSR in the Post-War Period" October 19, 1945), 3, 4, 9; Ibid., "Soviet Forces in Far East at 1 January 1945" (June 6,1944), 3; *O.S.S. / State Department Intelligence and Research Reports, Part 6: The Soviet Union, 1941-1949* (Frederick, MD: University Publications of America, 1977), "Military Potential of the Soviet Union, Part IV: Munitions" (November 11, 1942), 1.

4. A. M. Sokolov, "Sovetsko-germanskii front i voennye deistviia na zapade dekabr' (1944-janvar' 1945 gg.)," *Voprosy Istorii* (January 1985), 5.

5. L. I. Zorin, *Osoboe Zadanie* (Moscow: Izdatel'stvo Politicheskoi Literatury, 1987), 129.

6. *Joint Chiefs of Staff,* "Bradley Mission: Bombers for the Far East" (January 11, 1943), 1-2.

7. Wesley Frank Craven and James Lea Cate, eds., *The Army Air Forces in World War II,* vol. 6, *Men and Planes* (Chicago: University of Chicago Press, 1955), 212-214; "Report on War Aid," 18; "Report to Walsh of Meeting with General Nikitin" (July 24, 1944), Robert L. Walsh Papers, U.S. Army Military History Institute, Carlisle Barracks, PA, Archives; *History of the Great Patriotic War of the Soviet Union, 1941-1945* (Moscow: Voenizdat, 1960; OCMH translation), 3:216. Russian airfields were primitive. About half were designated as "landing grounds," with few facilities. Harry E. Goldsworthy, "A Toast from Stalin," *Aerospace Historian* 23 (Fall 1979), 163; *Joint Chiefs of Staff,* "Air Capabilities of the USSR in the Post-War Period" (October 19, 1945), 6. Lend-

Lease included 42.7 million square feet of landing mat. "History of the U.S. Military Mission," 353. This would have been enough for 150-170 small airstrips.

8. Zorin, *Osoboe Zadanie,* 122-23.

9. "Report on War Aid," 18; Craven and Cate, *Men and Planes,* 212; William H. Standley and Arthur A. Ageton, *Admiral Ambassador to Russia* (Chicago: Henry Regnery, 1955), 287; A. Galland, K. Ries, and R. Ahnert, *The Luftwaffe at War, 1939-1945* (Chicago: Henry Regnery, 1973), 133. Figures include planes sent to Britain and retransferred to the U.S.S.R.

10. Col. C. R. Bond to Walsh, "Memorandum for General Walsh" (October 18, 1944); Craven and Cate, *Men and Planes,* 211; "History of the U.S. Military Mission," 362-63; *Joint Chiefs of Staff,* "Air Capabilities of the USSR, Generally and by Areas" (October 31, 1945), 4-5; Higham and Kipp, *Soviet Aviation and Air Power,* 128; George C. Herring, *Aid to Russia, 1941-1946: Strategy, Diplomacy, and the Origins of the Cold War* (New York: Columbia University Press, 1973), 47; Edward R. Stettinius, Jr., *Lend-Lease: Weapon for Victory* (New York: Macmillan, 1944), 208; George Racey Jordan, *From Major Jordan's Diaries* (New York: Harcourt, Brace, 1952), 48; I. Mazurik, "Vozdushnaia trassa Aliaska-Sibir," *Voenno-Istoricheskii Zhurnal* (no. 3, 1977), 51; Reinhard Gehlen, *The Service: The Memoirs of General Reinhard Gehlen* (New York: World Publishing, 1972), 54; Craven and Cate, *Services around the World,* 159, 166; Spalding and Deane to AGWAR, June 21, 1944, Modern Military Records Division, R.G. 334, Box 13, Subject File October 1943-October 1945, Folder September 1943 through July 31, 1944, N.A.; *Joint Chiefs of Staff,* "Arrangements with the Soviets" (April 3, 1945). German intelligence was apparently aware of these problems.

11. Standley and Ageton, *Admiral Ambassador to Russia,* 287; *History of the Great Patriotic War,* 3:216.

12. "Report to Walsh of Meeting with General Nikitin" (July 24, 1944), Walsh Papers; Craven and Cate, *Men and Planes,* 198-99, 211; Stettinius, *Lend-Lease,* 208; Higham and Kipp, *Soviet Aviation and Air Power,* 214; *Joint Chiefs of Staff,* "Postwar Economic Policies and Capabilities of the USSR" (November 1, 1945), 10.

13. Walter Schwabedissen, *The Russian Air Force in the Eyes of German Commanders* (New York: Arno Press, 1960), 158; "Notes on Archangel-Murmansk Trip of General Spalding by Captain Ware" (January 1944): "Report of Trip to USSR by General Connolly," Modern Military Records Division, R.G. 334, Box 5, Subject File October 1943-October 1945, N.A.; Edward V. Rickenbacker, *Rickenbacker* (Englewood Cliffs, NJ: Prentice-Hall, 1967), 370; John Erickson, *The Road to Berlin: Continuing the History of Stalin's War with Germany* (Boulder, CO: Westview Press, 1983), 71; Memoirs, 88, Wellington Alexander Samouce Papers, U.S. Army Military History Institute, Carlisle Barracks, PA, Archives.

14. Schwabedissen, *Russian Air Force,* 158, 159; Klaus Uebe, *Russian Reactions to German Airpower in World War II* (New York: Arno Press, 1964).

9; "Lessons of ESCOM" (n.d.), 9, 10, Walsh Papers. For an example of the size and orientation of air operations, see: U.S.S.R. Red Army General Staff, *Collection of Materials for the Study of War Experience, No. 1* (Moscow: Voenizdat, 1942; U.S. Army Intelligence translation); Rickenbacker, *Rickenbacker,* 375.

15. *Joint Chiefs of Staff,* "Russian Combat Estimate" (April 1, 1942), 46; Sutton, *Western Technology and Soviet Economic Development, 1945 to 1965,* 11-12; Kenneth Macksey and John H. Batchelor, *Tank: A History of the Armoured Fighting Vehicle* (New York: Charles Scribner's Sons, , 1970), 105. The total does not include about 6,000 self-propelled guns, half-tracks, and armored scout cars.

16. U.S.S.R. Ministry of Foreign Affairs, *Correspondence between the Chairman of the Council of Ministers of the U.S.S.R. and the Presidents of the U.S.A. and the Prime Ministers of Great Britain during the Great Patriotic War of 1941-1945* (London: Lawrence & Wishart, 1958), 2:30; Georgii K. Zhukov, *The Memoirs of Marshal Zhukov* (New York: Delacorte Press, 1972), 392.

17. Memoirs, Oleg Pantuhoff Papers, U.S. Army Military History Institute, Carlisle Barracks, PA, Archives, 610; *History of the Great Patriotic War,* 3:214. Fifty-five percent of the U.S. tanks sent to the Soviet Union were light, 25 percent were medium.

18. Erickson, *Road to Berlin,* 83, 84; *History of the Great Patriotic War,* 3:214; Albert Seaton, *The Russo-German War 1941-1945* (New York: Praeger, 1972), 589; "The Armored and Mechanized Troops of the Soviet Armed Forces" (n.d.) (U.S. Army Intelligence translation), U.S. Army Military History Institute, Carlisle Barracks, PA, 7. According to this source, Russians invented the tank. Ibid., 12-14. Western tanks were again requested in 1944.

19. *History of the Great Patriotic War,* 3:214, 215.

20. "Armored and Mechanized Troops," 50, 69.

21. Sokolov, Sovetsko-germanskii front," 5.

22. Franz Halder, *The Halder Diaries: The Private War Journals of Colonel General Franz Halder* (Boulder, CO: Westview Press, 1976), 2:1336, 1481; "Report of Trip to USSR by General Connolly," 2; Spalding to Protocol Committee (July 25, 1944), Modern Military Records Division, R.G. 334, Box 13, Subject File October 1943-October 1945, Folder September 1943 through July 31, 1944, N.A.; *Joint Chiefs of Staff,* "Estimate of Soviet Postwar Military Capabilities and Intentions" (November 8, 1945), 2-3; Ibid., "Memorandum for Information: Russian Capabilities" (June 20 1942), appendix A, 1, appendix C, 1-2; *O.S.S.,* "Military Potential of the Soviet Union, Part IV: Munitions" (November 11, 1942), 2. British Valentine tanks were used in a few "senseless" mass assaults in 1941. American tanks were seen moving in the direction of the front, but nothing is known about their fate. German intelligence believed that 30 brigades were equipped with U.S. tanks, but this appears to have been a guess (and too high). Gehlen, *Service,* 54.

23. Boris Skomorovsky and E. G. Morris, *The Siege of Leningrad* (New York: E. P. Dutton, 1944), 184; Ivan Parotkin, ed., *The Battle of Kursk*

(Moscow: Progress Publishers, 1974), 144, 167, 207; F. W. von Mellenthin, *Panzer Battles: A Study of the Employment of Armor in the Second World War* (Norman: University of Oklahoma Press, 1971), 299, 301; *History of the Great Patriotic War,* 1:139; G. Titov, "The Entire Country to the Front," *Tyl i Snabzhenie Sovetskikh Vooruzhennykh Sil* (No. 5, 1975; U.S. Army Intelligence translation), 14-22; "History of the U.S. Military Mission," 354; *Joint Chiefs of Staff,* "Estimate of Soviet Postwar Military Capabilities and Intentions" (November 8, 1945), 2-3; Ibid., "Memorandum for Information: Russian Capabilities" (June 20, 1942), appendix C, 1-2.

24. Robert E. Sherwood, *Roosevelt and Hopkins,* vol. 2, *From Pearl Harbor to Victory* (New York: Bantam Books, 1950 [Harper & Brothers, 1948]), 235-36; Standley and Ageton, *Admiral Ambassador to Russia,* 307; Joel Sayre, *Persian Gulf Command: Some Marvels on the Road to Kazvin* (New York: Random House, 1945), 16.

25. M. M. Kozlov, ed., *Velikaia Otechestvennaia Voina, 1941-1945: Entsiklopediia* (Moscow: Soviet Encyclopedia, 1983), 400; Titov, "Entire Country," 14-22; I. Krupchenko, "Metodika chteniia lektsii 'voenno-politicheskie itogi velikoi otechestvennoi voiny,'" *Voenno-Istoricheskii Zhurnal* (No. 2, 1980), 69-74; Galland, Ries, and Ahnert, *Luftwaffe at War,* 240. Germany produced 113,515 aircraft, including 18,235 bombers and 66,088 fighters, but many of these were committed elsewhere. The Soviet Union produced between 108,000 and 137,000 aircraft. Soviet production of artillery and small arms was double that of Germany's.

26. "Report on War Aid," 21; "History of the U.S. Military Mission," 354, 462-65; *Joint Chiefs of Staff,* "Postwar Economic Policies and Capabilities of the USSR" (November 1, 1945), 10; Antony C. Sutton, *Western Technology and Soviet Economic Development, 1930 to 1945* (Stanford: Hoover Institution Press, 1971), 209-17. British naval aid included a battleship.

27. *Joint Chiefs of Staff,* "Security Measures Involving the Transfer of Naval Vessels to the USSR" (March 16, 1945), 6-8; Ibid., "Cover and Deception Ban for Milepost: Report by Joint Security Control" (March 20, 1945), 12-13. Domestic political considerations may also have played a role.

28. Sutton, *Western Technology and Soviet Economic Development. 1930 to 1945,* 218; *Joint Chiefs of Staff,* "Memorandum for Information: Russian Capabilities" (June 30, 1942), appendix B, 1; M. G. Saunders, *The Soviet Navy* (New York: Praeger, 1958), 74, 76. The Soviet Union usually refused technical assistance. When British ASDIC equipment failed to perform due to improper location, the Russians blamed the equipment. *Joint Chiefs of Staff,* "Post-War Economic Policies and Capabilities of the U.S.S.R." (November 1, 1945), 20. In 1937 the Soviet fleet totalled about 1.3 million gross tons. Wartime losses were somewhere from 630,000 to 700,000 tons; Lend-Lease vessels totalled 637,000 gross tons.

29. J. Halperin, "L'economie sovietique pendant la guerre," *Revue d'Histoire de la Deuxieme Guerre Mondiale* 2 (April 1952), 18; *Joint Chiefs of Staff,* "Postwar Economic Policies and Capabilities of the U.S.S.R." (November 1,

1945), 25; Ibid., "Russian Combat Estimate" (April 1, 1942), 152; Robert Huhn Jones, *The Roads to Russia: United States Lend-Lease to the Soviet Union* (Norman: University of Oklahoma Press, 1969), 216-17; U.S. President, *Reports to Congress on Lend-Lease Operations,* no. 11 (Washington, DC: Government Printing Office, 1943), 12, 27; Ibid., no. 13 (Washington, DC: Government Printing Office, 1943), 17; *History of the Great Patriotic War,* 2:521. In 1943, like 1942, grain production was only 31 percent of 1940. *Istoriia Vtoroi Mirovoi Voiny, 1939-1945,* vol. 8 (Moscow: Voenizdat, 1977), xiii.

30. Erich Klinkmueller, "Some Economic Reflections on the Great Patriotic War (1941-1952)," *Soviet Union* 4 (1977), 227.

31. *History of the Great Patriotic War,* 1:536-38; Erickson, *Road to Berlin,* 85. In 1941 Soviet agriculture had about 684,000 tractors and 228,000 trucks. The Red Army requisitioned 90 percent of the trucks and one-third of the tractors. Tractor production appears to have been substantial before the war. See G. Buehlmann, *The Supply Services of Foreign Armies (Economic Principles, Organization and Supplies, Transportation, and Problems of the Supply Services)* (Frauenfeld, CH: Huber & Co.,, 1949; U.S. Army Intelligence translation), 29.

32. Rickenbacker, *Rickenbacker,* 380; *History of the Great Patriotic War,* 2:520; Erickson, *Road to Berlin,* 84, 404; "History of the U.S. Military Mission," 371, 374; "Report of Trip to USSR by General Connolly," 8; *O.S.S.,* "Military Potential of the Soviet Union, Part IIb: The Food Problem under War Conditions" (November 30, 1942), 7, 8, 10, 37, 49, 68-69; Memoirs, Samouce Papers, 27, 28, 31. Rationing existed before the war as well. See Buehlmann, *Supply Services,* 61.

33. U.S. President, *Reports to Congress on Lend-Lease Operations,* no. 19 (Washington, DC: Government Printing Office, 1945), 16; "Report of Trip to USSR by General Connolly," 7-8; Seaton, *Russo-German War,* 590; Stettinius, *Lend-Lease,* 228; John R. Deane, *The Strange Alliance: The Story of Our Efforts at Wartime Cooperation with Russia* (New York: Viking Press, 1947), 94; John Frederick Gardner, "The Lend-Lease Program of World War II: Analysis and Appraisal" (Ph. D. dissertation, University of Pittsburgh, 1946), 128; Memoirs, Samouce Papers, 23-24. One author speculated that the food was used for the homeless. Buehlmann, *Supply Services,* 60.

34. N. Dunaeva, "Lend-Liz: Fakty i vymysly," *Voenno-Istoricheskii Zhurnal* (No. 3, 1977), 105; *O.S.S.,* "Russian Import Requirements for Major Foods for the Periods 1 July 1944 to 30 June 1945, and 1 July 1945 to 30 June 1946" (July 20, 1944), 2. The O.S.S. statistics may underestimate Soviet production.

35. Roger Munting, "Lend-Lease and the Soviet War Effort," *Journal of Contemporary History* 19 (1984), 502.

36. Klinkmueller, "Economic Reflections," 229; *History of the Great Patriotic War,* 2:521; "Armored and Mechanized Troops," 23; Jones, *Roads to Russia,* 228, 289. The boots were made to Russian specifications.

37. Halperin, "Economie sovietique," 18; M. S. Zinich, "Iz istorii stankostroeniia i tiazhelogo mashinostroeniia v pervyi period velikoi

otechestvennoi voiny," *Istoriia SSSR* (No. 6, 1971), 93; Rene Girault, "L'effort humain de l'arriere (1941-43)," *Revue d'Histoire de la Deuxieme Guerre Mondiale* 17 (October 1967), 15-31; "Armored and Mechanized Troops," 23. The decline in heavy industry was especially problematic, as heavy industry comprised 61.2 percent of industrial output. *History of the Great Patriotic War,* I: 521.

38. An evacuation committee was formed on June 24, 1941, consisting of Kaganovich, Kosygin, chvernik, and Kuzmin. In mid-July 1941 the commitee was reconstituted. Kaganovich and Kuzmin were removed, while Pervukhin, Mikoyan, and Zakharov were added. Girault, "Effort humain," 18. The eastward movement of industry began, however, before the war.

39. *Istoriia Vtoroi Mirovoi Voiny,* 355, and appendix, 13; Klinkmueller, "Economic Reflections," 229; Col. Karoly Janza, "The Material and War Economic Power of the Soviet Union," *Honved* (December 1949: U.S. Army Intelligence translation), 5. The value percentage somewhat overstates the Soviet economic recovery.

40. According to Faymonville, machine tools were "urgently needed." *O.S.S., "Military Potential of the Soviet Union, Part II: Basic Industries"* (November 25, 1942), 39-41; Ibid., "Military Potential of the Soviet Union, Part IV: Munitions" (November 11, 1942), 12-13; Erickson, *Road to Berlin,* 84, 404; U.S. Army, Assistant Chief of Staff (Intelligence), "History of the War in Eastern Europe, 1941-1945" (synopsis) (1953), 156, U.S. Army Military History Institute, Carlisle Barracks, PA; Sutton, *Western Technology and Soviet Economic Development, 1930 to 1945,* 125-26, 140, 149, 167-68, 184. Plant equipment and raw materials formed the bulk of Soviet requests. Leon Martel, *Lend-Lease, Loans, and the Coming of the Cold War: A Study of the Implementation of Foreign Policy* (Boulder, CO: Westview Press, 1979), 28. U.S. rubber plants produced a better-quality product than Soviet facilities.

41. "Report on War Aid," 16, 17. The 'portables' generated less than 1 million kilowatts, but one author has suggested that Lend-Lease electrical equipment was sufficient to replace wartime losses. Sutton, *Western Technology and Soviet Economic Development, 1930 to 1945,* 125-26, 140, 149, 167-68, 184.

42. *Joint Chiefs of Staff,* "Postwar Economic Policies and Capabilities of the USSR" (November 1, 1945), 13, 25; Ibid., "Soviet Supply Programs" (January 11, 1943), 2; *O.S.S.,* "Losses of Russian Industrial Production Resulting from the Eastward Movement of the War Front: General Geographic Distribution of Russian Industry" (September 19, 1941), 1; Munting, "Lend-Lease and the Soviet War Effort," 500 (42 percent); *O.S.S.,* "Military Potential of the Soviet Union, Part IV: Munitions" (November 11, 1942), 12-13 (about 40 percent); Jones, *Roads to Russia,* 220-21 (one-half). The United Kingdom supplied about 31,000 tons of tin, 45,000 tons of copper, and 36,000 tons of aluminum. Sutton, *Western Technology and Soviet Economic Development, 1930 to 1945,* 11-12. Except for aluminum, the nonferrous metals industries suffered little. A. Ivanov,. "Stalin's Industrial Base, *Posev* (1951; U.S. Army Intelligence translation), 3. Before the war Soviet shells contained TNT with a lower

percentage of ammonium nitrate. The Germans attributed the change to the loss of two-thirds of the coke works in the invasion. David Kahn, *Hitler's Spies: German Military Intelligence in World War II* (New York: Macmillan, 1978), 90.

43. One source estimates that the Caucasus supplied 84 percent of the Soviet Union's oil. Another estimate divides the sources as follows: Baku region, 75 percent: Grozny-Maikop field (which the Germans reached), 17 percent: Volga-Ural, 6.4 percent. *Joint Chiefs of Staff,* "Specific Action to Be Taken under Revised Policy with Russia: Memo, CG, USMMUSSR" (April 16, 1945), 35; *O.S.S.,* "The Effect of Territorial Losses on Russia's Petroleum Position" (May 20, 1942), v; Ibid., "Military Potential of the Soviet Union: Part III, Basic Industries" (November 25, 1942), 15; Ibid., "Losses of Russian Industrial Production Resulting from the Eastward Movement of the War Front: General Geographic Distribution of Russian Industry" (September 19, 1941), 6; "Military Notes from Around the World," *Military Review* 21 (October 1941), 48-49; Joseph E. Davies, *Mission to Moscow* (London: Victor Gollancz, 1942), 368; Jones, *Roads to Russia,* 224, 272; "History of the U.S. Military Mission," 355, 372; Kessler, "Report on Russian Trip," 8; Seaton, *Russo-German War,* 589; Sutton, *Western Technology and Soviet Economic Development, 1930 to 1945,* 90. The Red Army sometimes allocated all fuel to just a few units during an offensive. Raymond L. Garthoff, "The Soviet Manchurian Campaign, August 1945," *Military Affairs* 33 (October 1969), 319-20. A single offensive with 3,000 tanks and an operational depth of 100 kilometers would require a minimum of 1 million gallons for the tanks, and probably more. See *Brief Tactical-Technical Manual, 2d ed.* (Moscow: Voenizdat, 1945; U.S. Army Intelligence translation), 55. Lend-Lease petroleum amounted to about one-sixth or less of the Soviet total.

44. Sutton, *Western Technology and Soviet Economic Development, 1930 to 1945,* 86, 88-90; *O.S.S.,* "Russian Capabilities and Prospects: Basic Industries" (July 11, 1944), 73, 76.

45. "Report on War Aid," 16; Antony C. Sutton, *National Suicide: Military Aid to the Soviet Union* (New Rochelle, NY: Arlington House, 1973), 71; Memo, "For Discussion with General Arnold" (n.d.), Walsh Papers; "History of the U.S. Military Mission," 366-70, 372; Sutton, *Western Technology and Soviet Economic Development, 1930 to 1945,* 206.

46. See, for example, Kendall E. Bailes, "Soviet Science in the Stalin Period: The Case of V. I. Vernadskii and His Scientific School, 1928-1945," *Slavic Review* 45 (Spring 1986), 20-37.

47. *Joint Chiefs of Staff,* "Disclosure of Technical Information to the U.S.S.R.: Report by the Military Members of the JIC" (September 17, 1943), 2; "History of the U.S. Military Mission," 360-61.

48. *Joint Chiefs of Staff,* "Disclosure of Radar Information to the Russians and Chinese" (February 21, 1943), 3, 4; ibid., "Disclosure of Technical Information to the U.S.S.R." (September 17, 1943), 2; ibid., "Air Capabilities and Intentions of the USSR in the Post-War Period" (October 19, 1945), 12; ibid., "Release of Radar Information and Equipment to the U.S.S.R." (August 8, 1943), 1; ibid.,

"Disclosure of Information other than Radar to the U.S.S.R." (September 30, 1943), 1; "History of the U.S. Military Mission," 456; Final Report, 3: Maj. Gen. F. L. Anderson to Spaatz, "Report on Visit to Russia by Mission of USSTAF Officers" (May 21, 1944): "Conference with General Grendall" (May 11, 1944): "Lessons of ESCOM," 9, Walsh Papers.

49. *Joint Chiefs of Staff,* "Air Capabilities and Intentions of the USSR in the Post-War Period: Report by the Joint Intelligence Staff" (October 19, 1945), 12; Sutton, *Western Technology and Soviet Economic Development, 1930 to 1945,* 3. Aircraft showing substantial 'borrowing' included the Pe-2 and Pe-8 bombers. Kessler, "Report on Russian Trip," 8.

50. Sutton, *Western Technology and Soviet Economic Development, 1930 to 1945,* 206. Sutton has a point, although the actual effect of aid on postwar reconstruction is debatable.

51. Stalin said that "about two-thirds of all the large industrial enterprises in the Soviet Union had been built with United States help or technical assistance." This statement is sometimes quoted as an assessment of the impact of Lend-Lease. Herring, *Aid to Russia,* 116. In fact, Stalin was referring to the effect of all imports of industrial machinery and technology since the revolution.

9

Lend-Lease and the Soldiers

What effect did Lend-Lease have on Soviet tactics? Did American aid change the actual fighting in the field? Did our assistance alter or improve Soviet tactical methods? These are complicated questions because only a small part of Lend-Lease consisted of tactical combat equipment. The effect of American aid, if any, was therefore indirect, through improved command and control, better food and clothing for the troops, better flow of supply, augmentation of Soviet production, and (possibly) a boost to morale. On the other side of the coin, do Soviet tactics reveal anything about the effect of Lend-Lease? While Soviet tactics improved throughout the war, this alone proves nothing about Lend-Lease. The Red Army showed occasional tactical finesse even in 1941, although against a backdrop of fearful errors.

Analysis here is aimed mainly at the Red Army, because the other services functioned primarily in support of ground operations.[1] This does not mean that Western aircraft, aviation fuels, and technology did not influence Soviet air tactics. As noted earlier, Western aircraft composed a substantial part of Soviet military aviation, and the Soviet air force (VVS) operated mainly as an adjunct to the army.

The term "tactics" (as used here) includes both the method of employment of individual small units and the conduct of operations involving several small units, although the latter falls within the Soviet definition of 'operational art.' Unit coordination was as much a problem for the Red Army at the micro as at the macro level. Materiel alone cannot offset the need for competent junior and noncommissioned officers, which has risen as increasing firepower has fragmented battle into a series of small-unit encounters. An army saddled with a lack of competence at the lower levels needs even better command and control, or its tactical options are limited to unimaginative, crude, or unorchestrated attacks, capable of breakthroughs only at enormous cost.

Stalinist purges and the disaster inflicted during the opening phases of Barbarossa deprived the Red Army of many trained officers. Tactics were, as a result, less than perfect, although these problems have sometimes been exaggerated. Some Western writers depict the Great Patriotic War as a series of mass World War I-style attacks, successful only because of inexhaustible Russian human and material resources. There were indeed many incompetent attacks that make this generalization understandable. Two things tend to be overlooked, however. First, the well-documented labor and economic shortages present in the Soviet Union during the war deprived the Red Army of these advantages, especially as regards the former. Second, military authorities made widespread and systematic improvements in training, methods, and allocation of military resources and developed methodical approaches to tactics, operational art, and strategy. If Russian operations had been nothing more than wave attacks, it is doubtful that the Red Army could have defeated an army organized to frustrate precisely that type of offensive. Yet it did, contrary to many contemporary expectations, destroying German divisions which had acquitted themselves well elsewhere and inflicting devastating casualties.[2]

An assessment of Lend-Lease's impact on command and control of tactical units must take into account the effect of sending forward small units with set instructions, but with limited communications capability to monitor and direct them. As in World War I, exploitation of early successes would be minimal, since small units would have to act on their own initiative (not a notable strength of the Red Army), and the 'punch' of the attack would become so diffuse as to eliminate the advantage of initial numerical superiority. Such lack of control was a major factor leading to the use of the mass attack, although the Red Army did attempt to design careful, precise small-unit attacks, penetrations, and encirclements.[3]

The Red Army was hampered by a shortage of qualified personnel, a lack of initiative, and poor communications. The results were sometimes disastrous. The purge-decimated airborne force (a pet project of the executed Marshal Tukhachevskii), for example, was virtually destroyed in an otherwise well-planned operation at the Bukrin bridgehead.[4] To prevent such mishaps, the General Staff published and circulated detailed studies to teach its officers the 'correct' solution to almost every tactical problem (in a sense anticipating the more recent 'algorithm' approach). In 1941 the General Staff established a Section for the Utilization of Combat Experience which communicated information and conclusions to lower-echelon commanders and wrote a variety of instructions, orders and regulations. The Section began publishing *A Miscellany of Materials for Studying Combat Experience* in the fall of 1942, later superseded by the *Information Bulletin* and *Tactical Methods Miscellany*. Subjects included the destruction of surrounded enemy formations, the correct employment of tanks, amphibious operations, defense against tanks and aircraft, operational war games, problems of studying combat operations, reconnaissance, order of battle, methods of command and control, forcing rivers, and descriptions of interesting small-unit engagements.[5] The Russians were quick to copy basic lessons from German tactical methods, especially in regard to the handling of tanks and tank-infantry combinations.[6]

The Red Army had to do this because many of its junior officers lacked skill and experience. Losses in battle of trained personnel were heavy, and the communications net to closely manage tactical operations did not exist. The prevention of encirclement by an enemy had occupied the General Staff before the war; faced with the actual event again and again in 1941, the Red Army strove to extricate its trained cadres. Breakouts occurred as early as July of 1941, and by 1943 trapped Russian forces were able to avoid disorganization. Small units would enter the encirclements to bring out selected personnel.[7]

Russian coordination skills were evident, if not ubiquitous, even at the beginning of the war, especially regarding the use of artillery. As early as July 10, 1941, German field formations near Zhitomir were forced back by artillery fire alone.[8] The Spanish 'Blue Division' found its ammunition dumps under accurate artillery fire during the siege of Leningrad.[9] German officers complained about the effect of Russian fire on their troops and the danger of 'rolling' Russian artillery barrages, describing the enemy artillery as "good" and "unpleasantly effective."[10]

The Russian use of artillery became better as the war progressed. Surprise artillery attacks were first seen in 1943.[11] Offensives were supported by massive concentrations of gunfire. During the Russian breakout from the Kitska bridgehead in Romania, for example, the Germans were subjected to a 90-minute bombardment by 4,000 guns and mortars.[12] Russian offensives were spearheaded by artillery concentrations of 200 guns and mortars per half-mile of front, plus 150-300 rocket batteries. Not surprisingly, the resulting bombardments were described as "veritable drumfires of destruction."[13]

This massive deployment of artillery and the improvements in its coordination would not have been possible without good communications and the transport capacity to supply the guns with shells. Communications are essential to ensure that artillery fire begins (and ends) at precisely the planned time, as premature or delayed fire might dislocate the entire attack. As much as the Soviet artillery improved during the war, much of its 'method' consisted of lining up the guns hub to hub and firing together, concentrating mostly on frontline rather than rear-area targets. This suggests that the communications system had not reached a high level of proficiency by the end of the war. Nor were the artillery's problems limited to communications difficulties. Shells were often hand-carried to the gun sites, even in 1945. If artillery operations were then hardly perfect in 1945, without Lend-Lease communications gear and transport the Soviet artillery would have been in much worse shape.

Artillery represents only one facet of operations, although it was the mainstay of the Red Army. The army proved adept at combining many methods for the attack, such as mass, mobility, camouflage and deception, and skillful initiation.[14] If Soviet attacks seemed needlessly mass-oriented at times, this was because early war experience taught them that narrow breakthroughs did not lead to decisive victories.[15] Reconnaissance became a highly developed art. Minefield clearing also developed into a fairly exact science (although occasionally accomplished by sending a large mass of people through the minefield). Russian artillery would sometimes simulate a preparatory bombardment to locate German batteries and then shift fire to rear positions to lure German infantry from their dugouts. Such coordinated operations would have been impossible without a reasonably functional communications system.[16] Given that system's known shortcomings, it is questionable how well it would have functioned without foreign assistance.

Infiltration techniques were practiced by small units on a broad scale. Soviet formations would penetrate the thin German lines at night and dig in, undiscovered until morning. Feints would be made to distract attention from the operation, and reinforcements would move up quickly so that the bridgehead could be used as a jumping-off point for an offensive. The Germans feared these methods from the beginning and concluded that the Russians had an "unparalleled genius" for infiltration. In 1942, for example, Soviet units near Kursk quietly slipped behind the front and bested the Germans in a series of mobile engagements.[17] Lend-Lease cannot be credited for the success of these operations, but their coordination and reinforcement required sophisticated command and control resources, which American aid supplied.

Lend-Lease substantially aided offensive capacity, both at the tactical and strategic levels. The Red Army's defensive skills were good enough, however, to suggest that the Soviet Union survived without any outside assistance. Barely two weeks after the invasion, for example, half a German tank regiment was destroyed by cleverly hidden Russian tanks at Zhlobin.[18] The Germans described the Russians as "masters at digging in and erecting field fortifications."[19] The Russians demonstrated both ability and willingness to fight in cities where their communications problems, if not their casualties, were less. Cities were prepared for defense with careful attention to every detail.[20] Russian units could hold their positions obstinately, causing heavy losses and avoiding enemy capture of valuable equipment. On September 10, 1941, German General Franz Halder lamented that not a single intact T-34 tank had been captured.[21]

Soviet defensive preparations were as skilled and methodical as terrain and materiel permitted. At Kursk, for example, the Red Army constructed 40-kilometer-deep defensive zones with 'interlocking' defense and closely linked fire-points. The defense was based on hidden gun emplacements, switch positions, dummy installations to confuse attackers, minefields, antitank ditches, and alternate dug-in positions for both tanks and artillery. A typical battalion defense area had a front of 2-2.5 and a depth of 1.5-2 kilometers and contained strong points of companies and reserves united by a common system of fire and obstacles, organized for perimeter defense. Mobile obstacle-setting units were available in case of a German breakthrough. Tanks and guns in defensive positions were used to neutralize German armor. Zones of similar depth were constructed near Lake Balaton, Hungary, in 1945. These *pakfronts* were designed to take the 'sting' out of the German attack rather than stop it.[22]

That the Soviet forces proved methodical and resourceful in their approach to defense does not suggest that Lend-Lease was irrelevant. The immense concentration of force at Kursk required a good deal of coordination to function properly, not to mention transport resources adequate for assembly and supply. Nevertheless, the Red Army obviously had many skills and capacities that had nothing whatsoever to do with foreign aid. Consider, for example, the mounted band of Cossack troops who, armed with nothing but Molotov cocktails and small arms, destroyed most of a German tank unit during the Battle of Moscow (1941).[23] Even early in the war German officers were impressed by Soviet resourcefulness, a view reinforced by the Russian capture of a large quantity of secret German rocket material early in the war.[24] The Russians were so good at concealment, both in defense and attack, that the Nazis called them "masters of camouflage."[25]

The resourcefulness of many Soviet commanders and soldiers reinforces the view that survival, if not victory, would have been probable without aid. Soviet troops were less inhibited by terrain, time of day, or weather, than were the Germans. The German High Command was dumbfounded that the Red Army pressed its offensives despite appalling weather and terrain (although Russian history should have suggested this possibility to the Germans). Ironically, the German army twice wreaked havoc in the West by attacking through supposedly unsuitable terrain (the Ardennes), yet it failed to anticipate the ability of Russian forces to fight in places as diverse as Stalingrad and the Pripet Marshes. The peasant background of many Russian soldiers actually helped them survive, and the lack of specialized equipment was sometimes no hindrance.[26]

The Soviet forces were especially adept at river crossings. In 1943 Russian troops, while under fire, built a submerged infantry bridge across the Dnieper. Neither natural nor German obstacles deterred them. Russian engineers entered the cold Dniester river in early 1944 and neutralized German mines. In this context, it should be noted that Lend-Lease aid included over 4,000 amphibious vehicles, and that in 1944 alone the Soviet Union requested over a thousand "Duck" two-and-one-half-ton amphibians.[27]

Night fighting was a forte of the Russians. On December 3, 1941, Russian forces destroyed an entire battalion of the Fifth Grossdeutschland Division in a night attack. Night river crossings and harassing attacks were common. A whole series of successful after-dark attacks was made during the fighting in the Stalingrad 'corridor' in 1942. While it may be that winter fighting came naturally to the Russians, their successes can perhaps better be attributed to the reforms made after the Russo-Finnish war, which led to more systematic planning for such warfare, including the successful employment of ski troops.[28] Lend-Lease clothing and cloth shipments helped the Red Army somewhat during the cold months, as did food supplies (especially given the high individual calorie requirements in cold weather).

Tactical success had to become typical, rather than exceptional, for the Red Army to defeat the Nazis. Much depended on the courage and motivation of the individual soldier. Some motivational methods were crude, such as the use of N.K.V.D. troops and minefields in the rear to prevent unauthorized retreats. Vigorous measures, however, were necessary. Tactical misbehavior, such as *tankboyazn* (fear of tanks) or careless assembly on vulnerable high ground, was a chronic problem.[29] The Soviet command's massive, precisely orchestrated offensives were designed to shift the psychological balance to the Soviet forces by controlling and minimizing errors, forcing rapid advances, and dislocating German morale by controlling the *temp nastupleniia* (tempo of battle). The severity of the attack, spearheaded by Russian infantrymen (sometimes drunk) and supported by formidable artillery bombardments, sometimes drove some defenders insane; at the very least, it required great 'fire-discipline' to survive in the face of these orgasmic onslaughts.[30] These operations derived much of their "punch" from Lend-Lease transport, communications gear, and aviation fuels.

How did Lend-Lease affect the actual fighting, the operations of the small unit, and the situation of the individual soldier? In terms of combat equipment, very little, excepting aircraft (and, to a much lesser extent, tanks). The exact uses of the small quantities of combat equipment are not known because Western observers were not permitted to view the Red Army in action.[31] Western armored vehicles, not a particularly popular item to the Russians, constituted only a relatively small part of the Russian tank park, and were rarely noted by the Germans.[32]

Yet no matter how resourceful the lower-level Soviet officer became during the war, or how tenacious and heroic the defense was, without adequate communications and resupply the ability of the Red Army to sustain combat would have been severely curtailed. In the absence of Lend-Lease transport and communications gear, the Red Army would have had to rely on flexible, small-unit defense, rather than on high-concentration offensive warfare. Soviet NCOs and junior officers would have had to develop greater initiative and receive more freedom of action from the higher command. Did Lend-Lease, by encouraging aggressive, large-scale offensive operations, actually increase losses? The evidence suggests that this is a doubtful, although interesting, proposition. It is also entirely entirely academic, as the Soviet state showed its determination to expel the invader, regardless of cost, long before foreign aid became a reality.

NOTES

1. M. G. Saunders, *The Soviet Navy* (New York: Praeger, 1958), 74.

2. F. W. von Mellenthin, *Panzer Battles: A Study of the Employment of Armor in the Second World War* (Norman: University of Oklahoma Press, 1971), 283.

3. Gerald R. Kleinfeld and Lewis A. Tambs, *Hitler's Spanish Legion: The Blue Division in Russia* (Carbondale: Southern Illinois University Press, 1979), 249. The Waffen SS, for example, suffered disproportionate casualties on the Eastern Front. George H. Stein, *The Waffen SS: Hitler's Elite Guard at War, 1939-1945* (Ithaca: Cornell University Press, 1977), 134.

4. Graham H. Turbiville, "Paradrop at the Bukrin Bridgehead: An Account of the Soviet Dnieper Airborne Operation," *Military Review* 56 (December 1976), 26-40. Lest we exaggerate the Soviet parafumble, operations at Crete and Arnhem showed that other combatants had not mastered the intricate problems of executing, coordinating, and reinforcing parachute attacks. The disaster has been

blamed on "general inexperience." Richard Armstrong, "The Bukrin Drop: Limits to Creativity," Military Affairs 50 (July 1986), 127-132.

5. S. M. Shtemenko, *The Last Six Months: Russia's Final Battles with Hitler's Armies in World War II* (Garden City, NY: Doubleday, 1977), 11-14.

6. Heinz Guderian, *Panzer Leader* (New York: E. P. Dutton, 1952), 234-35; *World War II German Military Studies: A Collection of 213 Special Reports on the Second World War Prepared by Former Officers of the Wehrmacht for the United States Army*, 24 vols. (New York: Garland Publishing, 1974), 18:(VII)(D)(10), 125.

7. Franz Halder, *The Halder Diaries: The Private War Journals of Colonel General Franz Halder* (Boulder, CO: Westview Press, 1976), 2:1065; Mellenthin, *Panzer Battles,* 263; *German Military Studies,* 16:(VII)(C)(1), 91.

8. John Erickson, *The Road to Stalingrad* (London: Harper & Row, 1975), 169.

9. Kleinfeld and Tambs, Hitler's *Spanish Legion,* 221.

10. *German Military Studies,* 18:(VII)(D)(11), 19-20; Halder, *Halder Diaries,* 2:1145-46, 1150, 1166, 1188.

11. Ivan Parotkin, ed., *The Battle of Kursk* (Moscow: Progress Publishers, 1974), 208; *The Great March of Liberation* (Moscow: Progress Publishers, 1972), 96.

12. *Great March of Liberation,* 96.

13. Mellenthin, *Panzer Battles,* 299, 301.

14. German Army, "Fuehrung, Kampf und Kraftquellen der Roten Armee," lecture prepared by Foreign Armies East, 15 January 1945 (translated as "Leadership in the Red Army and the Sources of Power and Combat," U.S. Army Intelligence translation), 9.

15. Ibid., 6-7.

16. *German Military Studies,* 18:(VII)(D)(10), 25, 68-73, 163; *Great March of Liberation,* 97; Graham D. Vernon, "Soviet Combat Operations in World War II: Lessons for Today?" *Military Review* 60 (April 1980), 43.

17. *German Military Studies,* 16:(VII)(C)(1), 64; ibid., 18:(VII)(D)(10), 6, 103-6; Halder, *Halder Diaries,* 2:1352, 1369; Mellenthin, *Panzer Battles,* 185, 296.

18. *German Military Studies,* 18:(VII)(D)(10), 91-92.

19. Mellenthin, *Panzer Battles,* 162.

20. Ibid., 205; *Great March of Liberation,* 20; "Report of Trip to USSR by General Connolly," Modern Military Records Division, R.G. 334, Box 5, Subject File October 1943-October 1945, N.A., 3-4.

21. *German Military Studies,* 18:(VII)(D)(10), 4; Halder, *Halder Diaries,* 2:125; Augustin L. Guillaume, *The German Russian War* (London: War Office, 1956), 4.

22. *German Military Studies,* 16:(VII)(C)(2), 37; Parotkin, *Battle of Kursk,* 162-63; *Great March of Liberation,* 192-240; Mellenthin, *Panzer Battles,* 229-30.

23. Guillaume, *German Russian War,* 249.

24. *German Military Studies,* 18:(VII)(D)(10), 4; Halder, *Halder Diaries,* 2:1009, 1013.

25. Halder, *Halder Diaries,* 2:1079; Mellenthin, *Panzer Battles,* 219; Parotkin, *Battle of Kursk,* 167.

26. Halder, *Halder Diaries,* 2:1250; Mellenthin, *Panzer Battles,* 205.

27. Halder, *Halder Diaries,* 2:1156; Spalding to Protocol Committee (July 25, 1944), Modern Military Records Division, R.G. 334, Box 13, Subject File October 1943-October 1945, Folder September 1943 through 31 July 1944, N.A.; Mellenthin, *Panzer Battles,* 246; *Great March of Liberation,* 77; Robert Huhn Jones, *The Roads to Russia: United States Lend-Lease to the Soviet Union* (Norman: University of Oklahoma Press, 1969), 280-82.

28. *German Military Studies,* 16:(VII)(C)(1), 75, 185; ibid., 18:(VII)(D)(10), 39-40; Guillaume, *German Russian War,* 9; *Great March of Liberation,* 20; Kleinfeld and Tambs, *Hitler's Spanish Legion,* 112; Mellenthin, *Panzer Battles,* 196.

29. *German Military Studies,* 18:(VII)(D)(11), 21; Erickson, *Road to Stalingrad,* 143, 153; Mellenthin, *Panzer Battles,* 101; Vernon, "Soviet Combat Operations," 296.

30. Mellenthin, *Panzer Battles,* 247; Kleinfeld and Tambs, *Hitler's Spanish Legion,* 90, 106, 134; *Great March of Liberation,* 119; Eugene D. Betit, "The Soviet Manchurian Campaign, August 1945: Prototype for the Soviet Offensive," *Military Review* 56 (May 1976), 68.

31. "Report of Trip to USSR by General Connolly," 24.

32. Halder, *Halder Diaries,* 2:1386, 1441; Nikolai V. Sivachev and Nikolai N. Yakovlev, *Russia and the United States: U.S.-Soviet Relations from the Soviet Point of View* (Chicago: University of Chicago Press, 1979), 210.

10

Conclusion

On May 8, 1945, a Nazi delegation headed by Field-Marshal Wilhelm Keitel arrived at the headquarters of the first Byelorussian front to ratify the German surrender to the Allies. The fighting in Europe was over. Three months later the Soviet Union declared war against Japan, but for all intents and purposes its struggle for survival had successfully ended.

Soviet losses had been immense. Westerners were only dimly aware of the level of suffering in the Soviet Union during the war. Ironically, this was in part due to Soviet propaganda. The effort to lionize party leadership and prove the superiority of the system obscured the sheer chaos, suffering, and poverty caused or exacerbated by the war. Soviet authors do, of course, acknowledge serious problems and military and civilian mistakes during the war, but they do not dwell on the details. References in recent years to the heavy loss of life, while frequent, are often made as part of diplomatic or political-ideological statements which have limited appeal to Western audiences.[1] Specific criticisms of Stalin's wartime leadership are, however, becoming more frequent.[2]

Obviously, too much emphasis on domestic problems by Soviet historians might lead readers to conclude that the Soviet economy did not recover as quickly or as completely as most Soviet sources suggest. There is, in any event, much evidence that the economic situation remained poor, and that living conditions and food availability were minimal throughout the war. More significantly, in respect to this study, if the Soviet wartime economy was weaker than usually portrayed, then the relative value of Lend-Lease would be greater. Did some Soviet writers exaggerate the already-substantial wartime economic accomplishments in order to glorify the leadership and downplay foreign aid? Ironically, in doing so, they also downplayed the travails and even the achievements of the Soviet people.

Those travails were great indeed. The Nazi invaders leveled almost 32,000 industrial enterprises, including more than 900 factories. A hundred thousand farms and almost 3,000 machine-tractor stations were destroyed. The rail system lost 40,000 miles of rails and more than 4,000 stations. Twenty-five million people were made homeless as the war consumed some 70,000 villages, more than 1,700 towns, and 6 million buildings.[3]

The bare facts, however, tell only a small part of the story. During the war food and clothing were difficult to obtain, except through the expensive free legal market or the even more costly black market. At a time when the urban industrial worker earned about $60 per month, shoes, for example, cost $50 if bought legally, and ten times that amount on the black market. Meat, about $5-$10 per pound legally, was scarce; even on the black market a single roast goose cost as much as $150. Staples such as coal, oil, and penicillin were in short supply or unavailable.[4] Agricultural recovery in recaptured areas was necessarily slow. In the reconquered Ukraine there was "no evidence of the existence of any mechanical farm machinery, work animals, or dairy herds."[5] Local shortages were further exacerbated by transportation problems.[6] In April 1942 the American ambassador reported that "malnutrition was evident among the children and old people," while another envoy concluded in December that meager rations "unquestionably are resulting in general malnutrition verging on starvation." Molotov conceded that "nonessential" workers were "living on [a] restricted ration, one which provides them with a bare subsistence level of nutrition."[7]

By a mixture of skill, determination, courage, and foreign assistance, the Soviet Union survived. Industries moved to safer locales, private gardens sprouted, the *oblast* system was reorganized to simplify administration, and incentives were introduced in factories. "All for the front," (*vce dlia fronta*) was far more than simply a propagandistic device; it expressed the willingness of the state and its subjects to do whatever was necessary to expel the enemy.[8] "None can gainsay the gigantic effort by Soviet society nor gloss over the grievous hurts inflicted upon it, that numbing catalogue of bestiality, devastation, hardship and illimitable private griefs."[9] In the words of Winston Churchill, the Soviet Union, of which he was hardly an uncritical admirer, was an ally "which had broken the Germany Army as no other nation would have done."[10]

To recapitulate, given that the Soviet Union accomplished much and suffered greatly, to what extent did Lend-Lease contribute to victory or perhaps alleviate the suffering? Most judgments on this subject are at best generalizations and at worst misstatements borne of ideology or ignorance. As established earlier, American intelligence did not know what was done with Lend-Lease supplies and did not particularly care; its efforts were understandably focused on the enemy. War Plans Division officers tried to assess the use of various weapons, but as these officers did not influence American policy toward the U.S.S.R., they had no way of obtaining information.[11] The Soviet Union was rarely pressed for information and almost never volunteered it.

Stalin did suggest at Yalta that the absence of Lend-Lease might have "deferred" the victory, but he did not speculate for how long, or precisely why.[12] More recent Soviet spokesmen agree that Lend-Lease "positively influenced" the Soviet Union in its struggle and express gratitude for "moral and material" support during the war, but they generally argue that it did not "play a substantial role."[13] According to Mikhail Gorbachev, the "Soviet people remember the material help which the Allies gave this country. Though it was not as great as the West is wont to claim, we are nevertheless grateful for that help and regard it as a symbol of cooperation."[14] Western efforts to interpret Soviet generalizations have not always succeeded. The author of one of the best histories of the diplomacy surrounding Lend-Lease buttresses his conclusion regarding the importance of American aid by stating that "by Stalin's own admission, about two thirds of all major industrial enterprises had been rebuilt with equipment or technical assistance from the United States."[15] The "two thirds," however, includes 1920s and 1930s imports from the United States.[16]

Wartime American views, as has been suggested earlier, were a combination of ignorance, certainty that the aid was important, and a feeling that Lend-Lease was sufficiently important to justify the drain on the United States. As late as 1944 General Marshall, despite his earlier reservations about diverting U.S. Army supplies, concluded that "Lend-Lease food and transport played a vital role in Red Army successes, as did combat aircraft. If Russia suddenly lost Lend-Lease, the Nazis could probably still defeat her."[17] Ambassador Standley and General Walsh independently concluded that Lend-Lease was essential for the survival of the Red Army, but Harry Hopkins, speaking at a conference in Moscow shortly after the surrender, diplomatically suggested that "we had never believed that our Lend-Lease help had been the chief factor in the Soviet defeat of Hitler on the eastern front. This had been done by the heroism and blood of the Russian Army."[18] His position was echoed by the Foreign Economic Administration.[19] Contrasting these wartime opinions is academically interesting but substantively useless, as none was supported by meaningful data.

Germany was sufficiently concerned about the effect of aid to the Soviet Union on its own chances for success to attempt to disrupt the convoys bound for Murmansk and Archangel. These operations, successful in 1942 and 1943, absorbed much of the German navy's surface strength. Superficially this indicates that Germany was very much worried about Lend-Lease. Just before the ill-fated Christmas Day, 1943, anticonvoy raid, Admiral Doenitz informed the squadron that "The very considerable amount of war material that a convoy of some twenty ships could carry would add materially to Russia's offensive strength" and referred to these shipments as "attempting to frustrate the heroic struggle of our Eastern Armies." These operations did not take place, however, solely due to concern about Lend-Lease. The navy wanted to mute criticism that it was not contributing to the war effort. In addition, by 1942 there were few areas where German vessels could operate. In fact, in 1941 Doenitz (when still in charge of German submarines) protested the diversion of naval units to Norway, which he regarded as a "subsidiary" theatre.[20]

Did the Soviet Union survive because of Lend-Lease? No. Clearly the greatest crisis occurred in 1941-42, before Lend-Lease aid arrived in quantity. The military and economic situation of the country remained precarious, however, until the very end. Despite an economic recovery that must be judged impressive given the circumstances, the Soviet Union could barely feed its people, its transport system remained only marginally adequate to move troops, industrial goods, and staples, and its labor resources were very limited. In such an environment, every item of aid became important, perhaps more so than it would have been in the equipment-rich environment of U.S. and British forces.

Can that importance be measured or appraised meaningfully? Lend-Lease changed the way the war was fought, because American (and British) aid significantly increased Soviet offensive capacity. Transport and communications gear enabled the Red Army to concentrate rapidly and coordinate more effectively, which in turn increased the chance of launching successful surprise attacks. Lend-Lease helped ease the manpower situation, thereby making more men available for recruitment into the army.

Perhaps the Soviet Union would have fought offensively even without Lend-Lease. There is little evidence that Stalin ever planned for completely defensive warfare. The Red Army could not, however, have attacked as well or as often as it did without Lend-Lease. In 1943-45 the Soviet forces were almost continuously on the offensive, not blindly moving forward along a single predetermined axis, but using enhanced mobility and communications to orchestrate a series of attacks. The Germans were confused and disoriented by the Red Army's ability to reconcentrate rapidly and to mass troops and equipment at crucial points, none of which would have been possible without foreign transport and communications equipment.

As the frequency and momentum of the Soviet offensives in 1943-45 deprived the Wehrmacht of time, flexibility, and breathing space, the Nazis were delayed in deploying such promising weapons as the V-2 rocket, the four models of jet aircraft under development by war's end, and the Type XX and Type XXI submarines. By 1944 German resources were spread so thinly that shifting of large forces to win a decisive victory in any one theatre of war was probably impossible. While this was largely due to the size and power of the Red Army, there was more to it than that. If the Red Army had been unable to mount vigorous, frequent, overwhelming offensives throughout 1943-45, Germany could have significantly reduced its forces on the Eastern Front. Allied margins of victory in Sicily, Italy proper, the Battle of the Atlantic, and the air battles over Europe were often small. Any major shift of military resources by Germany would have had devastating results for the United Nations forces. It is for this reason that the argument occasionally made that Allied aid somehow contributed to the Soviet conquest of Eastern Europe fails. Lend-Lease did help Soviet forces advance; without this advance, however, the Germans might have been able to foil the Anglo-American liberation of Western Europe.

In the absence of Lend-Lease, the Anglo-American forces in other theatres of war would have been larger, and their timetable might have been advanced. Lend-Lease unquestionably hampered the Allied effort in North Africa and to a lesser extent in the Pacific, and it ironically delayed the opening of the "Second Front" so often demanded by the Soviet government. The single greatest problem was the shortage of shipping space. Shipping requirements for invasion preparations were immense. A single American division, for example, needed more than 120,000 tons to carry it and its supplies.[21] The 'run' to Soviet ports was a direct drain on shipping, as losses on the Murmansk route reached 20 percent.[22] These problems reached a head in 1942, when the Anglo-American invasion of North Africa (Torch) could only take place by diverting shipping from Lend-Lease and from preparations for the invasion of France. Even Churchill, a vigorous proponent of Torch, considered a postponement to avoid reducing shipments to the Soviet Union. Plans for a larger-scale invasion of North Africa (Super Gymnast) were abandoned because the Murmansk convoys would have had to be eliminated.[23] The British and American governments opposed, and the Soviet government discouraged, proposals to shift shipping space from Lend-Lease to preparations for the "Second Front."[24]

Support for aid to the U.S.S.R. was not unanimous. The cost, especially early in the war, was high. General Marshall's irritation with the Soviet ambassador's requests for scarce items in early 1942 led him to complain that "Mr. Oumansky will take everything we own."[25] The fulfillment of Soviet Lend-Lease obligations led the War Department to adopt a training schedule which gave U.S. forces only 50 percent of all needed equipment by June 30, 1942.[26] Aircraft were in particularly short supply in 1941-42.[27] Expressions of frustration and irritation with the Soviet Lend-Lease program were frequent.[28] In 1941-42 American officials feared that Lend-Lease supplies would fall into German hands if (as was expected) the U.S.S.R. lost the war.[29] Nor did the American military willingly part with valuable materiel which appeared to be useful mostly for postwar reconstruction.[30]

If all this were not enough, another complaint arose, primarily after the war. Roosevelt's critics charged that somehow the United States had handed over Eastern Europe to the Soviet Union. As a minor corollary to this "Yalta betrayal" theory, some of these critics charged that Lend-Lease had helped the Soviet Union in this. If Lend-Lease increased the offensive capacity of the Red Army, the argument goes, the Soviet forces finished the war somewhat further west than might otherwise have been the case.

As suggested earlier, this formulation ignores the question of whether Soviet weakness might have helped Nazi Germany to oppose the Anglo-American forces more effectively. But even if the critics are right in their contention, should, or could, the U.S. government have withheld Lend-Lease to prevent Soviet influence over Eastern Europe? Whether this would have had any effect late in the war beyond increasing Soviet hostility and suspicions is doubtful. Certainly by the time of the Yalta conference (February 4-11, 1945) the power of the Soviet forces was such that their advance through Eastern Europe could not have been stopped. More importantly, Lend-Lease hardly made up for the costs and suffering which the Soviet Union incurred during the war. No American city ever looked like Stalingrad, which, aside from one undamaged suburb, contained one habitable building at the end of the fighting there.[31] In addition, the Soviet Union did provide some "reverse Lend-Lease" aid, although this was necessarily quite small (table 46). Dollar figures on this topic meant little, as the Russians rarely furnished such data.[32] Recent Soviet valuations of wartime aid to America run into the billions, an estimate that cannot be taken seriously.[33] (Soviet and

American officials strenuously denied during the war that the Red Army had furnished brothels for American personnel.)[34]

In any event, criticisms of the Lend-Lease program for its positive effect on Soviet military operations ignore the reasons for which the program was established. Ambassador Harriman, for example, was "not at all anxious about [the Red Army] going too far. The farther they go, the more I like it." The United States should "give and give and give, with no expectation of any return, with no thought of a *quid pro quo.*"[35] Roosevelt demanded in 1942 that "all material promised to the Soviets" be shipped, "regardless of the effect . . . on any part of our war program."[36] Lend-Lease was designed "to strengthen our first line of defense while we could build up our woefully weak military forces."[37] America's aid was a tool to save Russia from defeat and "enable her to inflict telling blows on the enemy," and, just in case, to forestall the possibility that Hitler and Stalin might settle their differences, thereby making Britain's position untenable.[38]

In the context of these broad goals, was Soviet Lend-Lease a successful program for the United States? Yes. Critics who question Lend-Lease due to its drain on American forces and the advantages which accrued to the Soviet Union ignore both the basic American wartime strategy and the *zeitgeist,* the urgency and near panic regarding apparent Nazi invincibility from the spring of 1940 to El Alamein and Stalingrad. The United States used its powerful economy and relative invulnerability to aid its allies, an economic strategy that absorbed about 15 percent of American wartime expenditures.[39]

As much as American military leaders wanted to close with the enemy in battle, most recognized the wisdom of the Lend-Lease approach. In 1942 the army considered the need to aid the Russian front second only to the problem of organizing for worldwide force dispersion.[40] The War Department was willing to do everything possible to help the Soviet Union as long as preparations for the "Second Front" were not impeded.[41] The Joint U.S. Strategy Committee considered the Eastern Front important enough to justify not only as much Lend-Lease as possible, but also the planning of a diversionary offensive to relieve pressure on the Soviet forces.[42] Some military officers were sensitive to political advantages of programs like Lend-Lease and the ill-fated shuttle-bombing bases.[43] The military leadership recommended major increases in aircraft shipments to the Soviet Union early in the war, even though American combat units had to be "pared to the bare minimum" as a result.[44]

The American military demonstrated a less generous attitude during periods in 1941-42 when shortages were endemic and became parsimonious again as requirements for the Normandy invasion increased. The Soviet Union's demand for materiel did not slacken, however, until the very end. Perhaps the Soviet government's requests were a bit more tinged with desperation in 1941, when national survival was in doubt. While Soviet writers almost invariably note how small aid was at that critical time, they never speculate on the psychological boost given by Western assistance.[45] Whether or how much this affected the morale of the Soviet people may never be known.

Is there a clear connection between the increasing aid flow in 1943-45 and Red Army victories? Yes. It is true that Soviet sources argue that most shortages had disappeared, Soviet production had grown enough to support major military operations, and Lend-Lease was too small to have had much effect. The fact remains that many shortages were not eliminated, production had not completely recovered, and Lend-Lease aid fulfilled precisely the greatest needs. Lend-Lease supplies represented an important and possibly critical margin in many areas of the economy and also helped augment production.

Western technology proved a more subtle qualitative boost to the Soviet Union toward war's end. Britain and America furnished data in many areas, especially in the realm of industrial production. The fact that sophisticated equipment could quite legitimately be analyzed in the Soviet Union in order to improve domestic products as well as aid the war effort caused more anguish in high Allied military circles than the shipment of large quantities of less advanced devices.[46] American officers rejected any tripartite information-sharing agreements because the Soviet Union could then demand access to British-American technology transfers. This reticence was partly due to fears that the Germans might capture sensitive technology, but it was probably more a result of the virtually absolute refusal by Soviet authorities to supply data in return.[47] Nevertheless, the Americans rarely refused information about operational equipment.

Little information is available about Soviet use of foreign technology or about the actual use of Lend-Lease supplies. Soviet sources have to be reticent because accurate information about the use of Western goods would give away much information about the Soviet logistical system. The most visible statistics, Western figures for shipments and deliveries, do not account for waste and mismanagement.

Imprecise as they may be, the numbers nevertheless do indicate what the Soviet Union thought it needed to win the war. The intensity and frequency of Soviet requests for supplies and the angry rejection of all proposals to reduce aid bely the suggestion that Lend-Lease aid was a frivolous, irrelevant, or minor part of the Soviet arsenal. The Soviet forces benefitted from imported combat equipment, communications gear, and transportation machinery. Army and people alike were helped by Lend-Lease food supplies, raw materials, industrial machinery, and finished goods of all types. In one way or another, all these forms of aid helped the Soviet Union relieve the perilously tight manpower situation. The Soviet Union most likely would have survived without Lend-Lease, and eventually the United Nations would have prevailed. but the war would have been longer, the alliance less firm, and the victory possibly less complete.

NOTES

1. A discussion of this problem is beyond the purview of this chapter. The separation between what Westerners like to call "objective analysis" and

"ideological argument" does not exist within a system like Marxism in which 'Marxist analysis' is, by definition, perfectly objective.

2. The recent publication of previously omitted chapters of Marshal Zhukov's memoirs is an example of this. It remains to be seen whether *glasnost'* will lead to more specific information or simply continue the debunking of Stalin's wartime role.

3. Col Karoly Janza, "The Material and War Economic Power of the Soviet Union," *Honved* (December 1949; U.S. Army Intelligence translation), 5; M. S. Zinich, "Stankostroenie i tiazheloe mashinostroenin SSSR v 1941-1945 gg.," *Voprosy Istorii* (No. 5, 1973), 32-46; Oleg Rzheshevsky, *World War II: Myths and the Realities* (Moscow: Progress Publishers, 1984), 191. The educational system also suffered from the war. Students enrolled in the various institutions of higher education *(vuzy)* declined in number from 812,000 in the year before the war to 227,000 in the 1942-43 academic year. The prewar level was not regained during the war. William Moskoff, "Soviet Higher Education Policy during World War II," *Soviet Studies* 38 (July 1986), 409. The level of human suffering during the war is difficult to grasp. Homeless children fleeing the Nazis sang the following song: "Oh, I'll die, I'll die; I'll be buried and no one will know where my grave is." Margaret K. Stolee, "Homeless Children in the U.S.S.R., 1917-1957," *Soviet Studies* 40 (January 1988), 76-77. Not all the suffering was caused by the Germans. The *Gulag* did not cease to operate during the war. For one of the best recent reviews of the effects of the *Gulag,* see Steven Rosefielde, "Incriminating Evidence: Excess Deaths and Forced Labour under Stalin: A Final Reply to Critics," *Soviet Studies* 39 (April 1987), 292-313.

4. Wendell L. Willkie, *One World* (New York: Simon and Schuster, 1943), 59; Kemp Tolley, *Caviar and Commissars: The Experiences of a U.S. Naval Officer in Stalin's Russia* (Annapolis: Naval Institute Press, 1983), 270; Memoirs, Wellington Alexander Samouce Papers, U.S. Army Military History Institute, Carlisle Barracks, PA, Archives, 57; William H. Standley and Arthur A. Ageton, *Admiral Ambassador to Russia* (Chicago: Henry Regnery, 1955), 130, 165; Memoirs, Samouce Papers, 27, 28, 31; Oral history, John A. Heintges Papers, U.S. Army Military History Institute, Carlisle Barracks, PA, Archives, 423ff;. letter dated June 10, 1943, in "Letters from Iran," Olaf Osnes Papers, U.S. Army Military History Institute, Carlisle Barracks, PA, Archives. Toilet paper was also scarce.

5. Memoirs, Samouce Papers, 93.

6. In 1944 an American observer noticed that there were no food shortages in the Urals, indicating that perhaps the food problem was regional and related to transport problems (unless it was due to some unknown policy decision concerning distribution). Standley and Ageton, *Admiral Ambassador to Russia,* 442.

7. Ibid., 113, 162; Tolley, *Caviar and Commissars,* 270.

8. "Final Report," Robert L. Walsh Papers, U.S. Army Military History Institute, Carlisle Barracks, PA, Archives, 3; A. G. Kushnir, "Izmeneniia v administrativo-territorial'nom delenii SSSR v gody velikoi otechestvennoi voiny,"

Istoriia SSSR (No. 1, 1975), 128-32; Edward V. Rickenbacker, *Rickenbacker* (Englewood Cliffs, NJ: Prentice-Hall, 1967), 365-66, 378-79; Roger Munting, "Lend-Lease and the Soviet War Effort," *Journal of Contemporary History* 19 (1984), 499.

9. John Erickson, *The Road to Berlin: Continuing the History of Stalin's War with Germany* (Boulder, CO: Westview Press, 1983), 254.

10. Ibid., ix.

11. Ray S. Cline, *Washington Command Post: The Operations Division* (Washington, DC: Office of the Chief of Military History, 1951), 43.

12. R. W. Coakley, "Roosevelt et le pret-bail," *Revue d'Histoire de la Deuxieme Guerre Mondiale* 21 (April 1977), 96.

13. *Istoriia Vtoroi Mirovoi Voiny, 1939-1945,* vol. 8 (Moscow: Voenizdat, 1977), 387; Speech by Pavel D. Pavlov, Second Secretary of the Soviet Embassy to the United States, at the Student Conference on National Affairs, Texas A&M University, February 10, 1982. See also *Great Soviet Encyclopedia,* vol. 14 (New York: Macmillan, 1980), 351.

14. Mikhail S. Gorbachev, *A Time for Peace* (New York: Richardson & Steirman, 1985), 104-5.

15. George C. Herring, Jr., *Aid to Russia, 1941-1946: Strategy, Diplomacy, and the Origins of the Cold War* (New York: Columbia University Press, 1973), 116.

16. Antony C. Sutton, *Western Technology and Soviet Economic Development, 1930 to 1945* (Stanford: Hoover Institution Press, 1971), 3.

17. Robert Huhn Jones, *The Roads to Russia: United States Lend-Lease to the Soviet Union* (Norman: University of Oklahoma Press, 1969), 175.

18. "Lessons of ESCOM" (n.d.), Walsh Papers, 6; Standley and Ageton, *Admiral Ambassador to Russia,* 333; Robert E. Sherwood, *Roosevelt and Hopkins,* vol. 2: *From Pearl Harbor to Victory* (New York: Bantam Books, 1950 [Harper & Brothers, 1948]), 547. Britain contemplated an invasion of Norway (Operation Jupiter) to protect the convoy route. Maurice Matloff and Edwin M. Snell, *Strategic Planning for Coalition Warfare, 1941-42* (Washington, DC: Office of the Chief of Military History, 1953), 244n.

19. U.S. President, *Report on Operations of the Foreign Economic Administration* (Washington, DC: Government Printing Office, 1944), 29. The Joint Chiefs of Staff did point out that Lend-Lease composed almost all Soviet sea-going wartime trade. *Records of the Joint Chiefs of Staff: Part 1, 1942-1945: The Soviet Union* (Frederick, MD: University Publications of America, n.d.), "Postwar Economic Capabilities, Policies, and Capabilities of the U.S.S.R." (November 1, 1945), 21. Later American writers, especially veterans, were less forgiving than Hopkins about the minimization of the importance of Lend-Lease. See Harry E. Goldsworthy, "A Toast from Stalin," *Aerospace Historian* 23 (Fall 1979), 163. Emigres also emphasized the importance of aid. Victor A. Kravchenko, *I Chose Freedom: The Personal and Political Life of a Soviet Official* (New York: Charles Scribner's Sons, 1952), 401.

20. T. H. Vail Motter, *The Persian Corridor and Aid to Russia* (Washington, DC: Office of the Chief of Military History, 1952), 5; Patrick Beesly, *Very Special Intelligence: The Story of the Admiralty's Operational Intelligence Centre, 1939-1945* (London: Sphere Books, 1978), 274-77, 283, 284.

21. David Kahn, *Hitler's Spies: German Military Intelligence in World War II* (New York: Macmillan, 1978), 389.

22. U.S. Army, Assistant Chief of Staff (Intelligence), "History of the War in Eastern Europe, 1941-1945" (Synopsis) (1953), U.S. Army Military History Institute, Carlisle Barracks, PA, 158; U.S. Department of State, Protocol and Area Information Staff of the U.S.S.R. Branch of the Division of Research and Reports, "Report on War Aid Furnished by the United States to the U.S.S.R." (Foreign Economic Section, Office of Foreign Liquidation, November 28, 1945), 1, 9, 10, 14. The loss rate for all ships bound for the Soviet Union was less than 4 percent.

23. Beesly, *Very Special Intelligence,* 272; Matloff and Snell, *Strategic Planning,* 176, 310, 325; Sherwood, *Roosevelt and Hopkins,* 232; Mark A. Stoler, *The Politics of the Second Front: American Military Planning in Coalition Warfare, 1941-1943* (Westport, CT: Greenwood Press, 1977), 24.

24. Matloff and Snell, *Strategic Planning,* 119, 156, 191; Sherwood, *Roosevelt and Hopkins,* 158-59. Eisenhower saw shipments to Russia as second in importance only to maintaining existing American garrisons. Some authors definitely believe that Soviet Lend-Lease shipments delayed the "Second Front." See Jones, *Roads to Russia,* 115, 132-33.

25. Mark Skinner Watson, *Chief of Staff: Prewar Plans and Operations* (Washington, DC: Historical Division, Department of the Army, 1950), 329, 407. American officials believed that the Russians knew that many items they requested were in short supply. The U.S. Army faced a number of shortages, allegedly including machine tools, sugar, and aluminum (although this is disputed). U.S. Civilian Production Administration, *Historical Reports on War Administration: War Production Board, Documentary Publication No. 3: Minutes of the Supply Priorities and Allocations Board, September 2, 1941-January 15, 1942* (Washington, DC: Government Printing Office, 1946), 21-22, 30, 48, 60, 66; Margaret Saxton Haltom, "Discrepancies in the Lend-Lease Program," *Southern Quarterly* 4 (July 1966), 454.

26. Robert W. Coakley and Richard M. Leighton, *Global Logistics and Strategy, 1943-1945* (Washington, DC: Office of the Chief of Military History, 1968), 99. It would be inaccurate to suggest that U.S. forces were neglected. *The United States at War: Development and Administration of the War Program by the Federal Government* (New York: Da Capo Press, 1972), 49. The opening of the "Second Front" led to a decrease in the supply flow to the U.S.S.R. Georgii K. Zhukov, *The Memoirs of Marshal Zhukov* (New York: Delacorte Press, 1972), 493.

27. Early Soviet aircraft requests were met by stripping "every other Allied front." Antony C. Sutton, *National Suicide: Military Aid to the Soviet Union* (New Rochelle, NY: Arlington House, 1973), 82. About 14 percent of all aircraft

produced in America between October 1941 and June 1942 went to the Soviet Union, but Britain received almost three times as many planes during this period. Wesley Frank Craven and James Lea Cate, eds., *The Army Air Forces in World War II,* vol. 6, *Men and Planes* (Chicago: University of Chicago Press, 1955), 403. In 1943 the Soviet Union received 100 percent of all aircraft allocated to it by the United States, a greater percentage than either Britain or the USAAF. Craven and Cate, *Men and Planes,* 412. By March 1944 about 5 percent of all U.S. aircraft had gone to the Soviet Union, and 18.7 percent to Lend-Lease as a whole. Memoirs, Oleg Pantuhoff Papers, U.S. Army Military History Institute, Carlisle Barracks, PA, 669. Despite increasing production, however, munitions were inadequate to provide for both Lend-Lease and early, large-scale invasions. Cline, *Washington Command Post,* 60, 145, 148-49, 176.

28. Standley and Ageton, *Admiral Ambassador to Russia,* 240; Walsh to Major General V. N. Evstigneev, 25 July 1944, Walsh Papers; Matloff and Snell, *Strategic Planning,* 205.

29. In August 1941 Navy Secretary Frank Knox bet Treasury Secretary Henry Morgenthau that Petrograd [sic], Moscow, Kiev, and Odessa would be in German hands by September 1. In late November Roosevelt still thought that Moscow would fall. Paul Kesaris, ed., *The Presidential Diaries of Henry Morgenthau, Jr.* (Frederick, MD: University Publications of America, 1981), Book 4:951-52, 1020.

30. "History of the U.S. Military Mission to Moscow," Modern Military Records Division, R.G. 165, Box 146, OPD 336TS, N.A., 353. The U.S. government was well aware that some Lend-Lease materiel was for postwar use. *Joint Chiefs of Staff,* "Memorandum for Information No. 121: Strategy and Policy: Can America and Russia Cooperate?" (August 22, 1943), 3-5, 11, 14.

31. "History of the U.S. Military Mission," 3-4; I V. Kovalev, *Transport v Velikoi Otechestvennoi Voine (1941-1945)* (Moscow: Izdatel'stvo Nauka, 1981), 279.

32. Valuations of other countries' reverse Lend-Lease may also be questionable. Haltom, "Discrepancies," 448. Most came from the Commonwealth, which contributed an estimated $7.5 billion. Hessell Duncan Hall, *North American Supply* (London: Her Majesty's Stationery Office, 1955), 432.

33. M. M. Kozlov, ed., *Velikaia Otechestvennaia Voina, 1941-1945: Entsiklopediia* (Moscow: Soviet Encyclopedia, 1983), 400. The authors suggested a value of $7 billion due to scarcity of materials delivered. U.S. wartime estimates amounted to $2.2 million, mostly repairs made in Russian ports. U.S. President, *Reports to Congress on Lend-Lease Operations,* nos. 21 and 22 (Washington, DC: Government Printing Office, 1945-1946), no. 21: 19; no. 22: 20; U.S. President, *Foreign Economic Administration,* 34; John Frederick Gardner, "The Lend-Lease Program of World War II: Analysis and Appraisal" (Ph.D. dissertation, University of Pittsburgh, 1946), 92.

34. U.S. authorities suggested to Washington that censorship might prevent such rumors. Walsh to Marshall, July 27, 1944, Walsh Papers.

35. Larry I. Bland, "Averell Harriman, the Russians, and the Origins of the Cold War in Europe, 1943-1945," *Australian Journal of Politics and History* 23 (1977), 406. Apparently American officials hoped that the United States could influence which state had the most power in postwar Europe, which they expected to be Russia. *Joint Chiefs of Staff*, "Memorandum for Information No. 121: Strategy and Policy: Can America and Russia Cooperate?" (August 22, 1943), 3-5, 11, 14.

36. "History of the U.S. Military Mission," 352-53.

37. Gardner, "Lend-Lease Program," 6. There was, in some government circles, genuine emotional support for the Soviet Union as well.

38. *Joint Chiefs of Staff*, "Revision of Policy with Relation to Russia: Memo, Commanding General, USMM, USSR" (April 16, 1945), 1; *O.S.S./State Department Intelligence and Research Reports, Part 6: The Soviet Union, 1941-1949* (Frederick, MD: University Publications of America, 1977), "Russia and Germany in Winter and Spring: Allied Policy and a Separate Peace" (December 23, 1941), 3-5; U.S. President, *Foreign Economic Administration*, 30; Watson, *Chief of Staff*, 407.

39. R. M. Leighton, "Les armes ou les armees: origines de la politique d' 'arsenal de la democratie,'" *Revue d'Histoire de la Deuxieme Guerre Mondiale* 17 (January 1967), 9. Not all the brass favored the "economic approach," however. Ibid., 12-13; U.S. President, *Foreign Economic Administration*, 27-29; Leland M. Goodrich and Marie J. Carroll, *Documents on American Relations*, vol. 7, *July 1944-June 1945* (Princeton: Princeton University Press, 1947), 1954.

40. Stoler, *Politics of the Second Front*, 27.

41. Matloff and Snell, *Strategic Planning*, 206.

42. Ibid., 178. The general view was that the more Germans killed by Lend-Lease recipients, the fewer there would be to face American troops. See U.S. President, *Foreign Economic Administration*, 30.

43. The commander of the American air bases in the Ukraine thought that both Lend-Lease and his own operation were designed to impress the Russians. "Personal Report of Russian Assignment" (n.d.), Walsh Papers. Whatever political advantages there were to Lend-Lease, they failed to prevent friction during negotiations if any other problem cropped up (such as the controversy concerning the Warsaw uprising). Dean Acheson, *Present at the Creation: My Years in the State Department* (New York: W. W. Norton, 1969), 85.

44. *Joint Chiefs of Staff*, "Allocation of transport Airplanes for USSR" (April 20, 1942), 2; ibid., "Allocation of Aircraft under the Russian Protocol" (October 11, 1942); Gardner, "Lend-Lease Program," 182; Richard C. Lukas, *Eagles East: The Army Air Forces and the Soviet Union, 1941-1945* (Tallahassee: Florida State University Press, 1970), 15; Leon Martel, *Lend-Lease, Loans, and the Coming of the Cold War: A Study of the Implementation of Foreign Policy* (Boulder, CO: Westview Press, 1979), 37. In 1942 the military recommended an 18 percent increase in aircraft shipments to the Soviet Union, even though this would cost the USAAF 2 bomber and 2 fighter squadrons. Marshall later pointed

out that the number of American aircraft sent to Russia was twice the number in the Ninth Air Force, America's largest.

45. See Mikhail Soloviev, *My Nine Lives in the Red Army* (New York: David McKay, 1955), 259-60. See also Kravchenko, *I Chose Freedom,* 401.

46. In fact, secrecy was more important than domestic availability for determining whether the Soviet Union could obtain various items in 1943-45. *Joint Chiefs of Staff,* "Exchange of Technical Information with the U.S.S.R." (October 1, 1943), 1; ibid., "General Policy on Release of Nan Equipment and Related Technical Information to the U.S.S.R." (November 3, 1943), 1-2.

47. Such agreements would also have conflicted with the much stricter British policy on release of classified information. *Joint Chiefs of Staff,* "Memorandum for Information No. 25: British Army Policy on the Disclosure of Military Information to British, Allied, and Neutral Personnel" (December 9, 1943), 5; ibid., "Disclosure of Technical Information to the U.S.S.R." (January 21, 1944), 2;.ibid., "Disclosure of Technical Information to the U.S.S.R." (September 17, 1943), 1-2; ibid., "Disclosure of Information other than Radar to the U.S.S.R." (September 30, 1943), 1; ibid., "Exchange of Technical Information with the U.S.S.R." (October 1, 1943), 1; ibid., "Policy on Release of Nan Equipment to the U.S.S.R." (November 3, 1943); ibid., "Disclosure of Technical Information to the U.S.S.R." (June 3, 1944), 2. Discussion of the formation of a committee to deal with lists of secret information for exchange with the U.S.S.R. can be found in the following Joint Chiefs of Staff memoranda: *Joint Chiefs of Staff,* "Disclosure of Technical Information to the U.S.S.R.: Memorandum by the British Representatives" (n.d.); ibid., "Disclosure of Technical Information to the U.S.S.R." (October 11, 1943); ibid., "Disclosure of Technical Information to the U.S.S.R." (October 12, 1943); ibid., "Disclosure of Technical Information to the U.S.S.R." (n.d.), JIC 138/3. See also William Henry Chamberlin, "American-Russian Cooperation," *Russian Review* 3 (Autumn 1943), 5. Major George R. Jordan suggested in the 1950s that the Soviet Union obtained U.S. atomic secrets through the Lend-Lease program, and that it received jewelry and perfume, and that it used American aid to suppress opposition to Stalin. George Racey Jordan, *From Major Jordan's Diaries* (New York: Harcourt, Brace, 1952), 127-28, 268.

Appendix: Tables

TABLE 1
SUMMARY OF THE LEND-LEASE PROGRAM

Item	Dollar Value
Munitions, weaponry, etc.	22,101,721,000
Petroleum products	2,316,985,000
Machinery and raw materials	9,689,047,000
Agricultural products	6,088,924,000
Total transfers	40,196,677,000
Services rendered	3,755,128,000
Total charged to foreign governments	43,951,805,000
Costs not charged	2,088,249,000
TOTAL	46,040,054,000

SOURCE: U.S. President, *Reports to Congress on Lend-Lease Operations,* no. 21 (Washington, DC: Government Printing Office, 1945), 37. Figures are in 1945 dollars.

TABLE 2
BRITISH AID TO THE U.S.S.R., 1941-1945

Item	Quantity	Item	Quantity
Aircraft	7,000	Ammunition (rounds)	4.6 million
Tanks	5,000	Tin (tons)	31,420
Cable (mi.)	6,135	Copper (tons)	44,800
Camouflage net (mtrs)	2,000,000	Graphite (tons)	3,700
Industrial diamonds (£)	1,400,000	Aluminum (tons)	36,000

SOURCE: Antony C. Sutton, *Western Technology and Soviet Economic Development, 1945 to 1965* (Stanford: Hoover Institution Press, 1973), 11-12; Winston Churchill, *Triumph and Tragedy* (New York: Bantam Books, 1974 [Boston: Houghton Mifflin, 1974], 465, 467. Some miscellaneous items are not listed in the table.

TABLE 3
VOLUME OF MUNITIONS PRODUCED
(Billions of dollars)

Country	1935-39	1940	1941	1942	1943	1944
United States	1.5	1.5	4.5	20	38	42
Canada	-	-	0.5	1	1.5	1.5
Britain	2.5	3.5	6.5	9	11	11
U.S.S.R.	8	5	8.5	11.5	14	16
Germany	12	6	6	8.5	13.5	17
Japan	2	1	2	3	4.5	6

SOURCE: Hessel Duncan Hall, *North American Supply* (London: Her Majesty's Stationery Office, 1955), 421.

TABLE 4
INDEX OF COMBAT MUNITIONS PRODUCTION
(1944 = 100)

Country	1938	1939	1940	1941	1942	1943	1944
United States	2	2	5	11	47	91	100
Canada	0	2	6	27	73	102	100
Britain	4	10	34	59	83	100	100
U.S.S.R.	12	20	30	53	71	87	100
Germany	16	20	35	35	51	80	100
Japan	8	10	16	32	49	72	100

SOURCE: Hessel Duncan Hall, *North American Supply* (London: Her Majesty's Stationery Office, 1955), 420.

153

TABLE 5
LEND-LEASE EXPORTS BY REGION

Country/Region	Aid.(Billions of dollars)	Aid (% of total)
United Kingdom	13.8	43
Soviet Union	9.5	29
Africa and Middle East	3.4	10
China and India	2.4	7
Australia and New Zealand	1.5	5

SOURCE: U.S. President, *Reports to Congress on Lend-Lease Operations,* no. 21 (Washington, DC: Government Printing Office, 1945), 14, 18.

TABLE 6
AID TO BRITAIN AND THE U.S.S.R. IN CERTAIN CATEGORIES
(Percent of aggregate value of category received)

Item	Great. Britain	Soviet Union
Munitions	39	26
Petroleum products	74	5
Machinery and raw materials	45	29
Agricultural products	58	28

SOURCE: U.S. President, *Reports to Congress on Lend-Lease Operations,* no. 21 (Washington, DC: Government Printing Office, 1945), 39

TABLE 7
COMPARISON OF LEND-LEASE AID GIVEN TO BRITAIN AND THE U.S.S.R.
(Aid given in billions of dollars)

Category	British Empire		United Kingdom		Soviet Union	
	Aid	%	Aid	%	Aid	%
Exports	20.8	64	13.8	43	9.5	29
Aid	30.3	69	20.8	45	10.8	25
Aid adjusted for 'reverse' Lend-Lease	24	61	16.4	42	10.8	28
Aid adjusted for "reverse" Lend-Lease and British contributions to the Soviet Union	22.3	58	*15.3	*40	12.5	32

SOURCE: Table calculated on the basis of data in U.S. President, *Reports to Congress on Lend-Lease Operations, nos. 21 and 22* (Washington, DC: Government Printing Office, 1945-1946) no. 21: 11, 14, 18, 19, 22, 24; no. 22: 17-18, 20, 22, 28-29; Roger Munting, "Lend-Lease and the Soviet War Effort," *Journal of Contemporary History* 19 (1984), 507.

* Estimated.

155

TABLE 8
VALUE OF U.S. SHIPMENTS TO THE U.S.S.R.
(Billions of dollars)

Item	By 6/30/45	By end of program
Machinery & raw materials	2.945	3.040
Ordnance & ammunition	.811	.815
Aircraft & parts	1.602	1.652
Tanks & parts	.478	.478
Motor vehicles & parts	1.324	1.411
Watercraft	.284	.296
Petroleum products	.102	.111
Agricultural products	1.616	1.676

SOURCE: U.S. President, *Reports to Congress on Lend-Lease Operations,* no. 21 (Washington, DC: Government Printing Office, 1945), 19, 24, 25.

TABLE 9
SHIPMENTS FROM THE WESTERN HEMISPHERE TO THE U.S.S.R.
June 20, 1941-September 20, 1945
(Tons)

Item	Tonnage	Distribution (%)
R.R. transportation equipment	524,756	2
Trucks & other vehicles	2,565,730	13
Metals	4,004,094	20
Chemicals & explosives	1,285,496	6
Petroleum products	2,367,063	12
Machinery & equipment	1,397,590	7
Food	5,000,774	25
Other U.S. supplies	1,367,864	7
U.S. TOTAL	18,513,367	92
Canadian/British supplies	1,084,886	5
Other sources	2,793	0
SUBTOTAL	19,601,046	97
British petroleum shipments replaced with U.S. petroleum	621,826	3
TOTAL WESTERN HEMISPHERE	20,222,872	100

SOURCE: U.S. Department of State, Protocol and Area Information Staff of the U.S.S.R. Branch of the Division of Research and Reports, "Report on War Aid Furnished by the United States to the U.S.S.R." (Foreign Economic Section, Office of Foreign Liquidation, November 28, 1945), 8.

TABLE 10
DELIVERIES OF MILITARY EQUIPMENT TO THE U.S.S.R.

Item	Quantity	Item	Quantity
A. Aviation*			
Pursuit planes	9,438	Light bombers	2,908
Medium bombers	862	Heavy bombers	1
Cargo planes	708	Observation planes	19
Trainers	82	Navy patrol planes	**185
Landing mats (1,000 sq. ft.)	55,297	Link trainers	11
Total U.S. Aircraft	14,203		
B. Military Vehicles and Transport			
Tanks	6,196	SP guns	1,807
Misc. armored vehicles	4,158	Ordnance service	2,293
Jeeps	43,728	Amphibious jeeps	3,510
Trucks	363,080	Motorcycles	32,200
Trailers	105	Truck engines	2,000
Track-laying tractors	7,570	Railroad cars	11,075
Locomotives	1,966	Bridges	28
Construction equipment ($)	10,792,000	Portable pipelines	5
C. Other Weaponry			
AA guns	7,509	Rocket launchers	3,000
Antitank guns	35	Submachine guns	112,293
Pistols	11,500	Mortars	30
Smoke pots	1,423,000	Explosives (tons)	***325,784
D. Communications and Electronics			
Radio stations	35,089	Radio receivers	5,899
Radio locators & direction finders	1,053	Radio altimeters & beacons	601
Radio compasses	800	Other radio equipment ($)	7,526,000
Field telephones	380,135	Teletype ($)	4,470,000
Other telephone/telegraph ($)	14,419,000	Field telephone wire (mi.)	956,688
Flashlights	100,000		

SOURCE: U.S. Department of State, Protocol and Area Information Staff of the U.S.S.R. Branch
of the Division of Research and Reports, "Report on War Aid Furnished by the
United States to the U.S.S.R." (Foreign Economic Section, Office of Foreign
Liquidation, November 28, 1945), 18, 20,23-25; "History of the US Military
Mission to Moscow," Modern Military Records Division, R.G. 165, Box 146, OPD
336TS, N.A., 353-55.
* These figures do not include retransfers between Lend-Lease recipients.
** Sometimes given as 186, but one was lost in an accident before export. Wesley
Frank Craven and James Lea Cate, eds., *The Army Air Forces in World War II*,
vol. 6, *Men and Planes* (Chicago: University of Chicago Press, 1955), 405. Some
sources omit these planes altogether. See also Irving Brinton Holley, Jr., *Buying
Aircraft: Materiel Procurement for the Army Air Forces* (Washington, DC: Office
of the Chief of Military History, 1964).
*** Includes 10,048 tons from Britain.

TABLE 11
DELIVERIES OF FOOD, CLOTHING, AND MEDICINE TO THE U.S.S.R.

Item	Quantity	Item	Quantity

A. Foodstuffs
(tons)

Item	Quantity	Item	Quantity
Seeds	*39,744	Dried peas and beans	239,429
Wheat, grains, cereals	953,314	Sugar	672,429
Canned and dehydrated meat	782,973	Animal fats and oils	730,902
Dairy (incl. dried milk & eggs)	247,490	Vegetable oils	517,522
Dried soups	9,373	Dried vegetables and fruits	27,759
Other foodstuffs	61,483	Concentrated juices	1,799

B. Clothing

Item	Quantity	Item	Quantity
Cloth (1,000 yds)	162,811	Other textiles ($)	14,881,000
Leather (tons)	46,161	Boots (prs)	14,793,000
Boots & shoes ($)	4,378,000	Belts	2,577,000
Other clothing ($)	12,841,000	Buttons ($)	1,598,000
Relief supplies (tons)	19,155		

C. Miscellaneous related items

Item	Quantity	Item	Quantity
Soap (tons)	9,102	Red Cross aid (tons)	7,690
Red Cross aid ($)	22,859,979	Total war relief (tons)	31,094

SOURCE: U.S. Department of State, Protocol and Area Information Staff of the U.S.S.R.
Branch of the Division of Research and Reports, "Report on War Aid Furnished
by the United States to the U.S.S.R." (Foreign Economic Section, Office of Foreign
Liquidation, November 28, 1945), 21, 22, 28, 30.
* Includes seeds shipped by Russian War Relief, Inc.

TABLE 12
SHIPS AND EQUIPMENT DELIVERED TO THE U.S.S.R.

Item	Quantity	Item	Quantity
A. Noncombat vessels			
Dry cargo vessels	*102	Ocean-going tankers	*20
Tugs and icebreakers	23	Other tankers	9
Steam schooners	1	Pneumatic floats	2,398
Motor launches	1	Floating repair shops	2
B. Combat vessels			
Sub chasers	103	Torpedo boats	**199
Minesweepers	77	Escort vessels	28
Landing craft	62	Cargo barges	6
C. Equipment			
Marine engines	7,725	Outboard motors	2,150
Parts & equipment ($)	13,047,000	3" and 5" guns	617
Submarine batteries	40	Small-calibre guns	4,099

SOURCE: U.S. Department of State, Protocol and Area Information Staff of the U.S.S.R. Branch of the Division of Research and Reports, "Report on War Aid Furnished by the United States to the U.S.S.R." (Foreign Economic Section, Office of Foreign Liquidation, November 28, 1945), 22.

* Some of these were returned in 1945.
** Twentyfour of these came from Britain.

TABLE 13
MACHINERY AND EQUIPMENT DELIVERED TO THE U.S.S.R.
($)

Item	Value
Engines, turbines, compressors, pumps	39,287,000
Crushing, mixing, conveying gear	9,699,000
Winches, cranes, derricks, hoists	33,732,000
Industrial trucks & tractors	7,213,000
Electrical	215,829,000
Metalworking equipment	143,632,000
Machine tools	358,722,000
Agricultural (except tractors)	751,000
Mining, excavating, drilling	50,819,000
Scientific & professional instruments	10,469,000
Industrial & mining locomotives	2,788,000
Bearings	25,813,000
Textile, woodworking, & paper machinery	2,629,000
Tire & rubber machinery	8,790,000
Petroleum-refining equipment	43,138,000
Cartridge-manufacturing lines	29,855,000
Specialized equipment for glass, chemical, & gas production	15,808,000
Automatic signal system	10,880,000
Power boilers	15,970,000
Agricultural tractors	2,773,000
Hand tools, nonpowered	2,810,000
Fan & blower equipment	3,702,000
SUBTOTAL	$ 1,035,109,000
Other equipment and machinery	24,124,000
TOTAL	1,059,233,000

SOURCE: U.S. Department of State, Protocol and Area Information Staff of the
U.S.S.R. Branch of the Division of Research and Reports, "Report on
War Aid Furnished by the United States to the U.S.S.R." (Foreign
Economic Section, Office of Foreign Liquidation, November 28, 1945),
22-24.

160

TABLE 14
MATERIALS AND PRODUCTS DELIVERED TO THE U.S.S.R.
(Tons)

A. Metals

R.R. rails and accessories	687,491
Steel plate, all types	525,369
Aircraft steel	233,170
Pipe and tubing	278,952
Wheels and axles	121,840
Steel wire	160,745
Polished drill rods and tool steel	55,861
Other finished steel & steel alloy	453,939
Stainless steel	12,822
Nails, tacks, barbed wire staples	61,338
TOTAL STEEL PRODUCTS	2,591,527
Ferro-silicon	7,174
Other ferro-alloys	8,884
Copper: base alloys	339,599
Copper: cable, wire, electrolytic, tubes, etc.	76,340
Aluminum: ingots, wire bars, fabricated, foil	261,311
Zinc	54,826
Lead	20,139
Other metals (magnesium, nickel, nichrome, monel, tin, babbitt, cadmium, cerium, cobalt, mercury, sodium)	29,448
TOTAL FERRO-ALLOYS AND NONFERROUS METALS	797,721
Cable (except field telephone wire)	3,254
Molybdenum concentrates	18,379
Pig iron and misc. ores	8,213
Metal products	30,898
TOTAL MISC. METALS AND PRODUCTS	60,744
GRAND TOTAL, METALS	3,449,992

161

TABLE 14 (continued)

Item	Quantity
B. Petroleum, chemicals, and other products	
Aviation gas over 99 octane	1,163,463
Other aviation gas	156,824
Gas blending agents	834,427
Automotive gas	267,088
Fuel oil	287,262
Lubricating oil and grease	111,676
Additives	4,788
Other petroleum products	23,645
TOTAL PETROLEUM	*2,849,173
Caustic soda	98,210
Other basic inorganic products	23,696
Ethyl alcohol	379,742
Toluol	113,884
Phenol	38,549
Methanol	23,774
Glycerine	21,544
Hexamine (Urotropine)	14,381
Ethylene glycol	13,800
Acetone	12,264
Other basic organic products	53,958
Paints, pigments, etc.	11,552
Plastics	7,539
Misc. chemicals	7,529
TOTAL CHEMICAL	*820,422
Fish nets	1,395
Cordage & twine	15,356
Rubber & products	11,078
Abrasives	17,711
Graphite powder	3,017
Paper & products	15,515
TOTAL - OTHER PRODUCTS	64,072
TOTAL	3,733,667
GRAND TOTAL	7,183,659

SOURCE: U.S. Department of State, Protocol and Area Information Staff of the U.S.S.R. Branch of the Division of Research and Reports, "Report on War Aid Furnished by the United States to the U.S.S.R." (Foreign Economic Section, Office of Foreign Liquidation, November 28, 1945), 24-28.
* Includes British supplies later replaced by the United States.

TABLE 15

DELIVERIES TO THE U.S.S.R. NOT INVENTORIED BY WEIGHT

($ unless otherwise specified)

Item	Quantity
Insulated wire and cable	58,913,000
Other wire products	2,401,000
Other metal products	1,719,000
Compressed and liquefied gas	67,000
Misc. rubber	34,117,000
Abrasive products	15,497,000
Graphite and carbon electrodes	20,933,000
Misc. graphite products	1,532,000
Misc. paper products	58,000
Photographic film, paper, materials	1,876,000
Asbestos material	483,000
Other products	858,000
Webbing (1,000 yds)	53,803
Tarpaulin (1,000 yds)	13,528
Shock absorber cord (1,000 yds)	166
Tires (units)	3,681,000
Tubes (units)	3,676,000

SOURCE: U.S. Department of State, Protocol and Area Information Staff of the U.S.S.R. Branch of the Division of Research and Reports, "Report on War Aid Furnished by the United States to the U.S.S.R." (Foreign Economic Section, Office of Foreign Liquidation, November 28, 1945), 25-28. Numbers of tires and tubes taken from Patrick Beesly, *Very Special Intelligence: The Story of the Admiralty's Operational Intelligence Centre, 1939-1945* (London: Sphere Books, 1978), 173-74.

163

TABLE 16
SHIPMENTS FROM THE WESTERN HEMISPHERE TO THE U.S.S.R. BY ROUTE, JUNE, 22, 1941-
SEPTEMBER 20, 1945
(millions of tons)

Year	Persian Gulf		Far East		North Russia		Black Sea		Soviet Arctic		TOTAL
	Tons	%	Tons	%	Tons	%	Tons	%	Tons	%	Tons
1941	.02	3.7	.22	53.6	.17	42.7	.00	0.0	.00	0.0	.41
1942	.79	28.8	.82	29.9	1.06	38.7	.00	0.0	.07	2.6	2.74
1943	1.80	33.5	2.68	49.8	.76	14.2	.00	0.0	.13	2.5	5.37
1944	2.00	28.8	3.19	45.8	1.63	23.4	.00	0.0	.14	2.0	6.96
1945	.05	1.2	2.33	56.6	.81	19.8	.76	18.5	.16	3.9	4.11
Total	4.66	23.8	9.24	47.1	4.43	22.7	.76	3.9	.50	2.5	19.59
Lost	4		0		7		0		0		2
En route, 9/20/45	0		1		0		1		0		1

SOURCE: U.S. Department of State, Protocol and Area Information Staff of the U.S.S.R. Branch
of the Division of Research and Reports, "Report on War Aid Furnished by the
United States to the U.S.S.R." (Foreign Economic Section, Office of Foreign
Liquidation, November 28, 1945), 29; T. H. Vail Motter, *The Persian Corridor and
Aid to Russia* (Washington, DC: Office of the Chief of Military History, 1952),
481-83. These figures include all shipments from the Western Hemisphere,
including 538,000 tons lost en route (most in 1942), and 622,000 tons shipped
from British refineries in Abadan, Iran, and replaced by allocations from U.S.
supplies for British use. They exclude equipment shipped to shuttle-bombing
bases and Persian Gulf Command and later transferred to Soviet officials after
those commands were disbanded.

TABLE 17
ANNUAL LEND-LEASE SHIPMENTS TO THE U.S.S.R.
(Thousands of tons and percentage of Soviet total)

Year	Tons	%	Year	Tons	%
1941	404	2	1944	6,964	36
1942	2,747	14	1945	4,115	21
1943	5,370	27	TOTAL	19,600	100

SOURCE: Albert Seaton, *The Russo-German War, 1941-1945* (New York: Praeger, 1972), 588.

TABLE 18
QUARTERLY LEND-LEASE SHIPMENTS TO THE U.S.S.R.
(Millions of dollars/percentage of total Lend-Lease)

Year	I	II	III	IV	TOTAL
1941	-	-	-	1/0	1
1942	168/24	342/30	358/27	493/28	1,361
1943	584/31	536/22	858/27	988/34	2,966
1944	806/29	859/27	949/34	829/33	3,443
1945	680/33	713/35	315/28	-	1,708

SOURCE: U.S. President, *Reports to Congress on Lend-Lease Operations,* no. 21 (Washington, DC: Government Printing Office, 1945), 41.

TABLE 19
MONTHLY U. S. LEND-LEASE SHIPMENTS TO THE U.S.S.R.
(Rounded to the nearest million dollars)

Yr	Jan	Feb	Mar	Apr	May	June	July	Aug	Sept	Oct	Nov	Dec
41												1
42	15	55	97	164	70	110	103	150	102	128	191	167
43	174	193	217	217	178	141	234	316	308	263	345	380
44	313	232	260	254	315	286	335	305	205	258	299	268
45	212	229	223	241	336	130						

SOURCE: U.S. President, *Reports to Congress on Lend-Lease Operations*, nos. 13 and 20 (Washington, DC: Government Printing Office, 1943-45), no. 13, 57; no. 20, 41.

TABLE 20
U.S., BRITISH, AND CANADIAN ACTUAL DELIVERIES TO THE U.S.S.R. FROM THE WESTERN HEMISPHERE
(Thousands of tons)

Yr	Jan	Feb	Mar	Apr	May	June	July	Aug	Sept	Oct	Nov	Dec
41						3	31	109	43	69	62	71
42	78	88	164	268	148	155	195	216	202	256	185	264
43	235	199	276	371	382	309	376	511	572	483	628	704
44	668	373	379	454	619	586	698	629	650	610	633	633
45	455	487	545	605	850	368	457	226				

SOURCE: U.S. Department of State, Protocol and Area Information Staff of the U.S.S.R. Branch of the Division of Research and Reports, "Report on War Aid Furnished by the United States to the U.S.S.R." (Foreign Economic Section, Office of Foreign Liquidation, November 28, 1945), 15; T. H. Vail Motter, *The Persian Corridor and Aid to Russia* (Washington, DC: Office of the Chief of Military History, 1952), 481-83. Figures do not include 622,000 tons of petroleum products from the Abadan refineries or equipment transferred from the Persian Corridor command or the U.S. Army Air Forces Eastern Command. About 93,000 tons were still en route as of September 20, 1945.

TABLE 21
AIRCRAFT DELIVERIES VIA ALSIB ROUTE

Year	Jan	Feb	Mar	Apr	May	June	July	Aug	Sept	Oct	Nov	Dec	TOTAL
1942									50	43	48	7	148
1943	70	102	101	169	188	329	320	296	295	204	317	271	2,662
1944	244	178	298	318	246	292	304	403	350	93	192	246	3,164
1945	310	216	386	309	257	337	157	30					2,002

SOURCE: Wesley Frank Craven and James Lea Cate, eds., *The Army Air Forces in World War I,* vol. 7, *Services around the World* (Chicago: University of Chicago Press, 1958), 159, 165.

TABLE 22
U.S. SHIPMENTS TO THE U.S.S.R., 1941

A. Shipments, June 22, 1941-September 30, 1941
(Tons)

Vehicles	1,764	Metals	5,214	Chem. & Expl.	5,293
Petroleum	145,996	Machinery	17,758	Food	4,388
Other U.S.	2,938	Non-U.S.	2,793	TOTAL	186,144

B. Shipments to February, 1942
(thousands of dollars)

Ordnance & ammunition	5,092	Tanks & motor vehicles	20,335
Aircraft & parts	26,223	Machinery & parts	15,374
Agricultural products	3,241	TOTAL	70,265

SOURCE: U.S. President, *Reports to Congress on Lend-Lease* Operations, no. 15 (Washington DC: Government Printing Office, 1944), 25; U.S. Department of State, Protocol and Area Information Staff of the U.S.S.R. Branch of the Division of Research and Reports, "Report on War Aid Furnished by the United States to the U.S.S.R." (Foreign Economic Section, Office of Foreign Liquidation, November 28, 1945), 1.

TABLE 23
LEND-LEASE TO THE U.S.S.R., MARCH 1942-FEBRUARY 1943
(Thousands of dollars)

Ordnance & ammunition	262,372	Agricultural products	263,917
Aircraft & parts	347,342	Naval gear	17,081
Tanks & motor vehicles	355,673	Machinery & parts	387,763
	TOTAL	1,634,148	

SOURCE: U.S. President, *Reports to Congress on Lend-Lease Operations,* no. 15 (Washington, DC: Government Printing Office, 1944), 25.

TABLE 24
SHIPMENTS TO THE USSR, OCTOBER 1, 1941 - JUNE 30, 1942
(Tons)

Metals	475,468	Petroleum products	188,154
Food	341,641	Trucks & vehicles	239,864
Chemicals & explosives	62,728	Machinery & equipment	33,255
	Other U.S. supplies	85,371	
	US TOTAL	1,426,481	
	British & Canadian supplies	164,204	
	SUBTOTAL	1,590,685	
	LESS: losses en route	343,504	
	TOTAL	1,247,181	

SOURCE: U.S. Department of State, Protocol and Area Information Staff of the U.S.S.R. Branch of the Division of Research and Reports, "Report on War Aid Furnished by the United States to the U.S.S.R." (Foreign Economic Section, Office of Foreign Liquidation, November 28, 1945), 2. Twenty-two ships discharged cargo in Britain to await the safety of darkness on the Northern route.

TABLE 25
AMERICAN ESTIMATE OF SOVIET FORCES, JUNE 1942

Division type	Number	Av. strength	Tanks	Planes	Nazi divisions
Infantry	250	10,000			217
Cavalry	49	6,600			34
Armor (brig.)	51	3,500	150		38
Air	42	4,000		100-160	32

SOURCE: *Records of the Joint Chiefs of Staff: Part 1, 1942-1945: The Soviet Union* (Frederick, MD: University Publications of America, n.d.), "Memorandum for Information: Russian Capabilities" (June 1, 1942), 1. This table indicates what American analysts thought at this time about the Eastern Front. Red Army infantry divisions rarely had 10,000 men, and the armored brigades usually only had 65 machines at best. Wehrmacht divisions in 1942 had a TOE strength of 14,000-17,000 men, depending on type.

TABLE 26
LEND-LEASE SHIPMENTS TO THE U.S.S.R., MARCH 1943-FEBRUARY 1944
(Thousands of dollars)

Ordnance & ammunition	364,752	Watercraft	102,732
Aircraft & parts	488,428	Machinery & parts	938,312
Tanks & motor vehicles	542,125	Agricultural products	598,637
TOTAL			3,034,986

SOURCE: U.S. President, *Reports to Congress on Lend-Lease Operations,* no. 15 (Washington, DC: Government Printing Office, 1944), 25.

TABLE 27
PLANNED VS. ACTUAL SHIPMENTS, JULY-SEPTEMBER 1943
(Thousands of tons)

Month	Atlantic			Pacific			Total		
	Target	Actual	%	Target	Actual	%	Target	Actual	%
July	200.0	141.3	70.7	225.0	234.8	104.3	425.0	376.1	88.5
August	200.0	198.5	99.2	225.0	326.0	144.9	425.0	524.5	123.4
September	200.0	221.5	110.8	225.0	349.6	155.4	425.0	571.1	134.4
TOTAL	600.0	561.3	93.5	675.0	910.4	134.9	1275.0	1471.7	115.4

SOURCE: *Records of the Joint Chiefs of Staff: Part 1, 1942-1945: The Soviet Union* (Frederick, MD: University Publications of America, n.d.), "Convoys to North Russia" (October 2, 1943), 1.

TABLE 28
LEND-LEASE SHIPMENTS TO THE U.S.S.R., JULY 1942-JUNE 1943
(Thousands of dollars)

Ordnance & ammunition	266,684
Aircraft & parts	400,362
Tanks & parts	101,135
Watercraft	52,281
Motor vehicles & parts	256,120
Machinery & parts	524,295
Agricultural products	330,200
TOTAL	1,931,077

SOURCE: U.S. President, *Reports to Congress on Lend-Lease Operations,* no. 16 (Washington, DC: Government Printing Office, 1944), 30.

TABLE 29
SHIPMENTS TO THE U.S.S.R., JULY 1, 1942-JUNE 30, 1943
(Tons)

Metals	839,877
Petroleum products	239,107
Food	1,117,517
Trucks & vehicles	502,307
Chemicals & explosives	203,130
Machinery & equipment	188,684
Other U.S. supplies	266,309
U.S. TOTAL	3,356,931
Canadian & British supplies	63,885
TOTAL	3,420,816

SOURCE: U.S. Department of State, Protocol and Area Information
Staff of the U.S.S.R. Branch of the Division of Research
and Reports, "Report on War Aid Furnished by the United
States to the U.S.S.R." (Foreign Economic Section, Office
of Foreign Liquidation, November 28, 1945), 3.

TABLE 30
DELIVERIES TO THE U.S.S.R., OCTOBER 1, 1941-JULY 31, 1943

Item	Arrived	In transit
Pursuit planes	1,555	230
Bombers	1,901	17
Other aircraft	191	1
Tanks	2,411	---
AA guns	481	1,590
Small arms	109,609	---
Other guns	3,065	5,500
Motor vehicles	120,330	23,115
Field telephones	141,843	31,151
Field telephone wire (mi.)	538,383	30,371
Explosives (tons)	93,701	34,716
Leather (tons)	19,340	2,605
Boots (1,000 pr)	3,144	497,000
Cloth (1,000 yds)	6,886	1,853
Non-ferrous metals & products (tons)	270,620	31,743
Ferro-alloys (tons)	4,736	199
Steel & products (tons)	786,218	121,031
Petroleum products (tons)	360,142	138,481
Chemicals (tons)	120,688	21,792

SOURCE: "Status of the Soviet Aid Program as of July 31, 1943," Modern Military Records Division, R.G. 334, Box 13, File October 1943 to October 1945, N.A., 1-4.
American and Soviet small arms were not compatible. All major Soviet small arms were 7.62-mm. The most significant American weapons were .30-, .303-, .45- and .50-calibre, with some 7.92-mm and 9-mm weapons produced as well.

171

TABLE 31
SOVIET PRODUCTION, 1943

Item	Unit of measure	Jan-June	July-Dec	TOTAL
Electricity	Kwh, millions	14.9	17.4	32.3
Coal	Tons, millions	42.8	50.3	93.1
Petroleum	" "	8.8	9.2	18.0
Smelting iron	" "	2.5	3.1	5.6
Steel	" "	3.8	4.7	8.5
Rolled metal	" "		3.1	
Iron ore	" "		4.9	
Coke	" "		4.5	
Cement	" "		.7	
Aluminum	Tons, thousands		37.1	
Tanks	Thousands	11.2	12.9	24.1
Aircraft	Thousands	13.7	16.1	29.8
Guns over 76 mm	Thousands	23.8	24.6	48.4
Machine tools	Thousands		13.4	
Infantry weapons	Millions		2.8	
Shells & mines	Millions		120.1	
Nat'l production	Percentage of 1940			90.0
Freight transport	" " " "			61.0
Agr. economy	" " " "			37.0
Grain harvests	" " " "			31.0

SOURCE: *Istoriia Vtoroi Mirovoi Voiny, 1939-1945,* vol. 8 (Moscow: Voenizdat, 1977), 355, 357, Appendix.

TABLE 32
LEND-LEASE SHIPMENTS TO THE U.S.S.R., JULY 1943-JUNE 1944
(Thousands of dollars)

Ordnance & ammunition	398,502
Aircraft & parts	659,732
Tanks & parts	134,795
Motor vehicles & parts	500,607
Industrial machinery & parts	1,094,483
Agricultural products	610,114
Naval equipment	91,519
TOTAL	3,489,752

SOURCE: U.S. President, *Reports to Congress on Lend-Lease Operations,* no. 16 (Washington, DC: Government Printing Office, 1944), 30.

TABLE 33
WESTERN HEMISPHERE SHIPMENTS TO THE U.S.S.R., JULY 1943-JUNE 1944
(Tons)

R.R. transportation equipment		78,922
Metals		1,133,889
Petroleum		
Western Hemisphere	500,311	
from Abadan	186,322	
		686,633
Food		1,953,057
Trucks & vehicles		831,417
Chemicals & explosives		501,927
Machinery & equipment		546,001
Other U.S. supplies		529,724
TOTAL		6,261,570
Canadian & British supplies		370,040
TOTAL		6,631,610

SOURCE: U.S. Department of State, Protocol and Area Information Staff of the U.S.S.R. Branch of the Division of Research and Reports, "Report on War Aid Furnished by the United States to the U.S.S.R." (Foreign Economic Section, Office of Foreign Liquidation, November 28, 1945), 4.

TABLE 34
WESTERN HEMISPHERE SHIPMENTS TO THE U.S.S.R., JULY 1, 1944-MAY 12, 1945
(Tons)

R.R. transportation equipment	398,428	Trucks & vehicles	722,702
Petroleum; North America	838,589	Chemicals & explosives	447,268
Petroleum: Abadan	435,504	Machinery & equipment	532,722
Metals	1,257,308	Food	1,296,258
		Other U.S. supplies	347,761
US TOTAL	6,276,539		
		British/Canadian supplies	355,678
	TOTAL	6,632,217	

SOURCE: U.S. Department of State, Protocol and Area Information Staff of the U.S.S.R. Branch of the Division of Research and Reports, "Report on War Aid Furnished by the United States to the U.S.S.R." (Foreign Economic Section, Office of Foreign Liquidation, November 28, 1945), 5.

TABLE 35
SHIPMENTS FROM THE WESTERN HEMISPHERE TO THE U.S.S.R. AFTER THE SURRENDER OF GERMANY
(Tons)

Item	May 13-Sept. 2, 1945	Sept. 2-20, 1945	Total
R.R. transportation equipment	46,346	1,061	47,407
Trucks & vehicles	266,691	984	267,675
Metals	279,106	13,233	292,339
Chemicals & explosives	64,723	428	65,151
Petroleum products	454,906	0	454,906
Machinery & equipment	76,763	2,407	79,170
Food	289,185	8,808	297,993
Other US supplies	131,272	4,489	135,761
US TOTAL	1,608,992	31,410	1,640,402
Canadian and British supplies	117,712	13,366	131,078
TOTAL	1,726,703	44,776	1,771,480

SOURCE: U.S. Department of State, Protocol and Area Information Staff of the U.S.S.R. Branch of the Division of Research and Reports, "Report on War Aid Furnished by the United States to the U.S.S.R." (Foreign Economic Section, Office of Foreign Liquidation, November 28, 1945), 6, 7.

TABLE 36
SHIPMENTS OF CERTAIN ITEMS AS A PERCENTAGE OF SUPPLIES SENT TO THE U.S.S.R.
(Based on tonnage)

Item	Second Protocol		Third Protocol		Fourth Protocol	
	%	Rank	%	Rank	%	Rank
Agricultural products	33	1	31	1	21	1
Petroleum products	7	4	11	4	20	2
Metals	25	2	18	2	20	3
Vehicles	15	3	13	3	12	4

SOURCE: calculated data.

TABLE 37
SOVIET PER CAPITA FOOD PRODUCTION
(Kilograms per person)

Item	Pre-war	1944-45 Domestic	1944-45 Domestic plus Lend-Lease
Sugar	14.0	3.8	5.6
Meat	22.0	9.7	12.0
Vegetables	4.5	2.8	4.0
Animal fats	3.7	1.4	3.1

SOURCE: *O.S.S./State Department Intelligence and Research Reports, Part 6: The Soviet Union, 1941-1949* (Frederick, MD: University Publications of America, 1977), "Russian Import Requirements for Major Foods for the Periods 1 July 1944 to 30 June 1945, and 1 July 1945 to 30 June 1946" (July 20, 1944), 2.

TABLE 38
ESTIMATED SOVIET PRODUCTION CAPACITY
(Millions of tons)

Item	Prewar	After war loss	1945
Pig iron	17.6	5.5	9.9
Steel	20.7	9.7	17.1
Synthetic rubber	.139	.046	.1
Aluminum	.086	.043	.132
Sugar	2.8	.361	1.2
Lead	.083	.072	.139
Electricity (mw)	11.0	5.5	10.3
Grain	94.6	51.2	73.6
Coal	181.1	71.1	154.0

SOURCE: *Records of the Joint Chiefs of Staff: Part 1, 1942-1945: The Soviet Union* (Frederick, MD: University Publications of America, n.d.), "Postwar Economic Policies and Capabilities of the U.S.S.R." (November 1, 1945), 25.

TABLE 39
SUPPLIES CONSUMED BY 'AVERAGE' SOLDIER
(Long tons per soldier, per month)

Item	U.S. soldier	Soviet soldier
Rations	.0837	.042
QMO&E	.0117	.009
QM (generally)	.0045	.003
Ordnance vehicle replacement	.0081	.008
Engineering equipment	.0045	.003
Ordnance	.0036	.003
Chemicals	.0045	.002
Signal	.0045	.003
Medical	.0027	.007
Arctic fuel	.2295	.003
Medical	.0036	.003
Maintenance	.0027	.002
QM sales items	.0036	
Supply/replenish	.0387	.025
Engineering constr. materials	.1611	.056
Aircraft ammunition	.0614	.041
Other ammunition	.0782	.063
Gas, oil, grease	.1188	.130
TOTAL	1.0063	.552
TOTAL (less air supplies)	.764	.381

SOURCE: *Records of the Joint Chiefs of Staff: Part 1, 1942-1945: The Soviet Union* (Frederick, MD: University Publications of America, n.d.), "Specific Action to Be Taken under Revised Policy with Russia: Memo, CGUSMMUSSR" (April 16, 1945), 30. This data was repeated in other Military Mission reports. It is not indicated whether these were merely estimates or whether the Military Mission had unspecified sources inside the Soviet military. There is some corroborative evidence, however. The United States agreed to supply the Soviet Far Eastern forces in their war against Japan. The Soviet forces in the Far East were to consist of 1.5 million men, with 3,000 tanks and 5,000 aircraft. Two months of supplies were requested, totalling about 1 million tons. John Erickson, *The Road To Berlin: Continuing the History of Stalin's War with Germany* (Boulder, CO: Westview Press, 1983), 410. The per-soldier consumption figure indicated by these figures, about one-third of a long ton per soldier, is fairly close to the information contained in table 39. QM refers to Quartermaster; QMO&E refers to Quartermaster Organization and Equipment.

TABLE 40
AMERICAN ESTIMATE OF SOVIET DIVISIONAL STRENGTH, 1941-1942

Division type	Men	Guns	Vehicles	Misc.
Infantry, prewar	14,000-15,000			
Infantry, June 1941	17,750	253	685	6,000 horses, 58 dogs, 30 pigeons
Artillery		hundreds		
Motorized infantry	7,360			
Cavalry	6,600	150		6,640 horses

SOURCE: *Records of the Joint Chiefs of Staff: Part 1, 1942-1945: The Soviet Union* (Frederick, MD: University Publications of America, n.d.), "Russian Combat Estimate" (April 1, 1942), 32-34. This table says more about American knowledge than about Russian strength.

TABLE 41
AIRCRAFT DELIVERED TO THE U.S.S.R.

Model	Name(s)	Total delivered	Comments
P-40	Warhawk, Tomahawk, Kittyhawk	2,097	Britain exported 270 to Russia.
P-39	Airacobra	4,746	U.S.S.R. received half of all produced
P-63	Kingcobra	2,400	Represents most of production
P-47	Thunderbolt	197	
	Spitfire*	1,331	
	Hurricane*	2,952	
A-20	Boston, Havoc	2,908	
B-25	Mitchell	862	
B-24	Liberator	1 or 2	Stranded plane transferred to U.S.S.R.
B-29	Superfortress	4	Stranded; basis for Soviet bombers.
	Hampden*	46	
C-46	Commando	1	
C-47	Skytrain	862	Also produced in U.S.S.R.
O-52	Norseman	19	
AT6	Texan	82	
PBY-A	Catalina	48	
PBN	Nomad	138	

SOURCE: *Records of the Joint Chiefs of Staff: Part 1, 1942-1945: The Soviet Union* (Frederick, MD: University Publications of America, n.d.), "Air Capabilities of the U.S.S.R. Generally and by Areas" (October 31, 1945), 5; Richard C. Lukas, *Eagles East: The Army Air Forces and the Soviet Union, 1941-1945* (Tallahassee: Florida State University Press, 1970), 233-35; U.S. Department of State, Protocol and Area Information Staff of the U.S.S.R. Branch of the Division of Research and Reports, "Report on War Aid Furnished by the United States to the U.S.S.R." (Foreign Economic Section, Office of Foreign Liquidation, November 28, 1945), 18.
* British aircraft: numbers listed represented total shipped, not total that arrived.

TABLE 42
SOVIET AGRICULTURAL PRODUCTION, 1940-1945

	Grain		Meat		Milk		Aggregate value (Index)
	(Mt)	(Kg/pc)	(Mt)	(Kg/pc)	(Mt)	(Kg/pc)	
1940	96	519	5	26	34	183	100
1941	38.3	*251	*3	*16	*21	*113	62
1942	30	215	2	13	16	112	38
1943	29	233	2	14	16	132	37
1944	49	351	3	14	22	158	54
1945	47	296	3	16	26	165	60

Mt = millions of tons
Kg/pc = Kilogramms per capita, per year

SOURCE: *Great Soviet Encyclopedia,* vol. 14 (New York: Macmillan, 1980), 351; *Istoriia Vtoroi Mirovoi Voiny, 1939-1945,* vol. 8 (Moscow: Voenizdat, 1977), xiii; Erich Klinkmueller, "Some Economic Reflections on the Great Patriotic War (1941-1952)," *Soviet Union* 4 (1977), 229; "The Armored and Mechanized Troops of the Soviet Armed Forces" (n.d.) (U.S. Army Intelligence translation), U.S. Army Military History Institute, Carlisle Barracks, PA, 23.

* Estimated.

TABLE 43
SOVIET PRODUCTION, 1940-1944
(Millions of tons)

Item	1940	1941	1942	1943	Jan-June 1944
Cast iron	14.9	13.8	4.8	5.6	3.3
Steel	18.3	17.9	8.1	8.5	5.1
Coal	165.9	142.8	75.5	93.1	56.5
Elec. (billion kwh)	48.3		29.0	32.3	18.8

SOURCE: "The Armored and Mechanized Troops of the Soviet Armed Forces" (n.d.) (U.S Army Intelligence translation), U.S. Army Military History Institute, Carlisle Barracks, PA, 23; Rene Girault, "L'effort humain de l'arriere (1941-1943)," *Revue d'Histoire de la Deuxieme Guerre Mondiale* 17 (October 1967), 15-31; Erich Klinkmueller, "Some Economic Reflections on the Great Patriotic War (1941-1952)," *Soviet Union* 4 (1977), 229; *Istoriia Vtoroi Mirovoi Voiny, 1939-1945,* vol. 8 (Moscow: Voenizdat, 1977), xiii.

TABLE 44
INDEX OF INDUSTRIAL PRODUCTION BY REGION, 1940-1943

Area	1940	1942	1943
Ukraine	100	.4	1.2
"Central Zone"	100	67	85
Urals	100	280	330
Western Siberia	100	240	300

SOURCE: Rene Girault, "L'effort humain de l'arriere (1941-43)," *Revue d'Histoire de la Deuxieme Guerre Mondiale* 17 (October 1967), 19.

TABLE 45

LEND-LEASE RAW MATERIALS AS A PERCENTAGE OF SOVIET REQUIREMENTS

Item	Percentage of shortfall from estimated minimum requirements	Percentage of total supply of item
Aluminum	+100	60
Steel	45	8
Copper	+100	46
Lead	53	18
Zinc	+100	35
Tin	(exact figures unknown; imports far exceeded shortfall)	
Nickel	(exact figures unknown; imports far exceeded shortfall)	
Est. total	57	11

SOURCE: *O.S.S. State Department Intelligence and Research Reports, Part 6: The Soviet Union, 1941-1949* (Frederick, MD: University Publications of America, 1977), "Russian Capabilities and Prospects: Basic Industries" (July 11, 1944), 20, 27-38, 40-42; ibid., "Military Potential of the Soviet Union, Part III: Basic Industries" (November 25, 1942), 2-3. As many Soviet 'requirements' figures were deduced from Lend-Lease requests, these calculations give only a very general picture of the Soviet economic situation. The Soviet Union was never required to submit data to support its requests. Deane to AGWAR, "Lend-Lease to Soviet" (January 6, 1944), and Deane to AGWAR, "Soviet Aluminum and Nickel requirements" (January 14, 1944), Modern Military Records Division, RG 334, Box 13, Subject File October 1943-October 1945, Folder September 1943 through July 31, 1944, N.A.

TABLE 46
SOVIET "REVERSE LEND-LEASE" AID TO THE UNITED STATES

Item	Quantity
Chromium ore (tons)	300,000
Manganese ore (tons)	32,000
Platinum	*
Tin	*
Petroleum (tons)	1,070
Fruit (tons)	6
Vegetables (tons)	102
Meat (tons)	23
Eggs (doz.)	17,643
Railroad freight (ton-miles, est.)	9,538,050
Railroad passenger (passenger-miles, est.)	1,345,560
Truck freight (ton miles)	60,000
Labor ($)	280,000
Aggregate value (U.S. wartime est.)	$ 2,200,000

SOURCE: "History of the U.S. Military Mission to Moscow," Modern
Military Records Division, R.G. 165, Box 146, OPD 336TS,
N.A., 356-57; Oleg Rzheshevsky, *World War II: Myths and
the Realities* (Moscow: Progress Publishers, 1984), 190.
* Negligible quantities.

Bibliography

I. PRIMARY SOURCES

Public Documents

The German Army High Command, 1938-1945. Arlington, VA: University
    Publications of America, 1975.
Goodrich, Leland M., and Marie J. Carroll. *Documents on American*
    Foreign Relations. Vol. 7, *July 1944-June1945*. Princeton: Princeton
    University Press, 1947.
"History of the U.S. Military Mission to Moscow" (1945). Washington, DC.
    National Archives. Modern Military Records Division, Record
    Group 165, OPD 336TS.
Kessler, Col. Alfred A. "Report on Russian Trip." December 2, 1943.
    Washington, DC. National Archives. Modern Military Records
    Division, Record Group 18, Box 1045, File "Report on Russian
    Trip," Folder 333.1.
O.S.S./State Department Intelligence and Research Reports. Part 6: The Soviet
    Union, 1941 - 1949. Frederick, MD: Microfilm ed., University Publications
    of America, 1977.
Records of the Joint Chiefs of Staff: Part I, 1942-1945: The Soviet Union.
    Frederick, MD: Microfilm ed., University Publications of America, n.d.
U.S. Army. "Bases on the Siberian Coast." Memorandum for the Chief of Staff,
    May 5, 1941. U.S. Army Military History Institute, CarlisleBarracks, PA.
U.S. Army. "Persian Gulf Command" (1945). Pamphlet filed in Sidney
    Gruneck Papers, U.S. Army Military History Institute,
    CarlisleBarracks, PA, Archives.
U.S. Army. Assistant Chief of Staff (Intelligence). "History of the War in
    Eastern Europe, 1941-1945" (Synopsis) (1953). U.S. Army Military
    History Institute, Carlisle Barracks, PA.

U.S. Army. Assistant Chief of Staff (Intelligence). "Soviet Rear Services" (n.d.). U.S. Army Military History Institute, Carlisle Barracks, PA.

U.S. Civilian Production Administration. *Historical Reports on War Administration: War Production Board, Documentary Publication No. 1: Minutes of the Advisory Commission to the Council of National Defense,June 12, 1940, to October 22, 1941.* Washington, DC: Government Printing Office, 1946.

U.S. Civilian Production Administration. *Historical Reports on War Administration: War Production Board, Documentary Publication No. 3: Minutes of the Supply Priorities and Allocations Board, September 2, 1941-January 15, 1942.* Washington, DC: Government Printing Office, 1946.

U.S. Department of State. *Foreign Relations of the United States.* Vols. 1-4, 12. Washington, DC: Government Printing Office, 1958-1966.

U.S. Department of State. Protocol and Area Information Staff of the U.S.S.R. Branch of the Division of Research and Reports. "Report on War Aid Furnished by the United States to the U.S.S.R." Foreign Economic Section, Office of Foreign Liquidation, Department of State, November 28, 1945.

U.S. Military Mission to Moscow. October 1943-October 1945 (records).Washington, DC: National Archives. Modern Military Records Division, Record Group 334.

U.S. President. *Economic Report of the President.* Washington, DC: Government Printing Office, 1986.

U.S. President. *Report on Operations of the Foreign Economic Administration.* Washington, DC: Government Printing Office, 1944.

U.S. President. *Reports to Congress on Lend-Lease Operations.* Nos. 11, 13-16, 18-22, 33. Washington, DC: Government Printing Office, 1943-1952.

U.S. War Department. *Murmansk Railway and Kola Peninsula.* Washington, DC: Government Printing Office, 1918.

U.S.S.R. Ministry of Foreign Affairs. *Correspondence between the Chairman of the Council of Ministers of the U.S.S.R. and the Presidents of the U.S.A. and the Prime Ministers of Great Britain during the Great Patriotic War of 1941-1945.* 2 vols. London: Lawrence & Wishart, 1958.

Papers and Manuscript Collections (U.S. Army Military History Institute Archives, Carlisle Barracks, PA)

Sidney Gruneck Papers.
John A. Heintges Papers.
John W. O'Daniel Papers.
Olaf Osnes Papers.
Oleg Pantuhoff Papers.
Wellington Alexander Samouce Papers.
A. E. Schanze Papers.

Robert L. Walsh Papers.

Ivan Downs Yeaton Papers.

Diaries, Memoirs, Contemporary Accounts

Acheson, Dean. *Present at the Creation: My Years in the State Department.* New
     York: W. W. Norton, 1969.

Beesly, Patrick. *Very Special Intelligence: The Story of the Admiralty's
     Operational Intelligence Centre, 1939-1945.* London: Sphere Books, 1978.

Chuikov, V. I. *The End of the Third Reich.* Moscow: Progress Publishers,
     1978.

Churchill, Winston. *The Hinge of Fate.* 1953. New York: Bantam
     Books, 1974.

————. *Triumh and Tragedy.* 1953. New York: Bantam Books, 1975.

Davies, Joseph E. *Mission to Moscow.* London: Victor Gollancz, 1942.

Deane, John R. *The Strange Alliance: The Story of Our Efforts at Wartime
     Cooperation with Russia.* New York: Viking Press, 1947.

Galland, A., K. Ries, and R. Ahnert. *The Luftwaffe at War, 1939-1945.*
     Chicago: Henry Regnery, 1973.

Gehlen, Reinhard. *The Service: The Memoirs of General Reinhard
     Gehlen.* New York: World Publishing, 1972.

Guderian, Heinz. *Panzer Leader.* New York: E. P. Dutton, 1952.

Halder, Franz. *The Halder Diaries: The Private War Journals of Colonel General
     Franz Halder.* Boulder, CO: Westview Press, 1976.

Jordan, George Racey. *From Major Jordan's Diaries.* New York: Harcourt,
     Brace, 1952.

Kesaris, Paul, ed. *The Presidential Diaries of Henry Morgenthau, Jr.*
     Frederick, MD: University Publications of America, 1981.

Konev, I. *Year of Victory.* 1966. Moscow: Progress Publishers, 1984.
     Kravchenko, Victor A. *I Chose Freedom: The Personal and Political Life of
     a Soviet Official.* New York: Charles Scribner's Sons, 1952.

Lochner, Louis P., ed. *The Goebbels Diaries.* New York: Universal-
     Award House, 1971.

Manstein, Erich von. *Lost Victories.* London: Methuen, 1958.

Mellenthin, F. W von. *Panzer Battles: A Study of the Employment of
     Armor in the Second World War.* Norman: University of Oklahoma Press,
     1971.

Meretskov, K. *City Invincible.* Moscow: Progress Publishers, 1970.

Morgenthau, Henry M. *Morgenthau Diary (Germany).* Washington, DC:
     Government Printing Office, 1967.

Rickenbacker, Edward V. *Rickenbacker.* Englewood Cliffs, NJ: Prentice-Hall,
     1967.

Sayre, Joel. *Persian Gulf Command: Some Marvels on the Road to
     Kazvin.* New York: Random House, 1945.

Schellenberg, Walther. *Hitler's Secret Service*. New York: Jove Publications, 1977.

Scott, John. *Behind the Urals: An American Worker in Russia's City of Steel*. London: Martin Secker and Warburg, 1943.

Senger und Etterlin, Frido von. *Neither Fear Nor Hope: The Wartime Career of General Frido von Senger und Etterlin, Defender of Cassino*. New York: E. P. Dutton, 1964.

Sherwood, Robert E. *Roosevelt and Hopkins*. Vol. 2, *From Pearl Harbor to Victory*. 1948. New York: Bantam Books, 1950.

Shtemenko, S. M. *The Last Six Months: Russia's Final Battles with Hitler's Armies in World War II*. Garden City, NY: Doubleday, 1977.

————. *The Soviet General Staff at War, 1941-1945*. Moscow: Progress Publishers, 1975.

Skomorovsky, Boris, and E. G. Morris. *The Siege of Leningrad*. New York: E. P. Dutton, 1944.

Soloviev, Mikhail. *My Nine Lives in the Red Army*. New York: David McKay, 1955.

Stalin, Joseph. *The Great Patriotic War of the Soviet Union*. New York: International Publishers, 1945.

Standley, William H., and Arthur A. Ageton. *Admiral Ambassador to Russia*. Chicago: Henry Regnery, 1955.

Stettinius, Edward R., Jr. *Lend-Lease: Weapon for Victory*. New York: Macmillan, 1944.

————. *Roosevelt and the Russians: The Yalta Conference*. Garden City, NY: Doubleday, 1949.

Tolley, Kemp. *The Caviar and Commissars: Experiences of a U.S. Naval Officer in Stalin's Russia*. Annapolis: Naval Institute Press, 1983.

Willkie, Wendell L. *One World*. New York: Simon and Schuster, 1943.

Winn, Godfrey Herbert. *PQ 17: The Story of a Ship*. London: Hutchinson, 1947.

World War II German Military Studies: A Collection of 213 Special Reports on the Second World War Prepared by Former Officers of the Wehrmacht for the United States Army. 24 vols. New York: Garland Publishing, 1974.

Zhukov, Georgii K. *The Memoirs of Marshal Zhukov*. New York: Delacorte Press, 1972.

Zorin, L. I. *Osoboe Zadanie*. Moscow: Izadatel'stvo Politicheskoi Literatury, 1987.

Articles

Bobrov, B. D. "Combat of the Infantry Division under Conditions of Encirclement." *Military Review* 21 (January 1942): 13-18. Translated from *Voennaia Mysl* (April 1940).

Chamberlin, William Henry. "American-Russian Cooperation." *Russian Review* 3 (Autumn 1943): 3-9.

"Foreign Military Digests: New Aspects of the War in the West." *Military Review* 21 (October 1941): 59-61. Condensed and translated from *Krasnaia Zvezda,* 4 December 1940.

Goldsworthy, Harry E. "A Toast from Stalin." *Aerospace Historian* 23 (Fall 1979): 161-65, 170.

Konovalov, V. "Iz opyta popol'neniia sostava severnogo flota v gody velikoi otechestvennoi voiny." *Voenno-Istoricheskii Zhurnal* (No. 8, 1978): 107-10.

Litvinov, Maxim. "Ambassador Litvinov on Lend-Lease." *Soviet Russia Today* (May 1943): 24.

Mason, F. Noel. "Observing the Russians at War." *Military Review* 28 (May 1948): 100-107.

Mazurik, I. "Vozdushnaia trassa Aliaska-Sibir." *Voenno-Istoricheskii Zhurnal* (No.3, 1977): 48-52.

"Military Notes from around the World." *Military Review* 21 (October 1941): 47-51.

Mokov, A. "Planning of Signal Communications in a Tank Group in Offensive Battle." U.S. Army Intelligence translation from *Zhurnal Avtobronetankovykh Voisk* (Nos. 2-3, 1943).

Nikitin, B. "Za tysiachi mil' ot fronta." *Morskoi Sbornik* (No. 10, 1976): 55-58.

Zorin, L. I. "Osoboe Zadanie." *Voprosy Istorii SSSR* (No. 3, 1985): 75-87.

Miscellaneous (U.S. Army Military History Institute Library, Carlisle Barracks, PA)

"The Armored and Mechanized Troops of the Soviet Armed Forces" (n.d.). U.S. Army Intelligence translation.

Brief Tactical-Technical Manual, 2d ed. Moscow: Voenizdat, 1945. U.S. Army Intelligence translation.

German Army. "Fuehrung, Kampf und Kraftquellen der Roten Armee." Lecture prepared by Foreign Armies East, 15 January 1945. Translated as "Leadership in the Red Army and the Sources of Power and Combat." U.S. Army Intelligence.translation.

Kuznetsov, O. M. "Railway Stations of Army Group Lines of Communications" (n.d.). U.S. Army Intelligence translation.

Marshkov, I. "Liaison Officers' Service" (n.d.). U.S. Army Intelligence translation.

U.S. Army. Intelligence. "General Organization of the Rear Service" (n.d.). Translation of "Vooruzhennye Sili, Sluzhba Syla: Manuscript by a Displaced Person."

U.S. Army. Intelligence. "Organization of the Signal Communications in the
Soviet Army" (n.d.).

U.S.S.R. Red Army. General Staff. *Collection of Materials for the Study of
War Experience No. 1, April-May 1942.* Moscow: Voenizdat, 1942. U.S.
Army Intelligence translation.

U.S.S.R. Red Army. General Staff. *Collection of Materials for the Study of
War Experience No. 2, September-October 1942.* Moscow: Voenizdat,
1942. U.S. Army Intelligence translation.

II. SECONDARY SOURCES

Official U.S. Histories

Cline, Ray S. *Washington Command Post: The Operations Division.* Washington, DC: Office of the Chief of Military History, 1951.

Coakley, Robert W., and Richard M. Leighton. *Global Logistics and Strategy,
1943-1945.* Washington, DC: Office of the Chief of Military History, 1968

Craven, Wesley Frank, and James Lea Cate, eds. *The Army Air Forces in
World War II.* Vol. 6, *Men and Planes.* Chicago: University of Chicago
Press, 1955.

———. *The Army Air Forces in World War II.* Vol. 7, *Services around the
World.* Chicago: University of Chicago Press, 1958.

Holley, Irving Brinton, Jr. *Buying Aircraft: Materiel Procurement for the Army
Air Forces.* Washington, DC: Office of the Chief of Military History, 1964.

Leighton, Richard M., and Robert W. Coakley. *Global Logistics and Strategy,
1940-1943.* Washington, DC: Office of the Chief of Military History, 1955

Matloff, Maurice, and Edwin M. Snell. *Strategic Planning for Coalition
Warfare, 1941-42.* Washington, DC: Office of the Chief of Military
History, 1953.

Motter, T. H. Vail. *The Persian Corridor and Aid to Russia.* Washington, DC:
Office of the Chief of Military History, 1952.

Ruppenthal, Roland G. *Logistical Support of the Armies.* Vol. 1, *May 1941-
September 1944.* Washington, DC: Office of the Chief of Military
History, 1953.

*The United States at War: Development and Administration of the War
Program by the Federal Government.* New York: Da Capo Press, 1972.

Watson, Mark Skinner. *Chief of Staff: Prewar Plans and Operations.*
Washington, DC: Historical Division, Department of the Army, 1950.

Histories and General Accounts

Bekker, Cajus. *The Luftwaffe War Diaries*. Garden City, NY: Doubleday, 1968.

Bienstock, Gregory, Solomon M. Schwarz, and Aaron Yugow. *Management in Russian Industry and Agriculture*. New York: Oxford University Press, 1944.

Brzezinski, Zbigniew, ed. *Political Controls in the Soviet Army*. Ann Arbor: Edwards Brothers, 1954.

Buehlmann, G. *The Supply Services of Foreign Armies (Economic Principles, Organization and Supplies, Transportation, and Problems of the Supply Services)*. Frauenfeld, CH: Huber & Co., 1949. U.S. Army Intelligence translation.

Carell, Paul. *Scorched Earth: The Russian-German War, 1943-1944*. Boston: Little, Brown, 1970.

Conquest, Robert. *The Great Terror: Stalin's Purge of the Thirties*. New York: Macmillan, 1969.

Cookridge, E. H. *Gehlen: Spy of the Century*. New York: Pyramid Books, 1973.

Dawson, Raymond H. *The Decision to Aid Russia, 1941: Foreign Policy and Domestic Politics*. Chapel Hill: University of North Carolina Press, 1959; Westport, CT: Greenwood Press, 1974.

Deutscher, Isaac. *Stalin: A Political Biography*. London: Pelican, 1966.

Divine, Robert A. *Roosevelt and World War II*. Baltimore: Johns Hopkins University Press, 1969.

Erickson, John. *The Road to Berlin: Continuing the History of Stalin's War with Germany*. Boulder, CO: Westview Press, 1983.

———. The *Road to Stalingrad*. London: Harper & Row, 1975.

Gorbachev, Mikhail S. *A Time for Peace*. New York: Richardson & Steirman, 1985.

Gorshkov, S. G. *Sea Power and the State*. Annapolis: Naval Institute Press, 1976.

The Great March of Liberation. Moscow: Progress Publishers, 1972.

Greenfield, Kent Roberts. *American Strategy in World War II: A Reconsideration*. Baltimore: Johns Hopkins University Press, 1963.

Guillaume, Augustin L. *The German Russian War*. London: War Office, 1956.

Hall, Hessel Duncan. *North American Supply*. London: Her Majesty's Stationery Office, 1955.

Hall, Hessel Duncan, and C. C. Wrigley. *Studies of Overseas Supply*. London: Her Majesty's Stationery Office, 1956.

Heilbrunn, Otto. *The Soviet Secret Services*. Westport, CT: Greenwood Press, 1981.

Herring, George C., Jr. *Aid to Russia, 1941-1946: Strategy, Diplomacy, and the Origins of the Cold War*. New York: Columbia University Press, 1973.

Higham, Robin, and Jacob W. Kipp, eds. *Soviet Aviation and Air Power: A Historical Review*. Boulder, CO: Westview Press, 1977.

History of the Great Patriotic War of the Soviet Union, 1941-1945. 6 vols. Moscow: Voenizdat, 1960-1965. Translation by Office of the Chief of Military History.

Istoriia Vtoroi Mirovoi Voiny, 1939-1945. 12 vols.. Moscow: Voenizdat, 1973-1982.

Jones, Robert Huhn. *The Roads to Russia: United States Lend-Lease to the Soviet Union*. Norman: University of Oklahoma Press, 1969.

Kahn, David. *Hitler's Spies: German Military Intelligence in World War II*. New York: Macmillan, 1978.

Kerr, Walter. *The Secret of Stalingrad*. Chicago: Playboy Press, 1978.

Kesaris, Paul. *The Rote Kapelle: The CIA's History of Soviet Intelligence and Espionage Networks in Western Europe, 1936-1945*. Washington, DC: University Publications of America, 1979.

Kleinfeld, Gerald R., and Lewis A. Tambs. *Hitler's Spanish Legion: The Blue Division in Russia*. Carbondale: Southern Illinois University Press, 1979.

Koblyakov, I. K. *U.S.S.R: For Peace against Aggression, 1933-1941*. Moscow: Progress Publishers, 1976.

Kovalev, I. V. *Transport v Velikoi Otechestvennoi Voine (1941-1945)*. Moscow: Izdatel'stvo Nauka, 1981.

Kozlov, M. M., ed. *Velikaia Otechestvennaia Voina, 1941-1945: Entsiklopediia*. Moscow: Soviet Encyclopedia, 1983.

Larionov, V., et al. *World War II: Decisive Battles of the Soviet Army*. Moscow: Progress Publishers, 1984.

Lukas, Richard C. *Eagles East: The Army Air Forces and the Soviet Union, 1941-1945*. Tallahassee: Florida State University Press, 1970.

Martel, Leon. *Lend-Lease, Loans, and the Coming of the Cold War: A Study of the Implementation of Foreign Policy*. Boulder, CO: Westview Press, 1979.

Matsulenko, V. A. *Operativnaia Maskirovka Voisk*. Moscow: Voenizdat, 1975.

Moor, Jay H. *World War II in Alaska: The Northwest Route (Ferrying Lend-Lease Aircraft to the Soviet Union): A Bibliography and Guide to Primary Sources*. Alaska Historical Commission Studies in History No. 175. Juneau: Alaska Historical Commission, June 1985.

Morison, Samuel Eliot. *History of United States Naval Operations in World War II*. Vol. 10, *The Atlantic Battle Won, May 1943-May 1945*. Boston: Little, Brown, 1956.

Parotkin, Ivan, ed. *The Battle of Kursk*. Moscow: Progress Publishers, 1974.

Patrick, Stephen B, Edward McCarthy, Trevor N. Dupuy, James F. Dunnigan, and David C. Isby. *War in the East: The Russo-German War, 1941-1945*. New York: Simulations Publications, 1977.

Rozofarov, M. S. *Trudovoye Rezervye SSSR, Sbornik Ofitsialnykh Materialov*. Moscow: Gosudarstvennoe Izdatelstvo, 1950. U.S. Army Intelligence translation.

Rzheshevsky, Oleg. *World War II: Myths and the Realities*. Moscow: Progress
    Publishers, 1984.
Saunders, M. G. *The Soviet Navy*. New York: Praeger, 1958.
Schwabedissen, Walter. *The Russian Air Force in the Eyes of German
    Commanders*. New York: Arno Press, 1960.
Scott, Harriet Fast, and William F. Scott. *The Armed Forces of the U.S.S.R.*
    Boulder, CO: Westview Press, 1979.
————. *The Soviet Art of War: Doctrine, Strategy, and Tactics*. Boulder, CO:
    Westview Press, 1982.
Seaton, Albert. *The Russo-German War, 1941-1945*. New York: Praeger,
    1972.
Sevruk, Vladimir, ed. *Moscow 1941/1942 Stalingrad: Recollections, Stories,
    Reports*. Moscow: Progress Publishers, 1970.
Sivachev, Nikolai V., and Nikolai N. Yakovlev. *Russia and the United States:
    U.S.-Soviet Relations from the Soviet Point of View*. Chicago: University
    of Chicago Press, 1979.
Stein, George H. *The Waffen SS: Hitler's Elite Guard at War, 1939-1945*.
    Ithaca: Cornell University Press, 1977.
Stoler, Mark A. *The Politics of the Second Front: American Military Planning
    in Coalition Warfare, 1941-1943*. Westport, CT: Greenwood Press, 1977.
Sutton, Antony C. *National Suicide: Military Aid to the Soviet Union*. New
    Rochelle, NY: Arlington House, 1973.
————. *Western Technology and Soviet Economic Development, 1930 to
    1945*. Stanford: Hoover Institution Press, 1971.
————. *Western Technology and Soviet Economic Development, 1945 to
    1965*. Stanford: Hoover Institution Press, 1973.
Uebe, Klaus. *Russian Reactions to German Air Power in World War II*. New
    York: Arno Press, 1964.
Voznesensky, Nikolai A. *The Economy of the U.S.S.R. during World War II*.
    Washington, DC: Public Affairs Press, 1948.
Werth, Alexander. *Russia at War, 1941-1945*. New York: E. P. Dutton,   1964.
Woodward, Llewellyn. *British Foreign Policy in the Second World War*.
    1952. London: Her Majesty's Stationery Office, 1962.

Articles

Alexeyev, A. "Lend-Lease as 'Weapon of U.S. Imperialism.'" *Current Digest
    of the Soviet Press* 3 (September 1951): 8-10.
Allred, Kenny. "The Persian Corridor: Aid to the Soviets." *Military Review*
    64 (April 1985): 13-25.
Armstrong, Richard. "The Bukrin Drop: Limits to Creativity." *Military Affairs*
    50 (July 1986): 127-132.
Bailes, Kendall E. "Soviet Science in the Stalin Period: The Case of V. I.
    Vernadskii and His Scientific School, 1928 - 1945." *Slavic Review* 45

(Spring 1986): 20-37.

Bakaev, V. "Morskoi transport v velikoi otechestvennoi voine." *Morskoi Sbornik* (No. 6, 1976): 25-29.

Baranov, S. V. "Rost tekhnicheskoi osnashchenosti sovetskikh vooruzhennykh sil v gody velikoi otechestvennoi voiny." *Voprosy Istorii* (No. 5, 1975): 22-35.

Beachley, David R. "Soviet Radio-Electronic Combat in World War II." *Military Review* 61 (March 1981): 66-72.

Beleznay, Istvan. "The Logistical Service of the Soviet Army." *Honved* (December 1949). U.S. Army Intelligence translation and abstract.

Berczeli, Bela. "The Spine of Command of the Stalinian Army, the Communication Troops of the Soviet." *Honved* (December 1949). U.S. Army Intelligence translation.

Betit, Eugene D. "The Soviet Manchurian Campaign, August 1945: Prototype for the Soviet Offensive." *Military Review* 56 (May 1976): 65-73.

Bland, Larry I. "Averell Harriman, the Russians, and the Origins of the Cold War in Europe, 1943-1945." *Australian Journal of Politics and History* 23 (1977): 403-16.

Bronevskii, S. "Concerning the Operational Pursuit." *Voennaia Mysl* (No. 5, 1946). U.S. Army Intelligence translation.

Chaney, Otto P., Jr. "The Agony of Soviet Military Historians." *Military Review* 48 (June 1968): 24-28.

Coakley, R. W. "Roosevelt et le pret-bail." *Revue d'Histoire de la Deuxieme Guerre Mondiale* 21 (April 1977): 73-96.

Cohen, Stephen. "Stalin's Terror as Social History." *Russian Review* 45 (October 1986): 375-84.

Dunaeva, N. "Lend-Liz: fakty i vymysly." *Voenno-Istoricheskii Zhurnal* (No. 3, 1977): 102-6.

Ferro, Marc. "Une histoire Russe de la deuxieme guerre mondiale." *Revue d'Histoire de la Deuxieme Guerre Mondiale* 11 (January 1961): 29-40.

FitzGerald, Charles G. "Operation Bagration." *Military Review* 44 (May 1964): 59-72.

Fitzpatrick, Sheila. "New Perspectives on Stalinism." *Russian Review* 45 (October 1986): 357-73.

Garthoff, Raymond L. "The Soviet Manchurian Campaign, August 1945." *Military Affairs* 33 (October 1969): 312-35.

Girault, Rene. "L'effort humain de l'arriere (1941-43)." *Revue d'Histoire de la Deuxieme Guerre Mondiale* 17 (October 1967): 15-31.

Gorskii, V. "Concerning the Rear of an Army in a Defensive Operation." *Voennaia Mysl* (No. 7, 1949). U.S. Army Intelligence translation.

Halperin, J. "L'economie sovietique pendant la guerre." *Revue d'Histoire de la Deuxieme Guerre Mondiale* 2 (April 1952): 16-25.

Haltom, Margaret Saxton. "Discrepancies in the Lend-Lease Program." *Southern Quarterly* 4 (July 1966): 446-68.

Herndon, James S., and Joseph O. Bayle. "Colonel Phillip R. Faymonville and the Red Army, 1934-43." *Slavic Review* 34 (September 1975): 483-505.

Hines, John G. "The Principles of Mass in Soviet Tactics Today." *Military Review* 62 (August 1982): 13-23.

Ivanov, A. "Stalin's Industrial Base." *Posev* (1951). U.S. Army Intelligence translation.

Janza, Karoly. "The Material and War Economic Power of the Soviet Union." *Honved* (December 1949). U.S. Army Intelligence translation.

Kieser, Rolf. "Die Kriegswirtschaft der Sowjetunion im Grossen Vaterlaendischen Krieg--Beweis fuer die Gesetzmaessigkeit der Militaroekonomischen Ueberlegenheit des Sozialismus ueber den Imperialismus." *Zeitschrift fuer Militaergeschichte* 7 (1968): 86-91.

Kimball, Jeffrey. "1st Soviet-American Symposium on US-USSR Relations during World War II, Moscow, USSR, Oct. 20-29, 1986." *SHAFR Newsletter* 18 (June 1987): 42-45.

Klinkmueller, Erich. "Some Economic Reflections on the Great Patriotic War (1941-1952)." *Soviet Union* 4 (1977): 223-36.

Krupchenko, I. "Metodika chteniia lektsii 'voenno-politicheskie itogi velikoi otechestvennoi voiny.'" *Voenno-Istoricheskii Zhurnal* (No. 2, 1980): 69-74.

Kucherenko, M. M. "Podgotovka rabochego popol'neniia v gody velikoi otechestvennoi voiny." *Voprosy Istorii* (No. 5, 1979): 3-18.

Kudriavtsev, I. I. "Sborniki dokumentov po istorii velikoi otechestvennoi voiny, 1941-1945 godov." *Sovetskie Arkhivy* (No. 5, 1976): 95-100.

Kumanev, G. A. "Reshaiushchii vklad sovetskogo naroda v pobedu nad fashistskoi Germaniei." *Prepodavanie Istorii v Shkole* (No. 15, 1960): 10-19.

--------. "Zheleznodoroznyi transport SSSR nakanune velikoi otechestvennoi voiny." *Istoriia SSSR* (No. 1, 1975): 110-21.

Kushnir, A. G. "Izmeneniia v administrativo-territorial'nom delenii SSSR v gody velikoi otechestvennoi voiny." *Istoriia SSSR* (No. 1, 1975): 128-32.

Langer, John Daniel. "The Harriman-Beaverbrook Mission and the Debate over Unconditional Aid for the Soviet Union, 1941." *Journal of Contemporary History* 14 (July 1979): 463-84.

--------. "The 'Red General': Phillip R. Faymonville and the Soviet Union, 1917-1952." *Prologue* 8 (Winter 1976): 209-21.

Lavrov, K. "The Army Group Rear in Offensive Operations." *Voennii Vestnik* (No. 6, 1946). U.S. Army Intelligence translation.

Leighton, R. M. "Les armes ou les armees: origines de la politique d' 'arsenal de la democratie.'" *Revue d'Histoire de la Deuxieme Guerre Mondiale* 17 (January 1967): 7-24.

Lukas, Richard C. "Soviet Stalling Tactics in the Forties." *Aerospace Historian* 14 (Spring 1967): 51-56.

Marushkin, B. I. and N. N. Yakovlev. "Vopros o bzaimootnosheniiakh SSSR i SSHA v period vtoroi mirovoi voiny v amerikanskoi burzhuaznoi istoriografii." *Novaia i Noveishaia Istoriia* (No. 3, 1957): 147-66.

Matsulenko, V. A. "Velikaia pobeda sovetskogo naroda i ego vooruzhennykh
    sil." *Voprosy Istorii KPSS* (No. 9, 1963): 111-17.
Mertsalov, A. N. "O kritike burzhuaznoi istoriografii vtoroi mirovoi voiny."
    Voprosy Istorii (No. 12, 1987): 35-50.
Millar, James R. "Financing the Soviet War Effort in World War II." *Soviet
    Studies* 32 (January 1980): 106-23.
Moskoff, William. "Soviet Higher Education Policy during World War II."
    Soviet Studies 38 (July 1986): 406-15.
Munting, Roger. "Lend-Lease and the Soviet War Effort." *Journal of
    Contemporary History* 19 (1984): 495-510.
Narochnitskii, A. L. "Vneshniaia politika S.S.S.R. i problemy evropeiskoi
    bezopasnosti mezhdu dvumia mirovimi voinami." *Novaia i Noveishaia
    Istoriia* (No. 5, 1974): 16-24.
Nikolaieff, A. M. "The Red Army in the Second World War." *Russian Review*
    1 (Autumn 1947): 49-60.
Platonov, B. A. "Uzel sviazi general'nogo shtaba v gody velikoi
    otechestvennoi voiny." *Voprosy Istorii* (No. 2, 1978): 93-103.
Plotnikov, I. V., and I. N. Chaban. "Tyl sovetskikh vooruzhennykh sil v gody
    velikoi otechestvennoi voiny." *Istoriia SSSR* (No. 1, 1975): 3-22.
Prokhorov, V. S. "Trudovoi podvig rabochikh i inzhenerno-tekhnicheskoi
    intelligentsii podshipnikovoi promyshlennosti v gody velikoi
    otechestvennoi voiny (1943-1945 gg.)." *Vestnik Moskovskogo
    Universiteta, Seriia 8: Istoriia* (No. 6, 1985): 13-18.
————. "Trudovoi podvig rabochikh i inzhenerno-tekhnicheskoi intelligentsii
    podshipnikovoi promyshlennosti v pervyi period velikoi otechestvennoi
    voiny (1941-1942 gg.)." *Vestnik Moskovskogo Universiteta, Seriia 8:
    Istoriia* (No. 5, 1985): 22-28.
Ratley, Lonnie O., III. "Air Power at Kursk: A Lesson for Today." *Military
    Review* 58 (April 1978): 54-62.
Rosefielde, Steven. "Incriminating Evidence: Excess Deaths and Forced Labour
    under Stalin: A Final Reply to Critics." *Soviet Studies* 39 (April 1987):
    292-313.
Rzheshevsky, Oleg A, and Evgeni Kulkov. "Politik und Strategie der UdSSR
    und der Westmaechte gegenueber dem faschistischen Deutschland in
    den letzten Monaten des Krieges in Europa." *Militaergeschichte* 24
    (No. 1, 1985): 3-17.
Rzheshevsky, Oleg A., "Noveishaia burzhuaznaia istoriografiia o korennom
    perelome v khode vtoroi mirovoi voine." *Istoriia SSSR* (No. 3, 1985): 155-
    168.
Sekistov, V. A. "Kritika burzhuaznykh fal'sifikatsii itogov i urokov vtoroi
    mirovoi voiny." *Voprosy Istorii KPSS* (No. 4, 1975): 81-92.
Sivachyov, Nikolai. "Franklin Delano Roosevelt: On the Occasion of his 100th
    Birth Anniversary." *Soviet Life* (February 1982): 16. Excerpted from
    USA: Economics, Politics, Ideology.

Sokolov, A. M. "Sovetsko-germanskii front i voennye deistviia na zapade (dekabr' 1944-janvar' 1945 gg.). *Voprosy Istorii* (No. 1, 1985): 3-15.

"Soviets Honoring American Civilian Sailors Who Risked Lives to Help U.S.S.R. in World War II." *Birmingham News,* June 30, 1987.

"Stalin in Command." *Atlas* (May 1966): 269-72. Translated from *Oktiabr'* .

Stolee, Margaret K. "Homeless Children in the U.S.S.R., 1917-1957." *Soviet Studies* 40 (January 1988): 64-83.

Titov, G. "The Entire Country to the Front." *Tyl i Snabzhenie Sovetskikh Vooruzhennikh Sil* (No. 5, 1975): 14-22. U.S. Army Intelligence translation.

Turbiville, Graham H. "Paradrop at the Bukrin Bridgehead: An Account of the Soviet Dnieper Airborne Operation." *Military Review* 56 (December 1976): 26-40.

Vernon, Graham D. "Soviet Combat Operations in World War II: Lessons for Today?" *Military Review* 60 (April 1980): 41-49.

Volkotrubenko, I. I. "Boepripasy i artsnabzhenie v velikoi otechestvennoi voine." *Voprosy Istorii* (No. 11, 1972): 82-91.

Wilson, Thomas A. "Soviet Combat Operations in World War II: Lessons for Today?" *Military Review* 60 (March 1980): 30-40.

Witt, Alan F. "Hitler's Late Summer Pause in 1941." *Military Affairs* 45 (December 1981): 187-93.

Yakovlev, Nikolai. "USSR-USA: 50 Years of Diplomatic Relations." *Soviet Life* (November 1983): 5, 19, 37, 43, 57.

Zagyv, M. "Some Problems of the 'Rear.'" *Voennaya Mysl* (No. 9, 1946). U.S. Army Intelligence translation.

Ziemke, Earl F. "Franz Halder at Orsha: The German General Staff Seeks a Consensus." *Military Affairs* 39 (December 1975): 173-76.

Zilberman, A. O. "Velikaia otechestvennaia voina v bibliograficheskikh izdaniiakh: obzor." *Istoriia SSSR* (No. 3, 1980): 162-66.

Zinich, M. S. "Iz istorii stankostroeniia i tiazhelogo mashinostroeniia v pervyi period velikoi otechestvennoi voiny." *Istoriia SSSR* (No. 6, 1971): 93-99.

———. "Izuchenie trudovoi deiatel'nosti zhenshchin v gody velikoi otechestvennoi voiny (1941-1945)." *Istoricheskie Zapiski Akademii Nauk SSSR* 97 (1976): 237-62.

———. "Stankostroenie i tiazheloe mashinostroenin SSSR v 1941-1945 gg." *Voprosy Istorii* (No. 5, 1973): 32-46.

Theses and Dissertations

Gardner, John Frederick. "The Lend-Lease Program of World War II: Analysis and Appraisal." Ph.D. dissertation, University of Pittsburgh, 1946.

Kern, Jeffrey Arthur. "Soviet Command and Control in an Historical Context." M.A. thesis, Naval Postgraduate School, Monterrey, CA, 1981.

Langer, John Daniel. "The Formulation of American Aid Policy toward the
    Soviet Union, 1940-1943: The Hopkins Shop and the Department of
    State." Ph.D. dissertation, Yale University, 1975.

Reference Works

Esposito, Vincent J., ed. *The West Point Atlas of American Wars*. 2 vols.
    New York: Praeger, 1972.
Feldbrugge, F. J. M., ed. *Encyclopedia of Soviet Law*. 2 vols. Dobbs Ferry,
    NY: Oceana Publications, 1973.
Great Soviet Encyclopedia. 31 vols. New York: Macmillan, 1973-83.
Macksey, Kenneth, and John H. Batchelor. *Tank: A History of the Armoured
    Fighting Vehicle*. New York: Charles Scribner's Sons, 1970.

Miscellaneous

Howard, Michael, "Strategy and Politics in World War II: The British Case," in
    Arthur L. Funk, ed. *Politics and Strategy in the Second World War*. San
    Francisco: International Committee for the History of the Second World War,
    1975, 31-42.
Kumanev, G. "Soviet War Economy," in *The Great Patriotic War of the Soviet
    People and Our Times*. Moscow: USSR Academy of Sciences, 1985, 108-
    118.
Pavlov, Pavel D. Speech at the Student Conference on National Affairs, Texas
    A&M University, February 10, 1982.
U.S.S.R. "Tetrad' Po Voenni Administratsii." 1947. U.S. Army
    Intelligence translation. U.S. Army Military History Institute, Carlisle
    Barracks, PA.

Index

About the Author

HUBERT P. VAN TUYLL is Associate Professor of History at Union College, Barbourville, Kentucky. He has published articles in the *Social Science Perspectives Journal*.